Deaf Children in America

Deaf Children in America

Edited by
Arthur N. Schildroth
Center for Assessment and Demographic Studies

and

Michael A. Karchmer
Gallaudet Research Institute

Gallaudet College
Washington, DC

 College-Hill Press, San Diego, California

College-Hill Press
A Division of
Little, Brown and Company (Inc.)
34 Beacon Street
Boston, Massachusetts 02128

Library of Congress Cataloging-in-Publication Data
Main entry under title:

Deaf children in America.

Includes indexes.
1. Deaf—Education—United States.   2. Children,
Deaf—United States.   I. Schildroth, Arthur N.,
1927–   II. Karchmer, Michael A.
HV2430.D4   1986   371.91'2   86-6809

ISBN 0-316-483028

Printed in the United States of America

*Dedicated to the teachers, administrators, and staff
who serve hearing impaired children and youth
with much wisdom and perseverance
and still find the time to complete our Annual
Survey forms with a minimal amount of grumbling*

Contents

About This Book   ix

Introduction   xi

Chapter 1 **Characteristics of Hearing Impaired Youth in   1
            the General Population and of Students in
            Special Education Programs for the Hearing
            Impaired**
            Peter Ries

Chapter 2 **Etiological Trends, Characteristics, and   33
            Distributions**
            Scott Campbell Brown

Chapter 3 **Multihandicapped Students**   55
            Anthony B. Wolff and Judith E. Harkins

Chapter 4 **Residential Schools for Deaf Students: A   83
            Decade in Review**
            Arthur N. Schildroth

Chapter 5 **Issues in School Placement**   105
            Donald F. Moores and Thomas N. Kluwin

Chapter 6 **Patterns of Sign Use among Hearing   125
            Impaired Students**
            I. King Jordan and Michael A. Karchmer

Chapter 7   Deaf Children and Speech Intelligibility: 139
             A National Study
             Steve Wolk and Arthur N. Schildroth

Chapter 8   Patterns of Academic Achievement among   161
             Hearing Impaired Students: 1974 and 1983
             Thomas E. Allen

Chapter 9   Minimum Competency Testing Programs and   207
             Hearing Impaired Students
             Carol A. Bloomquist

Chapter 10   Postsecondary Educational Opportunities for   231
             Deaf Students
             Brenda W. Rawlings and Susan J. King

Conclusion   257

Appendix A   *Form, 1982–1983 Annual Survey of*   263
              Hearing Impaired Children and Youth

Appendix B   *Selected Readings: Center for Assessment and*   267
              Demographic Studies

Author Index   275

Subject Index   279

About This Book

CONTRIBUTORS

One of the unusual aspects of this book is that, of the 14 contributing authors, all but 4 are or were on the staff of Gallaudet College's Center for Assessment and Demographic Studies (CADS). The other 4 contributors are researchers within the Gallaudet community who, over the past several years, have worked closely with the staff at the center. Thus, this book is the product of a group of professionals who have worked collaboratively on many of the projects described in this book.

Senior editor *Arthur N. Schildroth* is a senior research associate at CADS. He has worked at the center since 1973 and has coordinated the Annual Survey of Hearing Impaired Children and Youth since 1975. Co-editor *Michael A. Karchmer* is the associate dean for research at Gallaudet College; in this role he administers the Gallaudet Research Institute, of which the center is a part. Dr. Karchmer was director of CADS from 1978 to 1985.

Peter Ries (Chapter 1) is a statistician at the National Center for Health Statistics in Hyattsville, Maryland. Mr. Ries formerly worked at the Office of Demographic Studies and, from 1972 to 1974, was its director. Chapter 2 was written by *Scott Campbell Brown*, a research scientist at the center. A demographer by training, Dr. Brown has been with the center since 1983. *Anthony B. Wolff* (Chapter 3) has worked part-time at CADS as a research scientist since 1982. Dr. Wolff also practices clinical psychology in Annapolis, Maryland. *Judith E. Harkins* (Chapter 3) is director of the Gallaudet Research Institute's Technology Assessment Program. Dr. Harkins has worked at the Research Institute since 1979. *Donald F. Moores* and *Thomas N. Kluwin* coauthored Chapter 5. Dr. Moores has been director of the Gallaudet Research Institute's Center for Studies in Education and Human Development since 1980, and Dr. Kluwin is a research scientist with the same center and has worked at Gallaudet since 1977.

I. King Jordan (Chapter 6) is currently serving as interim dean of Gallaudet's College of Arts and Sciences. Dr. Jordan is also a professor of psychology at the college. *Steve Wolk* (Chapter 7) is a professor of educational foundations and research at Gallaudet College and is also chair of that department. Dr. Wolk worked at CADS from 1978 to 1981 and was associate director of the center from 1979 to 1981. *Thomas E. Allen* (Chapter 8) has been the director of CADS since 1985. Dr. Allen has worked at the center since 1980 and was the project coordinator for the norming of the seventh edition of the Stanford Achievement Test for use with hearing impaired students.

Carol Bloomquist (Chapter 9) is a research scientist in the area of tests and measurements at CADS. Dr. Bloomquist began working at the center in 1984. *Brenda W. Rawlings* and *Susan J. King* together wrote Chapter 10. Ms. Rawlings is a senior research associate at the center; with the exception of a year and a half spent working in Australia, she has worked at the center continuously since 1968. Ms. King is presently the coordinator of data systems for the Gallaudet Research Institute; she worked at CADS from 1979 to 1985, serving much of that time as coordinator of data processing.

Finally, although her name does not appear as the author of a specific chapter, *Sue A. Hotto* has been an important contributor. As editorial assistant, Ms. Hotto has worked closely with the editors and with the chapter authors at every stage of this book's development and also assembled the selected readings in Appendix B. She has been a member of the staff of the center since 1979.

ACKNOWLEDGMENTS

The information in this book resulted from the joint efforts of a great number of people who have contributed, over a period of nearly two decades, to the success of the Annual Survey of Hearing Impaired Children and Youth and to the other projects of the Center for Assessment and Demographic Studies. We salute the many staff members—past and present—who have been a part of this enterprise. The center has had five directors in its existence; three (Ries, Karchmer, and Allen) are represented in this volume. We acknowledge the contributions of the other two to the work reported here: Augustine Gentile (1966 to 1972) and Raymond J. Trybus (1974 to 1978). Throughout many of its years, the center was guided by the advice of a National Advisory Committee. Thanks are due these prominent educators and researchers for their collaboration.

We gratefully acknowledge the steadfast support of Gallaudet College, which has funded the work of the Gallaudet Research Institute and the Center for Assessment and Demographic Studies. Thanks are due Dr. Jerry C. Lee, president, and the other past and present Gallaudet College administrators who have recognized the importance of collecting and disseminating national statistical data on this unique population of students. It should be noted that the conclusions and opinions of the editors and authors are their own and do not necessarily reflect official Gallaudet policies. Gallaudet College is an equal opportunity employer/educational institution. The programs and services of Gallaudet College receive substantial assistance from the U.S. Department of Education.

The research reported in Chapters 7 and 8 was supported in part by Grant No. G008300004 from the Office of Special Education. Also, we acknowledge the financial assistance from the Bureau for the Education of the Handicapped, which largely supported the Annual Survey and its predecessors until 1974.

Finally, we note that any royalties from this book are being donated to the Gallaudet Research Institute to support continued research on deaf children in America.

Introduction

The chapters of this book are based largely on information collected by the Center for Assessment and Demographic Studies in its Annual Survey of Hearing Impaired Children and Youth, a project that has its roots in recent history.

In March of 1964 leaders of various disciplines in the field of hearing impairment attended a national meeting entitled "Conference on the Collection of Statistics of Severe Hearing Impairments and Deafness in the United States" at the National Institute of Neurological Diseases and Blindness (NINDB) in Bethesda, Maryland. The purpose of the 2-day meeting was, in the words of the official proceedings, "to explore the possibilities of developing uniform statistics on incidence, prevalence, and causes of severe hearing impairments and deafness, as well as on the characteristics of . . . [hearing] impaired individuals." The document added: "The meeting was the first of its kind to be held in this country." Except for information collected on the deaf population during the decennial censuses between 1830 and 1930—information called "inadequate" by the conference proceedings—studies prior to 1964 were limited in scope and in geographical area.

The conclusion of the 1964 meeting was a unanimous recommendation that NINDB establish a program to gather uniform information on the numbers and characteristics of hearing impaired persons in the United States. Appendix G to the meeting proceedings contained a proposal by Dr. H. Goldstein, Chief of the Biometrics Branch of NINDB, for "collecting data on students in schools and classes for the deaf." In April 1964 the Conference of Executives of American Schools for the Deaf, responding to the March meeting, passed a resolution expressing its support for the establishment of a program to collect data on deaf students as well as on other hearing impaired children.

Although NINDB was unable to establish this data-gathering organization, another U.S. government agency, the Bureau of Education for the Handicapped of the Office of Education, recognized the need expressed at the NINDB conference, and in 1965 made a 2-year grant to Gallaudet College to investigate the feasibility of such a project and to develop methods and procedures for collecting nationwide information on hearing impaired children.

The resulting study, a pilot project involving the District of Columbia and four nearby states, collected demographic and audiological information during the 1966–1967 school year on 4301 hearing impaired students enrolled in residential and day schools and in special education classes. The success of this project led directly to the establishment on May 1, 1968, of the Office of the Annual Census of Hearing Impaired Children (later called the Office of Demographic Studies and now known as the Center for Assessment and Demographic Studies.) The office's major project, the Annual Census, became, after its first year of national operation in 1968–1969, the Annual Survey of Hearing Impaired Children and Youth. It was funded initially by the Bureau of Education for the Handicapped and then by the National Institute of Education. The Center and its Annual Survey, now supported by Gallaudet College as part of its Research Institute, have been in operation since that time, updating and managing the largest ongoing data base on hearing impaired children in the world.

This data base has been used for a wide variety of purposes—by educators of hearing impaired students, by legislators, and by researchers. It has provided a sampling framework for numerous studies in the field of hearing impairment, perhaps the most important of which has been the development of testing procedures and special norms for hearing impaired students on the Stanford Achievement Test in 1974 and again in 1983. From the Center's frequent contact with schools and programs serving hearing impaired students in the survey and testing areas, it has been able to focus its own research efforts more effectively and to clarify its research results. The experience and recommendations of teachers and staff directly involved with hearing impaired students have been invaluable in these efforts.

Although the Annual Survey is completely voluntary, it has enjoyed the generous cooperation of a very large number of schools and programs working with hearing impaired students. From the 25,363 students in its first national survey of 1968–1969, it has continued to grow; the 1982–1983 survey collected demographic, audiological, and other educationally related data on more than 55,000 hearing impaired students enrolled in 8000 schools and programs. During these 15 years the Annual Survey's chief task has been to collect, analyze, and disseminate data on hearing impaired children and youth rather than to take a partisan view on controversial issues.

From its beginnings the Annual Survey has attempted to be inclusive, rather than exclusive. Consequently, although a very large majority of the hearing impaired students reported to the survey are enrolled in special education classes across the United States, small numbers of children have also been reported by regular education classes, by speech and hearing clinics, and by state hospitals.

In addition to the national survey and its achievement testing programs, the Center has also been involved in numerous special projects. Contracts with the departments of education in Texas, Louisiana, and Nebraska have provided an opportunity to study hearing impaired students in greater detail than that offered by the Annual Survey and to use survey data for pupil and program management. Special studies conducted by the Center on communication, postsecondary programs for deaf students, writing assessment, and school graduates are extensions of the Center's work in the survey and assessment areas. The chapters in this book represent an effort by Center staff and others associated with it to review Annual Survey data and achievement test results collected by the Center and to examine their relationship to other recent research findings.

The chapters in this book are necessarily selective, that is, they examine only a portion of the data reported to the Annual Survey and represent the special competencies and interests of the individual authors. There are, obviously, other important demographic considerations and educational issues regarding hearing impaired children and youth not addressed in this volume.

The chapters reflect the demographic and assessment work of the Center. They give numbers and facts about hearing impaired children and youth—numbers regarding student enrollment in various types of educational settings, of causes and additional handicaps, of achievement test scores. Their arrangement is somewhat arbitrary, though in general this arrangement includes a demographic overview of the numbers and characteristics of hearing impaired children (Chapters 1, 2, and 3), a section on types of educational programs in which hearing impaired children are enrolled (Chapters 4 and 5), two chapters on communication (Chapters 6 and 7), two concerning test issues (Chapters 8 and 9); a final chapter (Chapter 10) deals with postsecondary opportunities for hearing impaired students.

Chapter 1 is somewhat technical in nature, reflecting the complexity of any attempt to establish population figures. It is intended to serve three purposes: (a) to estimate the number of hearing impaired youth in the general U.S. population and to describe them in terms of some basic characteristics, (b) to estimate the number and describe the characteristics of students receiving special educational services for the hearing impaired in the United States, and (c) to assess the degree to which the information on students in the Annual Survey reflects the size and characteristics of the two groups identified above.

Chapters 2 and 3 present Annual Survey data on the causes of hearing loss and the additional handicaps of hearing impaired students reported to the Annual Survey. Trends in the etiology of hearing loss during the past 10 years are explored, and some hypotheses are presented as to what causes may influence the hearing impaired school-aged population in the near future. The chapter on multiply handicapped hearing impaired students considers some implications for educational and clinical interventions.

Chapters 4 and 5 describe two types of programs in which hearing impaired students are being educated, the characteristics of the students in these programs, the services they are receiving, and changes that have occurred over the past decade. Chapter 4 examines the residential schools for deaf students; Chapter 5 explores the issue of mainstreaming of hearing impaired students in light of the authors' ongoing research in several large public school systems.

Chapter 6 deals with the broad issue of communication, both from an historical point of view and from the data reported to the 1982–1983 Annual Survey. It discusses the differences between students who use sign to communicate and those who rely solely upon speech.

An important communication variable of hearing impaired students is examined in Chapter 7, speech intelligibility. The authors investigate the relationship of speech intelligibility, as rated by teachers, to other student characteristics, including educational placement and primary communication method of the student (e.g., speech alone, signs and fingerspelling).

As indicated earlier, the Center for Assessment and Demographic Studies has been able to use the data file supplied by the Annual Survey to select its achievement testing sample and also to examine the test results of its two norming studies in light of the student characteristics reported to the survey. Chapter 8 compares the results of the 1974 and 1983 Stanford normings, showing that the 1983 hearing impaired students scored significantly higher than students in 1974. Explanations for this fact are discussed. The chapter also compares the achievement levels of various subgroups in the 1983 norming of the test (e.g., scores by region of the country, by minority status, and by program type).

During the past decade, 80 percent of the states have established minimum competency testing programs at the high school level. Important decisions about hearing impaired students are being made on the basis of these testing programs. Chapter 9 presents information that may be useful to educators wishing to ensure that these decisions are made within an informed context. The chapter includes an overview of statewide minimum competency programs and summarizes practices used in states implementing these programs with hearing impaired students.

In the last 20 years postsecondary opportunities for hearing impaired students have expanded greatly in terms of geographical location, program offerings, and special services. Chapter 10 examines the growth of these postsecondary programs and discusses their present status and possible factors that may affect their future.

Educators of deaf students would be the first to admit they do not have solutions to the problems of educating deaf children and youth. However, what has been obvious to these educators—these teachers and administrators and school staff—is also becoming obvious to government officials and other educators, many of whom are grappling for the first time with the day-to-day education of these students. It is becoming evident that deaf students usually cannot be educated—or integrated with hearing children—in exactly the same manner as, for example, orthopedically handicapped students. At the core of this book is the issue of education of hearing impaired students: The kind of education they receive depends on a knowledge by teachers and administrators of the numbers and characteristics of these students.

This book attempts to direct attention to hearing impaired students, to share information about their numbers and characteristics and the education they are receiving with educators and others interested in their development. It is hoped that what is said here will broaden the general knowledge about hearing impaired children and youth and improve their educational opportunities.

Chapter 1

Characteristics of Hearing Impaired Youth in the General Population and of Students in Special Educational Programs for the Hearing Impaired

Peter Ries

This chapter is intended primarily to serve three purposes: (a) to estimate the number of hearing impaired youth in the general population in the United States and to describe them in terms of some basic characteristics, (b) to estimate the number and describe the basic characteristics of students receiving special educational services for the hearing impaired in the United States, and (c) to assess the degree to which the information on students included in the data file of the Annual Survey of Hearing Impaired Children and Youth reflects the size and characteristics of these two groups.

Before proceeding to these tasks it will be useful to consider some issues that have important implications for the content of this chapter.

The first concerns the terminology used to indicate different types and degrees of hearing loss. Terms such as *deaf* and *hard of hearing*, because of their lack of precision, are avoided unless the estimates from the studies being considered are based on these terms. The terms *hearing impairment* and *hearing loss* are used interchangeably to indicate any significant long-term deviations of any degree below levels associated with normal hearing. Because qualifying phrases (e.g., profound bilateral hearing impairment) can become quite cumbersome, the context of the discussion is often used to indicate the type of hearing impairment under consideration, without spelling it out in each case.

Peter Ries is employed by the U.S. National Center for Health Statistics. However, this chapter was written under a private contract between the Center for Assessment and Demographic Studies and Mr. Ries. The views expressed in this chapter do not therefore necessarily represent those of the U.S. National Center for Health Statistics.

Since the primary interest is those youth whose hearing loss is of a significance that would make them likely candidates for special education, the focus is on youth with a *moderate-to-profound hearing loss*. A preliminary indication of what is meant by moderate-to-profound hearing loss may be gained by listing the various criteria used to define this type of loss in the studies that serve as the basis for discussion. The following criteria are used to indicate a *profound hearing loss*: "cannot hear and understand any speech," a better-ear average of 91 or more dB, and "deaf." To indicate a more inclusive range of hearing loss, the following criteria used in the studies indicate a moderate-to-profound hearing loss: "at best can hear and understand shouted speech," a better-ear average of 41 or more dB, and "hard of hearing or deaf." The rationale for equating these different terms in the manner just described is indicated as the different studies are discussed. Only passing attention is paid to youth with a less-than-moderate hearing loss.

A second issue involves the age factor. The studies considered include youth of different age ranges. Since frequent comparisons are made of the results of these studies, the data presented and the discussion are restricted to youth in the age range of 6 to 17 years. In this way spurious differences or similarities in estimates are avoided that might arise from comparing results for youth of different age ranges while still including the age range encompassing most of the school-age population.

The third issue to be considered concerns the time when the data were collected. Ideally the discussion would be based on recent studies conducted at about the same time. This is possible in the discussion of students receiving special educational services for the hearing impaired; the point of reference for this topic is 1982. However, because most of the major studies of the prevalence of hearing impairment in the general population were conducted in the 1970s, this part of the discussion uses the mid-70s as its temporal point of reference. This use of different temporal reference points imposes a definite limitation on the conclusions that can be drawn from the discussion. But it is unavoidable if conclusions are to be based on the best recent empirical evidence on the topics under consideration.

The final issue relates to the nature of the data that serves as the basis of discussion. A large proportion of these data is based on sample surveys. Survey data produce an estimate of the population characteristic being studied rather than a measure of the population characteristic itself. An estimate associated with any particular sample ordinarily differs to some degree from an estimate of the same characteristic associated with other samples that might have been drawn from the same population. From the nature of any particular sample, sampling theory can determine how probable it is that the estimates of a characteristic from all of the samples that might be drawn from the same population would fall within a specified range. The statement including the specific probability and the specific range associated with an estimate is the so-called confidence interval of the estimate.

The amount of sampling variation is determined mainly by the size of the sample from which an estimate is derived. Unfortunately, much of the data considered in this chapter is based on small samples and therefore has large sampling errors. In fact, some of the estimates related to profoundly hearing impaired youth have a 95 percent confidence interval, which is as large as the estimates themselves.

The most desirable way of dealing with a situation in which the results of any single study are inconclusive because of high sampling variability is to consider the results of other relevant studies. To the degree that these results are consistent (or at a minimum, not inconsistent), confidence in the precision of the estimates of any one of them is increased. However, comparing the results of several studies involves a new set of problems. Because almost invariably each of the studies uses somewhat different definitions or methods of measuring the concepts under investigation, the task of comparing the results carries with it the added complication of determining the comparability of the concepts used in each of the studies and of taking into account any differences between these concepts.

These problems of large sampling errors and of reconciling different definitions impose limitations on any conclusions that may be drawn. Those seeking a sharply etched portrait of the young people in the United States with a moderate-to-profound hearing loss may be disappointed. Under the circumstances, the best that can be expected is a sketch in broad strokes that resembles the actual characteristics of these youth to an acceptable degree.

The presentation begins with an attempt to estimate the number and characteristics of hearing impaired youth 6 to 17 years of age in the general population. This is followed by a discussion of the degree to which the students included in the Annual Survey are representative of these youth. Next, the chapter attempts to estimate the number and characteristics of the students in the country who are receiving special educational services for the hearing impaired. Finally, the chapter compares these students with those included in the Annual Survey in an attempt to determine how representative these survey data are of all youth receiving special education for the hearing impaired.

NUMBER AND CHARACTERISTICS OF HEARING IMPAIRED YOUTH IN THE GENERAL POPULATION

The U.S. National Center for Health Statistics (NCHS) is the major source in the United States of data on the prevalence of hearing impairment in the general population. Most of these data are obtained from two of its ongoing surveys: the National Health Interview Survey (NHIS) and the

National Health and Nutrition Examination Survey (NHANES). After a brief overall description of these surveys and the way each obtains data on a person's ability to hear, the chapter reviews some of their findings concerning the hearing ability of youth 6 to 17 years of age in the general population. This is followed by an attempt to reconcile the estimates based on the two very different methods of measuring hearing ability used in these studies and a discussion of real or apparent differences in the results.

Estimates from the National Health Interview Survey

NHIS is an annual survey of the civilian noninstitutionalized population of the United States. Interviewers from the U.S. Bureau of the Census visit a randomly drawn, stratified sample of about 40,000 households each year and administer a questionnaire designed by the Division of Health Interview Statistics to obtain the health-related and sociodemographic characteristics of each family member residing in the household. Because they are considered to be institutionalized, residential students in schools for the deaf are not included in the NHIS sample. Over the years the response rate for the NHIS has averaged about 97 percent. The results of the interviews are processed by NCHS, and the data are weighted so that they reflect the official census estimates of the age, sex, and racial composition of the U.S. population. (For a more detailed description, see Ries, 1982, Appendix I.)

Each year since 1978 (and periodically before 1978) the questionnaire has contained items intended to determine the number of persons in the general population who have a hearing problem. These estimates are derived from the following questions: "Does anyone in the family now have (1) deafness in one or both ears, (2) any other trouble hearing with one or both ears?" Further questions are asked about the nature of the hearing problem for those identified by these screening questions. Among these questions are some that determine whether the hearing problem is due to a short-term condition or is chronic.

While useful in producing an overall estimate of the number and characteristics of hearing impaired persons, these data do not produce results that allow these persons to be classified in terms of their ability to hear and understand speech. To overcome this limitation, a special supplement on hearing ability is periodically included in the NHIS. This supplement (Figure 1–1) consists of a question on hearing aid use*, a rating scale for each ear, and the Gallaudet Hearing Scale.

---

*Since in NHIS both scales are administered in terms of a person's hearing ability without the use of a hearing aid, Question 1 in Figure 1–1 ("Has . . . ever used a hearing aid?") is intended to indicate to the interviewer whether it is necessary to include the parenthetical questions about hearing aid use shown for each of the two scales. Of course, responses to this question can also serve as a basis for estimating hearing aid use in the general population.

The Gallaudet Hearing Scale (Question 3 in Figure 1-1) was developed to measure hearing problems ranging from a minimal degree of only having difficulty hearing and understanding whispered speech (a scale score of 1) to not being able to hear any sounds at all (a scale score of 8, indicating a *no* response was received to all seven items). An evaluation study conducted jointly by Gallaudet College and NCHS indicated that the scale was relatively consistent and that there was a satisfactory level of agreement between the scale score and the results of audiometric testing (Schein, Gentile, and Haase, 1970).

The rating scale (Question 2 in Figure 1-1) is used primarily to distinguish persons with a *bilateral hearing loss* (defined as persons having at least a little trouble hearing in each ear) from those with a *unilateral hearing loss* (defined as persons whose hearing is good in at least one ear).

The supplement including these three questions was included in the 1971 NHIS (Gentile, 1975) and most recently in the 1977 NHIS (Ries, 1982). Ordinarily the results of two surveys of the same population that contained the same questions would be used to describe both the subject under study at each of these times and the changes that had occurred in the interim. However, when the sampling variations of each of the studies are very large, comparisons over time may not be meaningful. An alternative is to reduce the amount of variation by pooling the results of the

HEARING SUPPLEMENT	R1	☐ No Hearing Problem *(NP)* ☐ A, B, or 33 in C2 *(1–3)*			
1. Has — — ever used a hearing aid?	1.	1 Y		2 N	
(Hand Card H) Please look at this card — 2a. Which statement best describes — —'s hearing in his LEFT ear (without a hearing aid)?	2a.	Good 1☐	Little trouble 2 ☐	Lot of trouble 3 ☐	Deaf 4 ☐
b. Which statement best describes — —'s hearing in his RIGHT ear (without a hearing aid)?	b.	1☐	2 ☐	3 ☐	4 ☐
3a. If age 3+, ask: (Without a hearing aid) Can — — usually HEAR AND UNDERSTAND what a person says without seeing his face if that person WHISPERS to him from across a quiet room?	3a.	☐ Under 3 *(R2)* 1 Y *(R2)*		2 N	
b. (Without a hearing aid) Can — — usually HEAR AND UNDERSTAND what a person says without seeing his face if that person TALKS IN A NORMAL VOICE to him from across a quiet room?	b.	1 Y *(R2)*		2 N	
c. (Without a hearing aid) Can — — usually HEAR AND UNDERSTAND what a person says without seeing his face if that person SHOUTS to him from across a quiet room?	c.	1 Y *(R2)*		2 N	
d. (Without a hearing aid) Can — — usually HEAR AND UNDERSTAND a person if that person SPEAKS LOUDLY into his better ear?	d.	1 Y *(R2)*		2 N	
e. (Without a hearing aid) Can — — usually tell the sound of speech from other sounds and noises?	e.	1 Y *(R2)*		2 N	
f. (Without a hearing aid) Can — — usually tell one kind of noise from another?	f.	1 Y *(R2)*		2 N	
g. (Without a hearing aid) Can — — hear loud noises?	g.	1 Y		2 N	

Figure 1–1. Questions asked of respondents in the 1971 and 1977 National Health Interview Survey who indicated a hearing problem.

Table 1–1.   Number and Percent Distribution of Youth 6 to 17 Years of Age by Age, Sex, and Race, According to Degree of Hearing Loss, United States, 1971 and 1977 Combined

Age, Sex, Race	All Hearing Levels	All Hearing Impaired	All Types*
	Number of Youth (in thousands)		
All youth			
(6–17 years of age)†	47,583	841	354
Age			
6–11 years	22,810	421	198
12–17 years	24,774	419	156
Sex			
Male	24,212	485	210
Female	23,372	355	144
Race			
White	40,143	724	302
Black	6,801	106	45
	Percent Distribution		
All youth			
(6–17 years of age)	100.0	100.0	100.0
Age			
6–11 years	47.9	50.1	55.9
12–17 years	52.1	49.8	44.1
Sex			
Male	50.9	57.7	59.3
Female	49.1	42.2	40.7
Race§			
White	85.5	87.2	87.0
Black	14.5	12.8	13.0

Source: National Health Interview Survey
*Includes unknown degree of bilateral hearing loss.
†Includes races other than white and black.
‡Indicates estimate has a relative standard error of more than 30 percent.
§Excludes races other than white and black.

two surveys and considering their average as reflective of a single group at the midpoint of the times the two surveys were conducted. Because the sampling variations of these two studies are extremely large for hearing impaired youth 6 to 17 years of age, this alternative is adopted in the following discussion.*

| Bilateral Hearing Impairment | | | Unilateral Hearing Loss |
| At Best Can Hear and Understand Shouted Speech | | Lesser Degrees of Hearing Impairment | |
All	Cannot Understand Any Speech		
Number of Youth (in thousands)			
129	22	221	487
68	11‡	129	223
61	11‡	92	264
76	10‡	133	275
53	12‡	88	212
104	16‡	194	423
21	5‡	24	61
Percent Distribution			
100.0	100.0	100.0	100.0
52.7	50.0‡	58.4	45.8
47.3	50.0‡	41.6	54.1
58.9	45.5‡	60.2	56.5
41.1	54.5‡	39.8	43.5
83.2	76.2‡	89.0	87.4
16.8	23.8‡	11.0	12.6

The combined result for the 1971 and 1977 hearing supplements are shown by age, sex, and race in Table 1-1. The categories of hearing impairment are based on the results for both of the scales included in the supplement. The results of the rating scale were used solely to classify persons

*An example of what is gained by the somewhat unusual step of combining the results of surveys conducted 6 years apart may help to justify this decision. For each of the surveys considered separately, an estimate of about 35,000 youth has a relative standard error (i.e., the quotient of the standard error of the estimate divided by the estimate) of about 30 percent. When the results of the two surveys are pooled, an estimate of 35,000 has a relative standard error of about 22 percent. While this reduction of the relative standard error by about one fourth does not solve the problems encountered because of large sampling errors, it does make them somewhat more manageable.

in terms of whether they had a unilateral or bilateral hearing loss. Those with a bilateral hearing loss were further classified according to their results on the Gallaudet Hearing Scale. Only three categories of bilateral hearing impairment are shown because the eight possible scores had to be grouped to produce a sufficient number of cases. As indicated earlier, both scales were administered to measure how a person hears without the use of a hearing aid.

Table 1-1 shows that there were an estimated 841,000 youth 6 to 17 years of age with some degree of hearing impairment in 1974, the midpoint of the two surveys. However, about 487,000 of these youth had trouble hearing in only one of their ears, and about 221,000 (shown in the column headed "Lesser Degrees of Hearing Impairment") could, according to their Gallaudet Hearing Scale scores, hear and understand normal speech. Few of the youth in either of these groups would have the type of moderate-to-profound hearing loss focused on in this chapter.

It is from the estimated 129,000 youth who fit the category of "At Best Can Hear and Understand Shouted Speech" (a Gallaudet Hearing Scale score of 3 to 8), that most of the students 6 to 17 years of age receiving special educational services for the hearing impaired would be drawn. This is not to imply, of course, that all youth with this level of hearing loss would require this type of special education; other factors ranging from the use of hearing aids to the educational philosophy of parents would be involved in determining the actual need or desirability for such special services.

While not conclusive because of the large sampling variation associated with the estimates, the distributions by age, sex, and race for the estimated 129,000 who could at best hear and understand shouted speech are at least suggestive. They indicate that in relation to all youth 6 to 17 years of age in the general population these hearing impaired youth were proportionately overrepresented among 6-to-11-year-olds (52.7 percent compared to 47.9 percent), males (58.9 percent compared to 50.9 percent), and blacks (16.8 percent compared to 14.5 percent). As noted, these relationships are only suggestive, because none of the stated differences reaches a 95 percent level of statistical significance.

Table 1-1 also shows that among these 129,000 youth an estimated 22,000 could not hear and understand any speech. The sampling errors of the estimates by age, sex, and race for this group are so large that not even tentative conclusions regarding their characteristics can be drawn based on these data alone.

Estimates from the National Health and Nutrition Examination Survey

Another regular source of estimates of the hearing ability of persons in the civilian noninstitutionalized population is the NHANES, which prior to 1974 was the Health Examination Survey. Household interviews are conducted on a stratified random sample of households chosen by the U.S. Bureau of the Census. At the conclusion of these interviews family members are asked to make appointments to appear at specially constructed mobile units where various examinations are conducted by medical teams, including doctors, nurses, and health technicians.

Because of the great expense involved in conducting such a survey, far fewer people are included in the NHANES sample than in the NHIS sample. Because relatively so few people are examined in a given year, data on specific topics are often collected on a specific subgroup of the population over a number of years (called *cycles*). This, of course, is done mainly to reduce the sampling error that would be associated with a single year's testing of a relatively small sample.

The second cycle of NHANES (NHANES II), conducted between 1976 and 1980, included a study to measure the hearing ability of youth 4 to 19 years of age. The sample included about 7300 such youth, of whom about 5900 were examined. Like the NHIS sample, the NHANES sample does not include residential students in schools for the deaf.

Health technicians trained by audiologists conducted the audiometric examinations of the youth. Extensive steps were taken to calibrate and maintain the equipment used throughout the country during the 4 years of testing. The results for the tested youth in the sample were weighted to correspond to the age, sex, and racial characteristics of the general population of the United States. (For a more complete description of NHANES II see McDowell, Engel, Massey, and Maurer, 1981.)

Table 1–2 shows the results of this study by age, sex, and race according to different levels of hearing loss measured in terms of better-ear averages. Broad groupings of decibel ranges are shown because of the large sampling errors associated with these data. An estimated 230,000 youth 6 to 17 years of age had a hearing level in the better ear of 26 dB or greater, and of these about 84,000 had a hearing level of 41 dB or greater. The estimates for higher degrees of hearing loss are not shown in Table 1–2 because the frequencies are too small to be distributed by any of the characteristics shown. The estimate of the number of youth 6 to 17 years of age with a hearing level of 91 dB or greater is 14,000.

Because of the magnitude of sampling errors associated with these estimates, even tentative conclusions cannot be drawn regarding the distribution shown in Table 1–2 for youth with a better-ear average of 41 dB or greater. The distributions for those with a hearing level of 26 dB or greater suggest that, in comparison to youth of the same age in the general population, they are proportionately overrepresented among the 12- to 17-year age group (60.4 percent compared to 53.6 percent), among males (67.0 percent compared to 50.9 percent), and among blacks (24.3 percent compared to 14.9 percent). Formally, however, none of these

Table 1–2. Number and Percent Distribution of Youth 6 to 17 Years of Age by Age, Sex, and Race, According to Better-Ear Average, United States: 1976 to 1980

Age, Sex, Race	All Averages†	Less than 26 dB	All	26–40	≥41
			26 dB and Greater		
		Better-Ear Average in Decibels*			
	Number of Youth (in thousands)				
All youth (6–17 years of age)‡	44,964	44,294	230	146	84§
Age					
6–11 years	20,880	20,597	92	76§	16§
12–17 years	24,084	23,697	139	70§	69§
Sex					
Male	22,886	22,477	154	100	54§
Female	22,077	21,818	77§	46§	31§
Race					
White	37,291	36,789	174	123	51§
Black	6,529	6,390	56§	23§	33§
	Percent Distribution				
All youth (6–17 years of age)	100.0	100.0	100.0	100.0	100.0
Age					
6–11 years	46.4	46.5	40.0	52.1§	19.0§
12–17 years	53.6	53.5	60.4	47.9§	82.1§
Sex					
Male	50.9	50.7	67.0	68.5	64.3§
Female	49.1	49.3	33.5§	31.5§	36.9§
Race‖					
White	85.1	85.2	75.7	84.2	60.7§
Black	14.9	14.8	24.3§	15.8§	39.3§

Source: Preliminary unpublished data from the National Health and Nutrition Examination Survey.
*Re: audiometric zero (ANSI, 1969).
†Includes unknown better-ear average.
‡Includes races other than white and black.
§Indicates estimate has a relative standard error of more than 30%.
‖Excludes races other than white and black.

differences reaches a 95 percent level of statistical significance.

Reconciliation and Summary of the Results

The data discussed in the previous two sections were intended to serve the same purpose: to estimate the number of hearing impaired youth in the general population and to describe them in terms of age, sex, race, and the degree of their hearing loss. However, the studies used radically different methods to measure the hearing ability of the youth included in the samples. Unless some type of correspondence can be established between these two types of measurement, the results of the studies cannot be compared. Specifically, the problem is to establish some type of equivalence between scores from the Gallaudet Hearing Scale and levels of better-ear averages determined by audiometric testing. If this can be done, the estimates from the two surveys can be compared, and if they are similar, greater confidence can be placed in the results of each.

Attempts have been made to equate levels of better-ear averages with degrees and types of limitation in the ability of persons to function in everyday activities (Committees, 1981) and in their ability to hear and understand speech (Davis and Silverman, 1970). The Health Examination Survey of NCHS summarized the survey's earlier finding on hearing loss in the general population in terms of the correspondence between decibel levels and speech comprehension established by the Committee on the Conservation of Hearing Loss (CCHL) (Roberts and Ahuja, 1975; Roberts and Huber, 1970). This equivalence between different levels in the ability to hear and understand speech and different degrees of hearing loss as measured in better-ear averages is shown in the right half of Table 1–3*

Most of the items of the Gallaudet Hearing Scale are phrased in terms of the ability to hear and understand speech (see Figure 1–1). If the various levels of the Gallaudet Hearing Scale can be equated with the descriptive statements shown on the right half of Table 1–3, then an indirect relationship would be established between the scale scores of the Gallaudet Hearing Scale and different levels of better-ear averages. On this basis the results of NHIS and NHANES discussed earlier could then be compared.

The CCHL statements are phrased in terms of a person's *inability* to hear and understand speech; the items from the Gallaudet Hearing Scale are phrased in terms of the *ability* to hear and understand speech. To minimize the effects of this difference in phrasing, the items of the Gallaudet Hearing Scale have been translated into statements regarding the *inability* to hear and understand speech. These translated statements along with their corresponding scale scores are shown in the left half of Table 1–3. The pairs of statements are arranged in a manner meant to indicate which ones are most similar.

This proposed statement-by-statement correspondence is, of course, not perfect. However, because the primary interest here is in only broad groupings of levels of hearing loss, it is important only that the categories correspond as closely as possible at the points distinguishing these groupings. A lack of correspondence of pairs of statements within a grouping will not affect the estimate associated with the overall grouping. The NHIS

---

*There is some ambiguity whether a threshold of 25, 26, or 27 dB should be used to demarcate the point at which a hearing handicap begins (Davis, 1965). This has no practical significance for this discussion, and 26 dB is used in this chapter in the discussion even if some of the cited data from other studies use 25 or 27 dB.

Table 1-3. Correspondence among Measured Degrees of Hearing Loss and Descriptions of Ability to Understand Speech

Gallaudet Hearing Scale Score	Summary Descriptions of Items Included in the Gallaudet Hearing Scale	Classification of Hearing Impairments by Speech Comprehension Groups with Different Levels of Better-Ear Averages Proposed by the Committee on Conservation of Hearing Loss	Better-Ear Average
1	Usually can hear and understand whispered speech	No significant difficulty with faint speech	Less than 26 dB
2	Difficulty hearing and understanding whispered speech	Difficulty only with faint speech	26–40 dB
3	Difficulty hearing and understanding shouted speech	Frequent difficulty with normal speech	41–70 dB
4	Difficulty hearing and understanding shouted speech, but can usually hear and understand words spoken loudly into the better ear	Understands only shouted or amplified speech	71–90 dB
5–8	Cannot hear and understand any speech	Usually cannot understand even amplified speech	91 dB or more

data were earlier discussed mainly in terms of scale scores 3 to 8 (*can at best hear and understand shouted speech*) and 5 to 8 (*cannot hear and understand any speech*). Within this context the only relevant question is whether the proposed correspondence is satisfactory at the points distinguishing these groups. In other words, if *difficulty hearing and understanding normal speech* means about the same as *frequent difficulty with normal speech*, and *cannot hear and understand any speech* means about the same as *usually cannot understand even amplified speech*, then a scale score of 3 corresponds to a better-ear average in the 41 to 70 dB range, and a scale score of 5 to a better-ear average of 91 dB or more. If this correspondence is accepted as approximately correct, then the NHIS results based on scale scores can be compared to the NHANES II results stated in terms of better-ear averages.

There is, of course, a much better way of establishing a correspondence between Gallaudet Hearing Scale scores and better-ear averages. This would involve administering both measures to a sample of the general population and then comparing the resulting scale scores and better-ear averages for each of the persons tested. Two such studies have been conducted. In relation to the primary interests of this chapter, they were not conclusive for two reasons: first, the populations studied included only adults; and second, the number of sample cases for those with moderate-to-profound hearing losses was small, and the sampling errors are therefore very large, making comparisons between the groups somewhat tenuous. Because these are the only results available, they are discussed briefly in spite of these limitations.

The results for a sample of adults 18 years of age and over from the Philadelphia metropolitan area studied in 1966 (Schein et al., 1970) indicated that a scale score of 3 was associated with a mean better-ear average of 44.4 dB, which is very close to the lower bound (41 dB) of the category with which it is associated in Table 1–3. Only four persons in the sample had a scale score of 5 or greater, making any comparison at this level of no practical significance.

A study conducted during 1974–1975 by NHANES on a sample of more than 3000 persons 25 to 74 years of age in the general population used both types of hearing loss measures on each person (Ries, 1985). A scale score of 3 was found to correspond to a better-ear average of 37.2 dB. As in the case of the study previously discussed, this is close to the lower bound of the category with which it is associated in Table 1–3. In this study none of the sampled persons had a scale score of 5; however, the mean better-ear average of persons scoring 6 to 8 on the Gallaudet Hearing Scale was 84.1 dB. This is somewhat lower than the corresponding category of 91 dB or more shown in Table 1–3. However, when sampling error is taken into account, the difference is not necessarily significant.

The results of these two studies do not, of course, prove that the correspondences shown in Table 1–3 are precise. At best they suggest that the correspondences are reasonably close; at a minimum they do not substantially contradict these correspondences, and the results do not rule out their use as a basis for comparing the estimates from the NHIS and NHANES II studies of hearing loss in the general population.

Before proceeding to this comparison, it should be recalled that neither the NHIS nor the NHANES samples included residential students in schools for the deaf. Thus, in order to compare these results, the residential students 6 to 17 years of age must be added to both sets of estimates. In 1978, the approximate midpoint of the period during which NHANES II was conducted, there were approximately 17,000 residential students in schools for the deaf who had a hearing level of 41 dB or greater; of these, about 10,000 had a hearing level of 91 dB or greater.

In 1974, the midpoint of the two NHIS surveys, there were approximately 11,000 resident students in schools for the deaf who had a hearing level of 41 dB or greater; of these about 7000 had a hearing level of 91 dB or greater. In the following discussion the NHANES and NHIS estimates discussed earlier have been augmented by the number of resident students given here.

The augmented NHIS estimate of youth in the general population 6 to 17 years of age who could at best hear and understand shouted speech (a Gallaudet Hearing Scale score of 3 or greater) is 140,000; the augmented NHANES estimate for those with an average hearing level of 41 dB or greater for the better ear is 101,000. These estimates are within each other's 95 percent confidence intervals, and the difference between them is not statistically significant.

The augmented NHIS estimate of the number of those youth who cannot hear and understand any speech (a Gallaudet Hearing Scale score of 5 or greater) is 30,000; the augmented NHANES estimate of those youth with a hearing level of 91 dB or greater for their better-ear average is 24,000.* Lest a false sense of precision be implied by the similarity of these estimates, it should be noted that the 95 percent confidence interval of the NHIS estimate ranges from about 18,000 to about 42,000, and that of the NHANES estimate is, relatively, even larger. On the other hand, the similarity of the two independent estimates suggests that the true num-

*Since a better-ear average of 91 dB or greater is frequently equated with the term *deaf*, these estimates may appear to be completely out of line with the estimate of about 86,000 deaf youth 6 to 16 years of age as reported by the National Census of Deaf People (NCDP) (Schein and Delk, 1974). However, beyond the slight difference in the age groups and the fact that sampling variation is associated with both the NCDP estimate and the estimates shown above, the major factor explaining the difference relates to definitions. The NCDP defined deafness in a manner that more closely resembles (but is not identical with) the concept of "can at best hear and understand shouted speech." As such, the NCDP results are not directly comparable with those under discussion here concerning profound hearing loss.

ber of these youth in the general population is closer to the estimates themselves than it is to either of the limits of the confidence interval just stated.

Regarding the characteristics of hearing impaired youth, whereas the distributions shown earlier for both NHIS and NHANES were not conclusive because of sampling error, they did agree that males and blacks were proportionately overrepresented. The two studies appear to disagree with regard to the age distributions: in comparison to the general population the NHIS results suggest that the 6- to 11-year-old hearing impaired youth were proportionately overrepresented, whereas the NHANES II results suggest that 12- to 17-year-old hearing impaired youth were proportionately overrepresented.

However, this difference can be explained in terms of the rubella epidemic of 1963 to 1965. According to Annual Survey data, during the 1970s the hearing impairment of about 18 percent of youth with a significant bilateral hearing loss was caused by rubella. In 1974, the temporal reference point of the NHIS results, this so-called "rubella bulge" was located among the 6- to 11-year-old youth. At the end of 1978, the temporal reference point of the NHANES results, these youth were in the 12- to 17-year-old range. Thus, however tenuous might be any conclusions drawn regarding the age distributions of these youth from either of the surveys, the difference of the estimates for the age group are in line with what might be expected as a result of the earlier rubella epidemic, as well as the different times the NHIS and NHANES surveys were conducted.

CHARACTERISTICS OF STUDENTS IN THE ANNUAL SURVEY OF HEARING IMPAIRED CHILDREN AND YOUTH IN RELATION TO HEARING IMPAIRED YOUTH IN THE GENERAL POPULATION

Only a small proportion of the research conducted on hearing impaired youth is based on a national probability sample of these youth. Most of the research is based on studies of those hearing impaired youth who are receiving special educational, rehabilitation, or clinical services in a local setting. This is, of course, highly desirable when the studies are intended to provide guidance in solving particular problems in a local setting. However, serious limitations may result from generalizing the results of these studies to all hearing impaired youth in the United States.

The Annual Survey of Hearing Impaired Children and Youth attempts to maintain an annually updated data base on all students who are receiving special educational services for the hearing impaired in the United States. Two questions naturally occur about such a data base. First, to what degree are the students reported to the survey representative of all hearing impaired youth in the country? Second, to what degree are they representative of all of the students receiving special educational services for the hearing impaired? The first question is considered in this section; the second, in a later section.

Because the degree of hearing loss of the students included in the Annual Survey is measured in terms of better-ear averages, it appears more reasonable to make the comparison in terms of the audiometric results from NHANES. However, because the sampling errors associated with the NHANES estimates are so much larger than those of the NHIS estimates, the comparison is made on the basis of the NHIS results. This follows the practice of the previous section of equating the category "at best can hear and understand shouted speech" with a better-ear average of 41 dB or greater and of equating the category "cannot hear and understand any speech" with a better-ear average of 91 dB or greater. To avoid the cumbersome phrases defining these categories, the former group is referred to as *moderately-to-profoundly hearing impaired* and to the latter group as *profoundly hearing impaired*.

Table 1–4 shows the distribution of hearing impaired youth 6 to 17 years of age included in the Annual Survey during the 1974–1975 academic year by age, sex, race, and degree of hearing loss. The first thing that is noticeably different about these students in comparison to the hearing impaired youth in the general population discussed earlier is their distribution by degree of hearing loss. As may be noted, only about 2000 of the approximately 39,000 students included in the Annual Survey had better-ear averages of less than 41 dB, whereas more than 34,000 had hearing levels of 41 dB or greater. Although this is not surprising for a group of students in educational programs for the hearing impaired, it reverses the relationship between degree of hearing loss and prevalence found in the general population, where prevalence tends to increase as the degree of hearing loss decreases.

For this reason, and because the total of about 39,000 students 6 to 17 years of age in the Annual Survey represents only a small fraction of the estimated 354,000 youth with a bilateral hearing impairment identified in Table 1–1, it is clear that studies based on Annual Survey data would not offer any basis for conclusions regarding all youth in the general population who have a bilateral hearing impairment. The same conclusion applies to the estimated 129,000 youth in the general population with a moderate-to-profound hearing loss (shown in Table 1–1), of whom only about 26 percent are included in the Annual Survey.

Given the relatively small number of youth in the general population who have a profound hearing loss and the relatively large number of such youth included in the Annual Survey, the question next arises whether

Table 1-4. Number and Percent Distribution of Students in the Annual Survey of Hearing Impaired Children and Youth by Age, Sex, and Race, According to Better-Ear Average, United States, 1974–1975

Age, Sex, Race	Better-Ear Average in Decibels*				Better-Ear Average in Decibels*			
	All Levels	Under 41	41–90	91 and Over	All Levels	Under 41	41–90	91 and Over
	Number of Students†				*Percent Distribution‡*			
All students (6–17 years of age)	38,521	2,413	17,245	17,166	100.0	100.0	100.0	100.0
Age								
6–11 years	21,373	1,326	9,614	9,480	55.5	55.0	55.7	55.2
12–17 years	17,148	1,087	7,631	7,686	44.5	45.0	44.3	44.8
Sex								
Male	20,802	1,366	9,539	9,008	54.1	56.7	55.4	52.5
Female	17,676	1,045	7,685	8,140	45.9	43.3	44.6	47.5
Race								
White	26,717	1,784	11,898	12,007	82.2	82.9	82.1	82.6
Black	5,770	367	2,601	2,525	17.8	17.1	17.9	17.4

*International Standards Organization.
†Totals include unknown sex, race, better-ear average, and other races.
‡Excludes unknowns and races other than white and black.

the survey data might serve as a basis for conclusions regarding profoundly hearing impaired youth in the general population.

Earlier it was estimated there were about 30,000 profoundly hearing impaired youth 6 to 17 years of age in the general population in 1974. Table 1–4 indicates that about 17,000 youth included in the Annual Survey have a hearing level of 91 dB or greater. This suggests that about 57 percent of the profoundly hearing impaired youth 6 to 17 years of age in the general population were included in the survey in the mid-1970s.

If this degree of inclusion is thought of as similar to a response rate in a survey, it is clearly near the lower bound of a generally acceptable range for drawing conclusions regarding a sampled population. However, when a nonresponse rate is as high as it is in this case (about 43 percent), an attempt should be made to compare the characteristics of respondents with those of the total population being studied to ascertain whether these two groups differ significantly. When they do, it is necessary to qualify the results of the survey in terms of possible biases related to these differences.

As noted earlier, because of sampling error nothing could be concluded about the characteristics of the estimated 30,000 youth 6 to 17 years of age with a profound hearing loss in the general population. As such, the characteristics of the students included in the Annual Survey cannot be directly compared to those youth. However, the characteristics of the broader group of moderately-to-profoundly hearing impaired youth were tentatively described. These youth were found to be proportionately over-represented among males, blacks, and the 6- to 11-year-old age group. This parallels the characteristics shown in Table 1–4 for students with a profound hearing loss who were included in the Annual Survey. Thus, at least in relation to these characteristics, there are no apparent significant differences between the profoundly hearing impaired youth included in the survey and in the general population.

There are other characteristics that might involve important differences (e.g., the age at onset of the hearing loss) of which nothing can be said because they are not included in the NHIS data. Finally, the fact that all youth included in the Annual Survey are receiving special education for the hearing impaired, whereas not all profoundly hearing impaired youth in the general population are receiving this type of education, may indicate that other differences exist between these two groups. However, within the context of these limitations it seems reasonable to conclude that the Annual Survey data can serve as a potentially useful basis for conclusions regarding profoundly hearing impaired youth in the general population.

CHARACTERISTICS OF STUDENTS RECEIVING SPECIAL EDUCATIONAL SERVICES FOR THE HEARING IMPAIRED

The third question raised in the introduction to this chapter was: How many youth in the United States are receiving special education for the hearing impaired? In discussing this issue three sources of information are considered: (a) data available from the Division of Educational Services for Special Educational Programs of the U.S. Department of Education; (b) recent results from the 1982 NHIS on youth receiving special educational services in the United States; and (c) evidence from the Center for Assessment and Demographic Studies (CADS), which, as one of its activities, conducts the Annual Survey.

Before considering the information from these sources, a possible conceptual issue should be clarified. The group being estimated and described in this section consists of students receiving special educational services for the hearing impaired and not of hearing impaired youth receiving special educational services. It may be assumed that any student receiving special educational services for the hearing impaired has some significant degree of hearing loss. However, it is incorrect to assume that a hearing impaired youth who is receiving special education is necessarily in a program for the hearing impaired. Because of another type of impairment that is more serious from an educational point of view than the youth's hearing impairment, a hearing impaired youth may be enrolled in a special program for another type of impairment.

This issue becomes particularly complicated when multiply handicapped youth and special educational programs for the multiply handicapped are considered. The number being estimated would include a hearing impaired student in a so-called multiply handicapped unit in a special educational program for hearing impaired youth. However, it would not include a hearing impaired student in a program for the multiply handicapped, unless such a program had a unit or made special provisions for its hearing impaired students. Only in this latter case would the youth be receiving special education for the hearing impaired.

As will become apparent, this issue has important repercussions regarding the estimates from the sources included in the following discussion.

Estimates from the U.S. Department of Education

The first source of information to be considered is associated with U.S. Public Laws 89-313 and 94-142. Both of these laws mandate federal support to the states for the education of handicapped youth. In return, the states are required to annually report information to the U.S. Department of Education on the students served and on the programs offering these educational services. The U.S. Department of Education processes and analyzes this information and, since 1979, has submitted an annual report to the U.S. Congress on the results.

The information on students is submitted on the basis of guidelines supplied by the U.S. Department of Education. However, the decisions on how these guidelines are applied are made in each of the 50 states. The students are classified in terms of 11 categories of handicaps—or perhaps more precisely 10, since one of the categories is multiply handicapped. The ten others include the categories deaf, hard of hearing, and deaf-blind. (For a more extensive discussion of the data collection procedure, see Stearns, Kaskowitz, and Norwood, 1977.)

Classification in terms of the nature of the handicap rather than in terms of the nature of the program in which the student is enrolled creates a difficulty in using this source to estimate the number of students receiving special education for the hearing impaired. However, it is reasonable to assume that because students are classified *not* by all the handicaps they might have but rather by their primary handicap, this primary handicap corresponds to the type of special education they are receiving. On the other hand, it should be recognized that students classified under some of the other categories not apparently related to hearing loss may indeed have some degree of hearing loss. Although these hearing impaired students are receiving special educational services, they should not be included in the number being estimated for those receiving services for the hearing impaired.

The issue is particularly complicated in relation to the approximately 64,000 students 6 to 17 years of age classified in the 1982 report to the U.S. Congress as multiply handicapped. Some of these students may be in units for the hearing impaired, in which case they should be included in the estimate. On the other hand, others among them with a hearing impairment may not be receiving special educational services focused on their hearing impairment. These students should not be included in the number being estimated. Because these 64,000 multiply handicapped students cannot be classified in terms of this distinction on the basis of the U.S. Department of Education report, none of them is included in the following estimates. This suggests that in relation to this factor these estimates may underrepresent to some degree the actual number of students receiving special education for the hearing impaired.

With these limitations in mind, the published data for the 1981–1982 school year (Division of Educational Services, Special Education Programs, 1983) indicate that there were about 68,000 youth 6 to 17 years of age receiving special education for the hearing impaired. Of these, about 23,000 were classified as deaf or deaf-blind, and about 45,000 as hard of hearing.*

Estimates from the 1982 National Health Interview Survey

Each year the U.S. Division of Health Interview Statistics classifies persons included in its survey according to whether they have any long-term limitations of activity. In 1982 a new item was included in that part of the questionnaire that serves as the basis for classifying young persons in this area. The question asks: "Does _____ attend a special school or special classes because of any impairment or health problem?" When a positive response to this question is obtained, the respondent is asked to name all of the conditions or impairments that cause the limitation. If more than one is named, the respondent is asked to indicate the health problem or impairment that is the major cause of the limitation. For youth under 18 years of age the respondent is ordinarily an adult family member (usually a parent or guardian) living in the same household.

Table 1–5 shows the preliminary unpublished results for this item for hearing impaired youth 6 to 17 years of age who were limited in activity. The data are categorized by age, sex, race, how the hearing impairment was causally related to the limitation, and whether the youth were attending a special school or classes. Columns 2 and 3 show that of the estimated 156,000 who were limited in activity at least in part by a hearing impairment about 99,000 were attending special schools or classes.

This latter estimate appears high in relation to the U.S. Department of Education estimates discussed earlier. However, it should be noted that both of the estimates given include youth for whom a hearing problem is not the major cause of the limitation and who are receiving some type of special education. It would include, for instance, a youth with a profound learning disability and a mild hearing loss who was enrolled in a special educational program for learning disabilities.

In the previous section it was assumed that students with more than one handicap were classified in terms of their major handicap and that this would tend to correspond to the type of special education they were receiving. The data shown in columns 4 and 5 of Table 1–5 are for students whose hearing impairment was reported as the major cause of their limitation. The estimates associated with this classification indicate that of the 135,000 youth 6 to 17 years of age whose hearing impairment was

---

*The data are collected on students 3 to 21 years of age. Only the data related to U.S. Public Law 94-142 are reported by age, and it was therefore necessary to take the percentage of these students who were 6 to 17 years of age and apply this factor to the total of students 3 to 21 years of age reported in relation to U.S. Public Law 89-313 to arrive at the grand total of about 68,000 for the 6- to 17-year-old age group being aided under both laws.

Table 1-5. Number and Percent Distribution of Youth 6 to 17 Years of Age with Hearing Losses, by Age, Sex, Race, Whether the Hearing Loss Is the Major Cause of the Limitations, and Program Type; United States, 1982

Age, Sex, Race	All Youth 6–17 Years of Age	Hearing Loss Is One of the Causes of Limitation		Hearing Loss Is the Major Cause of Limitation	
		All	Attends Special School or Classes	All	Attends Special School or Classes
		Number of Youth (in thousands)			
All youth (6–17 years of age)*	41,999	156	99	135	82
Age					
6–11 years	19,756	88	56	73	43
12–17 years	22,243	68	43	62	39
Sex					
Male	21,487	99	61	79	45
Female	20,512	57	38†	56	36†
Race					
White	34,508	128	78	110	63
Black	6,153	29†	21†	25†	19†
		Percent Distribution			
All youth (6–17 years of age)	100.0	100.0	100.0	100.0	100.0
Age					
6–11 years	47.0	56.4	56.6	54.1	52.4
12–17 years	53.0	43.6	43.4	45.9	47.6
Sex					
Male	51.2	63.5	61.6	58.5	54.9
Female	48.8	36.5	38.4†	41.5	43.9†
Race‡					
White	84.9	81.5	78.8	81.5	76.8
Black	15.1	18.5†	21.2†	18.5†	23.2†

Source: Preliminary unpublished data from the National Health Interview Survey.
*Includes races other than white and black.
†Indicates estimate has a relative standard error of more than 30%.
‡Percent distributions for race exclude races other than white and black.

the major cause of their limitation, about 82,000 were attending special schools or classes. On the basis of the assumption stated previously, it is reasonable to infer that most of these youth were in programs for the hearing impaired. However, some may not be, and to this degree the NHIS estimate would tend to slightly overrepresent the number of students receiving special education for the hearing impaired.

As was the case in the earlier discussion of NHIS results, the estimates being discussed here do not include resident students in schools for the deaf. In the 1981–1982 school year there were approximately 8000 such students with a hearing level of 41 dB or greater. Adding these students to the NHIS estimate produces an overall estimate of about 90,000 students in special educational programs for the hearing impaired.

This estimate is higher than the corresponding estimate of about 68,000 students derived from the U.S. Department of Education data discussed in the previous section. However, this latter estimate is within the 95 percent confidence interval of the NHIS estimate, even when the possible effect of the under- and overrepresentation of the two estimates noted previously—which would decrease the difference between them—is ignored.

The hearing supplement was not included in the 1982 NHIS, and the degree of hearing loss of the estimated 82,000 students was distinguished only in terms of the general information asked about all conditions reported in the survey. On this basis (and including the residential students identified) about 31,000 of the 90,000 were classified as "deaf" and the remaining 59,000 as "other kinds of hearing loss." Given the amount of sampling error associated with these estimates, they are relatively close to those cited in the previous discussion of the U.S. Department of Education estimates (23,000 deaf and 45,000 hard of hearing).

Because the 1982 NHIS results include only 1 year of data, less can be said about the distribution of the students by age, sex, and race than could be said of the NHIS results discussed earlier, which were based on 2 years of data combined. Table 1–5 suggests that 6- to 11-year-old, male, and black hearing impaired youth were proportionately overrepresented among those attending special schools or classes in comparison to all youth in the general population. However, because of the very large sampling errors associated with these estimates, the relationships are, at best, suggestive.

Estimates from the Center for Assessment and Demographic Studies

The Center for Assessment and Demographic Studies has been in continuing contact with the administrative and professional staffs of most of the special educational programs for hearing impaired youth in the United States since its origin in 1968. This has been necessary in order to elicit staff support in submitting data on their students on an annual basis. Programs are continually being created, merged, closed, or redefined; and because these changes have important implications for maintaining and improving the data base of the Annual Survey, a significant portion of the staff's activities is devoted to maintaining an up-to-date account of such programs, including those who do not submit data on their students on an annual basis.

The usual reason for a program's failure to participate in the Annual Survey is a lack of the personnel or resources needed to complete an annual questionnaire on each of the program's students. In most cases, however, the programs are at least willing to indicate the number of students they are serving. As such, aside from the data available in their data file, the survey staff is able to maintain a running estimate of the number of students in known programs that are not included in the survey.

Such an estimate cannot, of course, include students in programs unknown to the Annual Survey. However, even here some idea about the size of this *unknown* group is obtained through another of CADS's activities. From time to time particular states initiate a cooperative project with CADS to make a special effort to identify every special educational program for the hearing impaired in their state, regardless of the size of the program. These intense efforts inevitably discover some programs that, on the basis of the previous efforts, were not known to CADS. These are ordinarily part-time programs including only a small number of students with lesser degrees of hearing loss who may receive as little as a few hours a week of special assistance from an itinerant teacher of the deaf.

As a result of such special state projects the number of students in a given state in programs known to CADS before the project can be compared to the total number of students, including those students identified as a result of the project. The difference between these numbers for each of these states can be averaged and this average used to project a national total of students receiving special education for the hearing impaired. Such a procedure assumes, of course, that the percentage of undercoverage is similar in the states in which such special projects have been conducted and in those in which no such projects were conducted.

Based on these sources of information, CADS estimates that in the 1982–1983 school year there were 75,000 to 80,000 students 3 to 21 years of age receiving special educational services for the hearing impaired in the United States. The rounded midpoint of this range estimate is 78,000. About 83 percent of the students 3 to 21 years of age in the U.S. Department of Education study were 6 to 17 years of age. Applying this percentage to the CADS estimate (i.e., $0.83 \times 78,000$) produces an estimate of about 65,000 students 6 to 17 years of age who received special education for the hearing impaired in the 1982–1983 school year.

CHARACTERISTICS OF STUDENTS IN THE ANNUAL SURVEY OF HEARING IMPAIRED CHILDREN AND YOUTH IN RELATION TO STUDENTS RECEIVING SPECIAL EDUCATIONAL SERVICES FOR THE HEARING IMPAIRED

To compare the hearing impaired students included in the Annual Survey with all students receiving special education for the hearing impaired, it is desirable to have a single estimate for each of the characteristics to be considered. Given the differences in the methods used to produce the estimates from the three sources just discussed, there is little justification in attempting to formally pool the results from each of the studies. Rather, because they are based on a census procedure and therefore do not contain the sampling variability of the 1982 NHIS estimates, and are not lacking a formal statistical basis as does the expert opinion that served as the basis of the CADS estimate, the U.S. Department of Education estimates of the number of students receiving special education for the hearing impaired and the numbers who are deaf and hard of hearing are used in the following comparison. Aside from methodological consideration, the fact that the estimate from this source (68,000) falls between the estimates from the other two sources (90,000 based on the 1982 NHIS and 65,000 from CADS) suggests a further reason for this choice.

The distributions of the students 6 to 17 years of age included in the Annual Survey during 1982–1983 by age, sex, and race according to their degree of hearing loss are shown in Table 1–6. The total of about 39,000 students represents about 57 percent of the 68,000 students estimated from the U.S. Department of Education data as enrolled in special education for the hearing impaired. This percentage of coverage is low enough so that the distributions of the characteristics of the students included in the Annual Survey have to be considered before it can be concluded that these students are representative of all students receiving special education for the hearing impaired.

As noted before, the age, sex, and race distribution of the 1982 NHIS estimates shown in the previous section were too uncertain to serve as a basis for describing all of the students in the United States receiving special educational services for the hearing impaired. However, in relation to sex and race, each of the studies considered in this chapter indicates that, in comparison to the general population, males and blacks are proportionately overrepresented among youth with a moderate-to-profound

Table 1-6. Number and Percent Distribution of Students in the Annual Survey of Hearing Impaired Children and Youth by Age, Sex, and Race, According to Better-Ear Average, United States, 1982–1983

Age, Sex, Race	Better-Ear Average in Decibels*				Better-Ear Average in Decibels*			
	All Levels	Under 41	41–90	91 and Over	All Levels	Under 41	41–90	91 and Over
	Number of Students				Percent Distribution‡			
All students (6–17 years of age)	38,790†	5,915	15,907	16,234	100.0	100.0	100.0	100.0
Age								
6–11 years	16,567	2,969	6,698	6,586	42.7	50.2	42.1	40.6
12–17 years	22,223	2,946	9,209	9,648	57.3	49.8	57.9	59.4
Sex								
Male	20,784	3,241	8,649	8,520	53.9	55.6	54.6	52.7
Female	17,777	2,591	7,189	7,649	46.1	44.4	45.4	47.3
Race								
White	25,673	3,976	10,532	10,749	79.8	81.8	79.4	79.6
Black	6,510	885	2,730	2,763	20.2	18.2	20.6	20.4

*International Standards Organization.

†Includes unknown sex, race, better-ear average, and races other than white and black.

‡Excludes unknowns.

hearing impairment. It is, therefore, highly likely that the overrepresentation for males and blacks shown in Table 1-6 reflects the actual distribution of these characteristics for hearing impaired youth in the general population and in special education for the hearing impaired.

With regard to the age distribution shown in Table 1-6, no comparison with age distribution of the 1971 and 1977 NHIS and the 1976 to 1980 NHANES II shown earlier is possible because the so-called "rubella bulge" was included in the 6- to 17-year-old age range in the mid-1970s, whereas only the tail end of this bulge was included in the 1982 data. The age distribution shown in Table 1-5 for moderately-to-profoundly hearing impaired students receiving special education is, as has been noted, of little consequence because of the sampling errors associated with those estimates. Thus, in terms of the data discussed in this chapter, nothing can be concluded about the representativeness of the age distribution of students described in Table 1-6.

The previous section did offer estimates of the number of deaf and hard-of-hearing students receiving special education for the hearing impaired. To compare those estimates with the data shown in Table 1-6, the problem of making different measures of hearing loss comparable must be addressed once more. The following discussion assumes that "deaf" corresponds to a better-ear average of 91 dB or greater and that "hard of hearing" corresponds to all lesser degrees of hearing loss.

The approximately 16,000 students shown in Table 1-6 as having a hearing level of 91 dB or greater represent about 70 percent of the previously estimated 23,000 deaf students receiving special education for the hearing impaired. The approximately 22,000 students with a level less than 91 dB shown in Table 1-6 represent about 49 percent of the 45,000 students identified in the previous section as hard of hearing. It should be noted that none of these estimates has sampling errors associated with them, and therefore differences between them cannot be explained in terms of sampling variability.

This indicates that, in relation to all of the students receiving special education for the hearing impaired in the United States, profoundly hearing impaired students are overrepresented in the Annual Survey. It would thus appear that for attributes associated with the degree of hearing loss, results based on Annual Survey data may be somewhat biased in the direction of the attributes of profoundly hearing impaired students. This conclusion is consistent with a point made earlier in relation to the CADS estimate of students receiving special education for the hearing impaired. There it was noted that the types of programs discovered by CADS in those states where a special effort was made to find all special educational programs for the hearing impaired not included in the Annual Survey were almost inevitably part-time programs. Because students in part-time programs have a lesser degree of hearing loss than do those in full-time programs (Rawlings, 1973), it is reasonable to expect that the Annual Survey file contains proportionately fewer students with lesser degrees of hearing loss and more students with profound hearing losses than are found in the population of all special educational programs for the hearing impaired.

In light of these considerations, conclusions based on Annual Survey data are more likely to be unbiased when they are restricted to conclusions on specific subgroups of the students defined in terms of levels of hearing loss or in terms of whether they are full-time or part-time special education students. Other possible biases would, of course, have to be considered in the context of the major variables included in any particular study using these data.

When the limitations noted here are heeded, it appears that the Annual Survey data offer a good basis for drawing conclusions about students receiving special educational services for the hearing impaired in the United States. However, conclusions regarding profoundly hearing impaired students and students in full-time special education for the hearing impaired will have a firmer basis than conclusions regarding students with lesser degrees of hearing loss or those receiving part-time services.

SUMMARY AND CONCLUSIONS

Precise figures on the number and characteristics of hearing impaired youth in the United States in the general population or in special educational programs for the hearing impaired do not exist. By using data from several different sources it is possible to draw some tentative conclusions about these youth. However, because much of these data are derived from surveys based on relatively small samples, the sampling variation associated with the estimates is very large. Also, the fact that such an endeavor must rely on the results of several surveys—most of which use different definitions and different methods of measuring hearing loss and were conducted at different times—necessitates a considerable effort to reconcile the results.

With these limitations in mind, the following description of hearing impaired youth in the general population has emerged from the discussion. In the mid-1970s there were about 354,000 youth 6 to 17 years of age who had a bilateral hearing loss. Of these, about 140,000 could at best hear and understand shouted speech, and about 30,000 of this latter group could not hear and understand any speech, including shouted speech.

In relation to the general population males and blacks were proportionately overrepresented among these hearing impaired youth.

Additional problems arise in attempting to estimate the number and characteristics of students receiving special educational services for hearing impaired youth. One major difficulty is determining what type of special education a youth with a hearing impairment is actually receiving. Complications arise particularly in the case of multiply handicapped children whose other handicapping conditions are equal to or more serious than their hearing impairment. It is often difficult to determine whether these youth are receiving special education for the hearing impaired or, alternatively, special education for a different handicap.

Given these added limitations, it was estimated that in 1982 there were about 68,000 youth 6 to 17 years of age receiving special educational services for the hearing impaired. Of these, about 23,000 were classified as deaf. The remaining 45,000 students had lesser degrees of hearing loss. Although the data on these students' characteristics were inconclusive, it appears that males and blacks were proportionately overrepresented among these hearing impaired students.

The other question that received considerable attention in the discussion was the degree to which the students 6 to 17 years of age represented in the yearly updated data file of the Annual Survey represent hearing impaired youth in the general population and in special education for the hearing impaired.

In relation to the general population, it was concluded that the Annual Survey data should not be used to describe all hearing impaired youth or even all bilaterally hearing impaired youth. Most of these youth in the general population have a mild-to-moderate hearing loss; the overwhelming majority of the students included in the Annual Survey have a severe-to-profound hearing loss. However, because so many youth with a profound hearing loss are included in the survey, the data on these youth can be used as a basis for drawing conclusions about profoundly hearing impaired youth in the general population. Since only about 6 out of 10 of these youth were included in the Annual Survey, care would have to be taken, of course, to qualify results derived from the survey data in relation to possible biases. In relation to sex and race, the distributions of students included in the Annual Survey appear to be similar to those of hearing impaired youth in the general population. The situation in regard to age is somewhat complicated by the fact that the so-called ''rubella bulge'' was moving through the age group under consideration during the period including the studies that have been discussed. As such, no conclusions could be drawn about the representativeness of the Annual Survey students along this dimension.

These conclusions are based on data from the mid-1970s and they apply to more recent years only to the degree that any changes in the number and characteristics of profoundly hearing impaired youth in the general population have been reflected by corresponding changes in the Annual Survey data.

The situation is somewhat more complicated *in relation to students in special educational programs for the hearing impaired*. Even though the 1982–1983 Annual Survey file appears to include about 6 of every 10 of these students, the students included in the Annual Survey do not appear to be representative of all students receiving special education for the hearing impaired. The students included in the survey are probably proportionately overrepresented among those with a profound hearing loss and those receiving full-time special educational services. (The Annual Survey file contains about 7 of 10 students with a profound loss and those in full-time special education programs, compared to about 5 of 10 for students with a moderate hearing loss or those attending part-time special educational programs for the hearing impaired.) Because of this, conclusions based on these data are more likely to be accurate when framed in terms of subgroups defined by their degree of hearing loss or by whether they are receiving full- or part-time special education rather than for the group as a whole.

These summary judgments are, of course, based on considerations related only to age, sex, race, degree of hearing loss, and the extent of the services received. Particular studies based on the Annual Survey data involving characteristics highly associated with factors not discussed (e.g., age at onset) would have to consider how representative the Annual Survey data were in relation to these factors.

However, the limitations associated with the use of the national data base of the Annual Survey would appear to be small compared to those of basing generalizations about all hearing impaired youth in the country or in special education for the hearing impaired on small local groups of these youth.

REFERENCES

Committees on the Definition of Hearing Handicap. (1981). On the definition of hearing handicap. *ASHA, 23* (4), 293–297.

Davis, H. (assisted by the Subcommittee on Hearing in Adults for the Committee on Conservation of Hearing of the American Academy of Ophthalmology and Otolaryngology). (1965). Guide for the classification and evaluation of hearing handicap in relation to the international audiometric zero. *Transactions of the American Academy of Ophthalmology and Otolaryngology, 69,* 740–751.

Davis, H., and Silverman, S. R. (1970). *Hearing and deafness* (3rd ed.). New York: Holt, Rinehart and Winston.

Division of Educational Services, Special Education Programs. (1983). *Fifth annual report to Congress on the implementation of Public Law 94-142: The education for all handicapped children act*. Washington, DC: U.S. Department of Education.

Gentile, A. (1975). *Persons with impaired hearing: United States, 1971* (Series 10, No. 101, DHEW Publication No. HRA 76-1528). Washington, DC: National Center for Health Statistics, Vital and Health Statistics.

McDowell, A., Engel, A., Massey, J. T., and Maurer, K. (1981). *Plan and operation of the second National Health and Nutrition Examination Survey, 1976-80* (Series 1, No. 15, DHHS Publication No. PHS 81-1317). Washington, DC: National Center for Health Statistics, Vital and Health Statistics.

Rawlings, B. (1973). *Characteristics of hearing impaired students by hearing status, United States: 1970-71* (Series D, No. 10). Washington, DC: Gallaudet College, Office of Demographic Studies.

Ries, P.W. (1982). *Hearing ability of persons by sociodemographic and health characteristics: United States* (Series 10, No. 140, DHHS Publication No. PHS 82-1568). Washington, DC: National Center for Health Statistics, Vital and Health Statistics.

Ries, P.W. (1985). The demography of hearing loss. In H. Orlans (Ed.), *Adjustment to adult hearing loss* (pp. 3–21). San Diego: College-Hill Press, Inc.

Roberts, J., and Ahuja, E.M. (1975). *Hearing levels of youths 12-17 years: United States* (Series 11 No. 145, DHEW Publication No. HRA 75-1627). Washington, DC: National Center for Health Statistics.

Roberts, J., and Huber, P. (1970). *Hearing levels of children by age and sex* (PHS Publication No. 1000, Series 11, No. 2). Washington, DC: National Center for Health Statistics.

Schein, J.D., and Delk, M.T. (1974). *The deaf population of the United States*. Silver Spring, MD: National Association of the Deaf.

Schein, J.D., Gentile, A., and Haase, K.W. (1970). *Development and evaluation of an expanded hearing loss scale questionnaire*, Series 2, No. 37. Rockville, MD: National Center for Health Statistics, Vital and Health Statistics. Government Printing Office.

Stearns, M.S., Kaskowitz, D., and Norwood, C. (1977). *A methodological report*. Prepared for Bureau of Education for the Handicapped, U.S. Office of Education, Washington, DC.

Chapter 2

Etiological Trends, Characteristics, and Distributions

Scott Campbell Brown

Hearing impairments arise from many causes, some of which are known and others not known. This wide variety of causes yields a heterogeneous hearing impaired population in at least two ways. First, different causes can attack people of different locations, ages, sexes, and ethnicities, yielding a demographically diverse hearing impaired population. Second, causes can vary in the degree of hearing loss and in the presence of, number of, and type of additional handicaps that they bring about, resulting in a hearing impaired population that is diverse in its handicap-related characteristics.

This chapter does not attempt to explain why such differences occur. Rather, it first presents the distribution of reported causes of hearing loss in impaired school-aged children and youth during the 1982–1983 school year. Then, demographic and handicap-related similarities and differences associated with particular causes among the students are examined. Finally, important trends in the etiology of hearing loss during the past 10 years are explored, and some speculations on the causes that will have significant effects on the hearing impaired school-aged population in the future are considered.

The etiological trends and characteristics reported here indicate general tendencies. The findings do not provide diagnoses that apply to each hearing impairment due to a particular cause. However, to the extent that patterns do emerge, the etiology of hearing loss can be indicative of the characteristics and trends that occur overall among hearing impaired children and youth.

SOURCE AND QUALITY OF DATA

The data cited here were obtained primarily from the Annual Survey of Hearing Impaired Children and Youth for the 1982–1983 school year. The question on cause of hearing loss contained four sections, of which only one was to be completed. (The questionnaire appears in Appendix A.) The question on cause of hearing loss reads:

A. If onset at birth, what was the probable cause(s)?
   Maternal rubella
   Trauma at birth
   Heredity
   Prematurity
   Rh incompatibility
   Other complications of pregnancy
   Other
B. If onset after birth, what was the probable cause(s)?
   Meningitis
   High fever
   Mumps
   Infection
   Measles
   Otitis media
   Trauma
   Other
C. Cause cannot be determined (though attempt was made)
D. Data not available in student's record

More than one probable cause could be circled. This happened in very few cases. Of the 55,136 students included in the survey, only 4 percent had more than one cause circled. These students do not appear to have important characteristics and trends that warrant lengthy analysis.

Examination of reported etiology of hearing loss that uses data from the Annual Survey of Hearing Impaired Children and Youth is colored by one important fact: In the survey, there is always a large group of students for whom the cause of hearing impairment is unknown. In 1982–1983, these youth accounted for 39.5 percent of the students in the Annual Survey.

In the 1982–1983 survey, students for whom cause of hearing loss was unknown made up three subgroups. The largest group of those with an unknown cause was those who had a cause that could not be determined, even though an attempt was made (10,332 students). Almost as large was a group for whom the reporting source stated that there were no data available in the students' records (9771 students). The smallest group contained students for whom no answer was given, i.e., the question on the cause of hearing loss was left blank (1656 students).

Students for whom the cause of hearing loss was reported as unknown may have actual causes that are associated with the variables under study. For example, if there was a tendency for the cause of hearing loss for black children who inherit their deafness to be classified as unknown, then there may be a danger of erroneously concluding that the children who inherited their hearing loss were more likely to be nonblack. Several methods can be employed to estimate the cause of hearing loss among those for whom the etiologies are unknown.

One technique is to distribute them based upon other characteristics known to be associated with particular causes. The weakness in such an approach is that one cannot then use the imputed data to demonstrate a relation between a cause and the very same characteristics used to impute that cause to an unknown. Such a classification of the *unknowns* diminishes the quality of the *known* cause data.

Another method is to obtain a sample of the students whose cause of hearing loss is unknown, attempt to determine the causes medically, and impute the distribution of these diagnoses to all of the hearing losses for which the cause is unknown. The resources to accurately perform such a procedure were not available at the time of this writing.

Although a large proportion of hearing impaired students in the Annual Survey had a cause reported as unknown, the actual cause of a substantial majority of these students was probably either genetic or congenital rubella syndrome (CRS). According to Nance and Sweeney (1975), hereditary factors are known to account for no less than half of all prelingual hearing loss. As demonstrated later, the overwhelming majority of students in the survey had such a hearing loss. Given that genetic causes account for less than half of the reported known causes in the Annual Survey, they must account for over half of the unknown causes. Moreover, given that the rubella epidemic occurred between 1963 and 1965 and that the number of students born in 1964 and 1965 reported in the Annual Survey with unknown causes is higher than for the years immediately following, it is likely that maternal rubella was the cause of hearing loss for many of these students.

When data for all students with hearing losses are presented, it is useful to remember that this unknown group made up a large part of the total in the 1982–1983 Annual Survey. It is also important to remember that the data were reported by the schools themselves and not medical authorities. This is a possible source for error, given that the schools were reporting *probable* causes. More potential for error exists because of the nature of special education programs. Some students may have been enrolled in these programs because of a handicap other than a hearing loss; yet, because they had a slight hearing loss, they were included in the Annual Survey.

These problems represent only limitations to be kept in mind when analyzing Annual Survey data. These data are the best available because no other data sources exist with the detail of information on etiology of hearing loss that is in the Annual Survey. Data for the 1982–1983 school year are important for study because by the end of that year many of the students with hearing loss caused by maternal rubella began to leave special education services. Hence, the 1982–1983 Annual Survey affords the final opportunity to examine the large number of children and youth with impairments due to congenital rubella syndrome. Moreover, the Annual Survey provides a good indication of future trends among students with hearing impairments. For these reasons, the 1982–1983 Annual Survey is an important source of information about the etiological trends, characteristics, and distributions of hearing impaired children and youth.

REPORTED ETIOLOGICAL DISTRIBUTIONS

Of the reported causes in the 1982–1983 Annual Survey, four stand out as warranting separate attention in this chapter: maternal rubella, heredity, meningitis, and otitis media. There are at least three important reasons for focusing on these causes. First, these four causes are somewhat more clearly defined than the other causes in the Annual Survey. Second, students with these causes tended to have unique traits. Third, as demonstrated by Figure 2-1, there were relatively large numbers of students for whom maternal rubella, heredity, and meningitis were reported as the probable cause of hearing loss. Each of these three causes was indicated for more than 4000 students, whereas the other causes were indicated for fewer than 2500 students each.

Of the reported causes, more students were reported to have hearing losses caused by maternal rubella than any other cause. Rubella, known to many people as German measles, usually results in minimal signs and symptoms: a slight backache, fever, a swelling of the neck, some muscular pain, a rash, cough, and nasal congestion (Masland, 1968). Gregg (1941) discovered the relation between maternal rubella and congenital birth defects. Calvert (1969) showed that when rubella occurs during the first month of pregnancy, there is a high probability that the child will have birth defects, a probability that lessens as the pregnancy advances. Shaver, Boughman, Kenyon, Mohanakumar, and Nance (1984) noted that the condition is really CRS, as the fetus actually contracts the disease. Hearing loss is one of many aspects of the syndrome that can occur. "The congenital rubella syndrome (CRS) is characterized by auditory, ocular, cardiac and neurologic defects which result from fetal infection with the

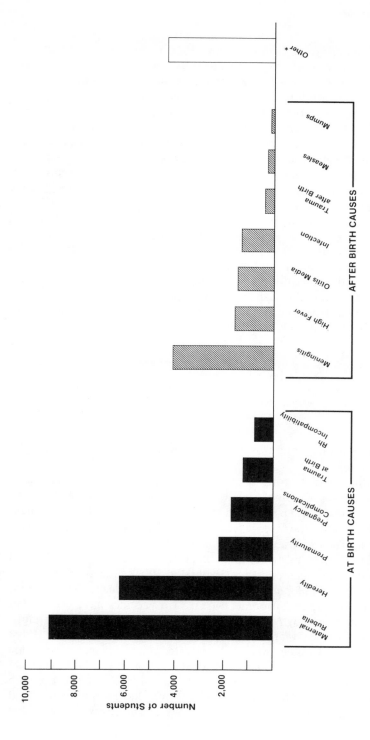

*Age at onset of hearing loss unknown.

Figure 2–1. Distribution of known causes of impairment for hearing impaired students.

rubella virus during early gestation'' (p. 382). Vernon (1967) placed opinion on the prevalence of hearing impairments among rubella births between 12 percent and 19 percent. Other anomalies, such as visual problems and heart disorders, are also associated with maternal rubella.

Epidemics of rubella are cyclic, tending to reach epidemic proportions every 6 to 10 years (Jensema, 1974; Stuckless and Hinman, 1983). The most recent one occurred between 1963 and 1965, resulting in a "deaf baby boom.'' Since the licensing of the vaccine against rubella in 1969, another epidemic has not occurred. By 1982–1983, the children whose hearing loss was caused by the 1963 to 1965 rubella epidemic were beginning to leave special education programs.

Among hearing impaired children in the 1982–1983 Annual Survey, those whose hearing loss was caused by maternal rubella tended to form a more cohesive group than those whose loss was from other causes. This cohesiveness, combined with the fact that this numerous group is leaving special education programs, makes the children whose impairment was caused by maternal rubella an important group to examine in this research.

Unlike maternal rubella, hereditary causes of deafness can be quite diverse. Rose, Conneally, and Nance (1977) have stated:

> The heterogeneity of genetic deafness can be demonstrated by clinical examination, family histories, or population data, or by a combination of these approaches. On the basis of the type of hearing loss, age at onset, severity, genetic mode of transmission, and associated clinical findings (pleiotropisms), over 50 types of hereditary hearing loss have been delineated. (p. 19)

This heterogeneous group was the second largest in size in the 1982–1983 Annual Survey.

The third largest group consisted of those children with meningitis reported as the known cause. Meningitis, an inflammation of the meninges, is usually the result of an infection by bacteria or viruses. (The meninges are the membranes, the three layers of animal tissue that serve as a covering or lining for the brain and spinal cord.)

Meningitis usually strikes after birth. Like heredity, meningitis can induce deafness in different ways (Paparella, 1977). One prevalent cause of meningitis is *Hemophilus influenzae* type B (Schlech, Ward, Band, Hightower, Fraser, and Broome, 1985). Two vaccines have been tested for meningitis caused by *Hemophilus influenzae* type B in 61 healthy adults of both sexes, 20 to 30 years of age. Lepow, Samuelson, and Gordon (1984) reported, "Both vaccines were well tolerated with no fever or systemic reactions. There were no significant local reactions" (p. 402). The vaccine has been licensed, and universal vaccination by 2 years of age with additional vaccination for certain at-risk groups has been recommended (Cochi, Broome, and Hightower, 1985). Wolff and Brown (in preparation) have argued that such universal vaccination at 18 months could prevent roughly 120 cases of hearing loss caused by meningitis.

Numerically, maternal rubella, heredity, and meningitis were the most important of the known reported causes of hearing loss in the Annual Survey. Though the number of students with a fourth reported cause, otitis media, is not large, these students also make up a subgroup of hearing impaired children and youth with unique characteristics and are discussed later in the chapter. Otitis media, an inflammation of the middle ear, occurs after birth, in early childhood. The highest incidence is found among children less than 10 years of age (McEldowney and Kessner, 1972). Lim (1977) reported that otitis media was likely to occur during colder seasons of the year and in colder areas.

In general, maternal rubella and heredity tend to be causes of hearing loss that occur at birth, or at least by the time of birth. Meningitis and otitis media occur after birth. Although other causes occurring both at birth and after birth may not warrant independent analysis, a brief discussion of them may prove useful.

Causes of hearing loss that can occur at birth are prematurity, pregnancy complications, trauma, and Rh incompatibility. With the possible exception of Rh incompatibility, these reported causes may actually represent other causes. The definition of each tends to be imprecise.

Three of the causes of hearing loss after birth—high fever, infections, and trauma—do not have precise definitions and could represent symptoms of other diseases. Trauma after birth could also be indicative of accidents, as well as childhood diseases.

Two other causes of hearing loss after birth have more precise definitions: measles and mumps. Measles or rubeola virus can invade the inner ear directly via the bloodstream or secondarily from the central nervous system (Bergstrom, 1977). Mumps, a seasonal and cyclic disease, invades the bloodstream and can enter the parotid glands, causing swelling below the ears (Horstmann, 1971; Jensema, 1975). It is possible that some of the students with losses caused by maternal rubella were erroneously reported as having measles as the cause of their hearing loss. There is no compelling need to try to adjust the data for possibly erroneous reporting of measles and mumps because the combined numbers of students reported for both these causes accounted for only 1 percent of all causes.

However defined, 13 specific causes were included on the Annual Survey form. Unfortunately, a very large group of students were those with unspecified causes of hearing impairments (i.e., the particular causes of hearing loss for these students were not specified on the questionnaire, being simply reported as *other*). For most of the following discussion of the impact of etiology on demographic and handicap-related characteristics of hearing impaired students, those whose hearing losses were caused by maternal rubella, heredity, meningitis, or otitis media are compared to each other and to the total for all hearing impaired children and youth reported to the Annual Survey.

REPORTED ETIOLOGICAL CHARACTERISTICS

Different causes of hearing loss attack different people at different times and in different locations. These causes of hearing impairment, some of which occurred long ago, influenced differences between causes in the geographical, age, sex, and ethnic distributions among students reported in the 1982–1983 Annual Survey.

The geographical distribution of hearing impaired children and youth reported in that survey appears to be more a function of the distribution of the general population rather than of any genetic or epidemiological factors associated with hearing loss. In general, this is also true for children with different causes of hearing loss within the hearing impaired population. This is because there are no extreme differences in the geographical distributions of the students by cause.

There are some differences worth noting, however. When the country is divided into the 10 U.S. Bureau of the Census divisions, as in Table 2–1, higher percentages of students with congenital rubella syndrome were reported to be enrolled in schools in New England and in the Pacific states than for the total of hearing impaired students in the Annual Survey.

On the other hand, those with genetic hearing losses were more likely than other students in the Annual Survey to be reported enrolled in schools in the East North Central division. This probably was a function of the concentration of the other causes in areas outside these states, rather than any tendency toward genetic defects within this division.

Children and youth whose hearing loss was caused by meningitis were clustered in the South Atlantic and West South Central states, possibly reflecting the fact that those reported with this cause were more likely than other hearing impaired students to be black, a minority group heavily concentrated in the southern region of the country.

Students with losses caused by otitis media were found in the Middle Atlantic and West North Central states. The clustering in the Middle Atlantic states was the most extreme of any cause. Although cold winters in these states may be partially responsible for this pattern, those with losses caused by otitis media were not clustered in other areas that have equally cold winters.

Differences in age by cause are primarily a function of the 1963 to 1965 rubella epidemic. More than 6 out of every 10 of these students were reported to be 16 to 18 years old in the 1982–1983 Annual Survey, clearly

Table 2-1. Percentage Distribution of U.S. Bureau of the Census Divisions by Cause of Impairment for Hearing Impaired Students

Census Division	Total (all causes)	Maternal Rubella	Heredity	Meningitis	Otitis Media
Total, all divisions	100.0	100.0	100.0	100.0	100.0
New England	4.2	6.3	4.7	4.2	2.3
Middle Atlantic	17.4	14.7	18.1	12.1	27.5
East North Central	16.0	15.0	19.9	15.4	13.7
West North Central	7.8	5.6	8.1	7.3	11.4
South Atlantic	18.1	18.7	15.1	20.3	18.0
East South Central	5.2	4.4	5.4	6.5	3.1
West South Central	12.5	13.1	11.2	17.0	7.6
Mountain	5.5	5.0	6.5	5.9	4.6
Pacific	12.8	16.0	10.6	10.7	11.9
Other	0.5	1.2	0.3	0.4	—

reflecting the rubella epidemic between 1963 and 1965. As shown in Table 2-2, the role of maternal rubella in causing hearing impairment subsided after this period, due undoubtedly to the vaccine against rubella.

Children and youth with genetic causes of hearing loss had a relatively even age distribution, with some concentration in the 13- to 15-year-old age group, over one fifth of the group. Meningitis and otitis media had their concentrations among students of different age groups, the first with one fourth under 7 years of age, the second with close to one half among those 7 to 12 years of age.

There were also sex differences among hearing impaired children and youth. Although females were 46.1 percent of all hearing impaired students in the Annual Survey, this percentage varied by cause. Although females accounted for 48.3 percent and 47.2 percent, respectively, of students with hearing loss caused by maternal rubella and heredity, they accounted for only 40.0 percent and 41.0 percent of those with losses caused by meningitis and otitis media.

As in the general population, the hearing impaired 1982–1983 Annual Survey population was predominately white, regardless of cause. As noted earlier, those whose losses were caused by meningitis were more likely to be black than were other hearing impaired students; the percentage of black children among those whose loss was caused by meningitis was 26.2 percent. The percentage for those with deafness caused by maternal rubella, 15.8 percent, was close to the average, 17.9 percent. Those with losses caused by heredity, 9.9 percent, and otitis media, 11.0 percent, were much less likely to be black.

The percentage of blacks among all children and youth with hearing losses is relatively high. Note that those with reported unknown causes

42   S. C. Brown

Table 2-2. Percentage Distribution of Age Groups by Cause of Impairment for Hearing Impaired Students

Age Group	Total (all causes)	Maternal Rubella	Heredity	Meningitis	Otitis Media
Total, all ages	100.0	100.0	100.0	100.0	100.0
Under 4 years	5.0	1.0	6.8	8.4	3.8
4–6 years	11.3	2.4	13.5	16.6	14.8
7–9 years	15.1	4.7	17.4	18.8	21.0
10–12 years	17.5	8.8	20.4	19.0	23.7
13–15 years	19.2	15.9	21.0	16.8	18.3
16–18 years	27.4	63.2	17.7	16.7	13.1
19 years and over	4.5	4.0	3.2	3.7	5.2

of hearing loss make up a large portion of the total and that there is a heavy concentration of minorities in the unknown category. If these unknowns really had losses due to heredity, then the proportion for those whose reported cause of hearing loss was heredity may be artificially low.

Despite such problems with unknowns, the differences in the concentration of blacks for the causes of maternal rubella, meningitis, and otitis media appear to be substantial. With the exception of the tendency of maternal rubella to have caused hearing loss among those born between 1964 and 1966, the differences in the concentration of blacks are probably the most significant of all of the demographic factors. The age patterns appear to be more pronounced than the gender patterns. Geographical differences appear to be small compared to the other demographic differences.

Along with variation in demographic aspects of etiology, there were also differences in the handicap-related consequences reported in the 1982–1983 Annual Survey. The results of each cause reached far beyond the fact that hearing loss occurred. Hearing threshold levels, as well as the numbers and types of additional handicaps, varied by cause of hearing loss.

In the Annual Survey, degree of hearing loss is reported by hearing threshold level. Pure-tone threshold in the better ear is measured at 500, 1000, and 2000 cycles per second and the arithmetic mean of these three values constitutes the pure-tone average. A *profound hearing loss* is defined as an attenuation in the pure-tone average greater than 90 dB, while a *severe loss* falls within a range of 71 to 90 dB (Davis, 1965).

The measure of hearing loss used in this study, although commonly used and widely accepted, may underestimate the actual degree of hearing loss. For understanding speech, the critical range of frequencies is thought to be 500, 1000, and 2000 Hz (Schein, 1981); significant hearing decrements among these frequencies will affect understanding of spoken communication. However, there is some disagreement over the choice of this particular range of frequencies. Use of this range is thought to result in conservative estimates of hearing impairment (Singer, Tomberlin, Smith, and Schrier, 1982).

It is difficult to determine whether those whose impairment was caused by maternal rubella or those whose impairment was caused by meningitis had the greater degree of hearing loss. Of all students in the Annual Survey with loss caused by meningitis, 63.5 percent had profound hearing losses, and 18.4 percent had severe losses. For the students with maternal rubella reported as the cause of hearing loss, the corresponding figures are 58.6 percent and 28.9 percent. Thus, the children and youth whose hearing loss was caused by meningitis were the most likely of all the groups to have a profound loss; those whose loss was attributed to maternal rubella were more likely to have at least a severe loss. The most important fact is that both groups had losses far greater than the average among all hearing impaired students in the survey, of whom 44.2 percent had profound hearing losses and 21.4 percent had severe losses.

Those with genetically caused hearing loss had hearing threshold levels similar to those for all hearing impaired children and youth reported to the Annual Survey: 47.7 percent had profound losses, a figure only slightly greater than that for the total, and 19.8 percent had severe hearing losses, a little less than the total. The percentages of the heredity group with severe-to-profound losses were substantially less than those percentages for the meningitis and maternal rubella groups.

In such comparisons of hearing threshold levels, the otitis media children and youth stand out: only 9.0 percent had profound losses and 7.0 percent had severe losses. Thus, 84.0 percent of students with hearing impairment caused by otitis media had less-than-severe losses. Clearly this group had the lowest average hearing threshold level of all of the groups.

Though otitis media resulted in milder hearing losses than other causes, it was more likely than other causes to result in the presence of a handicap in addition to hearing impairment. To a lesser extent, maternal rubella also had an association with additional handicaps (see Table 2–3). Conversely, those with genetically caused hearing loss tended not to have another handicap. Presence of additional handicaps was also relatively low among the students with meningitis-caused impairments.

Students losing their hearing because of maternal rubella were the most likely of those with any of the four causes examined to have two or more additional handicaps. Fully 16.2 percent of these children and youth had two or more such handicaps, as compared to 9.5 percent for all students in the Annual Survey. The corresponding percentages for students with hearing losses caused by heredity, meningitis, and otitis media are 4.2 percent, 7.4 percent, and 8.7 percent.

The Annual Survey handicaps can be divided into two broad categories: physical and cognitive-behavioral. Physical handicaps include visual

Table 2–3. Percentage of All Hearing Impaired Students with Additional Handicapping Conditions by Cause of Impairment

Additional Handicapping Condition	Total (all causes)	Maternal Rubella	Heredity	Meningitis	Otitis Media
With at least one additional handicapping condition	30.4	38.6	17.8	25.5	42.0
Physical	15.2	24.9	8.0	12.5	11.1
Legal blindness	2.0	6.6	0.7	0.7	1.1
Uncorrected visual problems	4.0	8.2	2.6	2.0	2.6
Brain damage or injury	2.1	2.8	0.9	2.4	1.4
Epilepsy	1.3	0.8	0.5	2.5	1.4
Orthopedic	2.6	2.6	1.3	2.7	2.5
Cerebral palsy	2.9	3.6	0.6	1.9	1.4
Heart disorder	2.0	6.6	0.6	0.3	1.2
Other health impaired	3.8	3.5	2.8	3.6	4.1
Cognitive-Behavioral	21.3	24.3	12.0	17.7	37.0
Mental retardation	8.5	10.1	3.4	6.4	17.9
Emotional/behavioral problem	5.6	9.4	3.9	4.5	4.9
Specific learning disability	8.1	8.0	4.9	7.1	14.2
Other	2.2	1.6	1.5	2.0	2.5

losses, brain damage or injuries, epilepsy and convulsive disorders, ortho-pedic disorders, cerebral palsy, heart disorders, and other health impair-ments. Cognitive-behavioral handicaps consist of mental retardation, emotional and behavioral problems, specific learning disabilities (includ-ing perceptual-motor problems), and other cognitive-behavioral impair-ments. The definitions of these handicaps and the problems in their reporting are dealt with more extensively in Chapter 3.

In the 1982–1983 Annual Survey, maternal rubella was associated with a variety of additional handicaps, especially visual losses and heart dis-orders. Roughly 15 percent of the hearing impaired children and youth with impairments caused by maternal rubella had some sort of visual prob-lem. These students were also much more likely than other hearing impaired students to have emotional problems. There was also some associ-ation between maternal rubella and mental retardation.

For those with genetically caused hearing loss, the proportions in all of the additional handicapping conditions were always lower than the cor-responding proportions for the total of all hearing impaired students in the Annual Survey. In general, these proportions were the lowest of the four causes profiled in this chapter.

The students with hearing impairments caused by meningitis had simi-lar patterns in regard to additional handicapping conditions as those who inherit hearing loss; both groups tended not to have additional handicaps. However, the proportions of students in most of the additional handi-capping categories were higher for those with hearing losses caused by meningitis than for those who inherited their hearing loss. Moreover, the percentages of the meningitis group with brain injury or epilepsy appear to be slightly higher than those for other groups.

Those who lost their hearing as a result of otitis media tended to have only one additional handicap. This handicap was likely to be either men-tal retardation or specific learning disability. Percentages of otitis media students with these handicaps were higher than those for any other group. (This association, however, does not mean that the presence of these addi-tional handicapping conditions was caused by otitis media.) Also, as noted before, the average degree of hearing loss was low for this group. There-fore, it is probable that the tendency of many students in this group to have cognitive-behavioral handicaps accounted for their placement in spe-cial education programs; their hearing losses were only incidental to such placement. In this sense, the youth with losses caused by otitis media are quite unique.

The age at onset of hearing loss also resulted in differences within the hearing impaired population reported to the Annual Survey. Whether or not a child loses hearing by 3 years of age is important because after that age significant language development takes place (Ries and Voneiff, 1974).

In the 1982–1983 Annual Survey, almost 3000 students were reported to have lost their hearing after age 3. This number accounts for 5.3 percent of all of those in the Annual Survey. Any examination of the association of cause with age at onset of hearing loss should, of course, examine those causes that, by definition, can occur after birth: meningitis, otitis media, high fever, infections, trauma after birth, measles, and mumps.

For these causes of hearing loss that occur after birth, percentages of students losing their hearing after age 3 were lowest for the meningitis, high fever, and measles groups: 13.5 percent, 14.0 percent, and 14.8 percent, respectively. The percentage for otitis media was higher—at 29.6 percent. The highest percentages were for those whose losses were due to trauma, 37.9 percent, and mumps, 42.9 percent. The actual numbers of students for many of these causes were quite small.

The differences in age at onset by cause of hearing loss were not as substantial as the other differences by cause shown in this chapter. However, etiology does appear to have important influences on the other two handicap-related aspects of hearing loss: hearing threshold levels and additional handicapping conditions. These findings imply that any changes in the distribution of the etiology of hearing loss could influence both the demographic and the handicap-related characteristics of hearing impaired children and youth.

PAST AND FUTURE TRENDS IN ETIOLOGY

When using Annual Survey data to study trends among hearing impaired children and youth, it is useful to keep in mind the reporting mechanism of this survey. Over the years, coverage of the Annual Survey has improved; therefore, reported numerical increases between Annual Surveys can represent improvements in coverage and not actual trends. Thus, both numbers and percentages should be analyzed to ascertain changes among the students.

One very substantial change in the distribution of causes of hearing loss among hearing impaired children and youth over the past 10 years of Annual Surveys has been the decline in the percentage of those for whom the cause of hearing loss is unknown. In the 1972–1973 school year, such students accounted for almost half of those reported in that year's survey. As mentioned previously, they accounted for 4 out of 10 students in 1982–1983.

The group that showed the largest rise over the 10-year period was those with unspecified causes of hearing impairments (i.e., students for whom the *other* category on the form was checked). In 1982–1983, the number of children and youth with these *other* causes was four times greater than the number 10 years previously. As a percentage of all hearing impaired children and youth in the survey, these students have more than tripled. As Table 2-4 reveals, no specific reported known cause has grown or declined so dramatically.

The decrease in the percentage of hearing impaired children and youth for whom maternal rubella was reported as the cause of hearing loss was not as substantial over the 10-year period as was the drop in the percentage with a cause reported as unknown. However, in terms of a continuing trend, the decline in maternal rubella may be more important. This is because, over the past decade, the large numbers of students with CRS have influenced much of the planning in special education programs for the hearing impaired.

Annual Survey increases in the numbers and percentages of hearing impaired children and youth for whom the causes of hearing loss were heredity, meningitis, and otitis media are not as great as the increases for those whose loss was attributed to unspecified causes. Over the 10-year period, the numbers of students in the Annual Survey with either heredity or meningitis reported as the cause of their hearing loss grew by more than 70 percent; the number for otitis media more than doubled. Such growth is a function of better coverage of the Annual Survey in recent years.

The trends in causes other than the four focused on in this chapter are also of some interest. The childhood diseases of mumps and measles have almost disappeared because of vaccines against these two diseases. Numbers of hearing losses attributed to the ill-defined causes of pregnancy complications, trauma at birth, high fever, and infections have grown. Perhaps the most dramatic change is the decline in hearing impairment caused by Rh incompatibility, probably because of improvements in blood transfusion techniques.

Predicting future trends in cause of hearing impairment is difficult. Such trends will be a function both of demographic changes in the general population and of genetic and epidemiological variables that affect that population. Future demographic characteristics of hearing impaired children and youth will probably tend to reflect the demographic trends in the general population, regardless of the selectivity of causes. Handicap-related characteristics will more likely reflect changes in the distribution of causes of hearing loss.

It is possible, however, to pose educated hypotheses as to what some of the characteristics of hearing impaired children and youth will be by 1990. Those born prior to 1966, inclusive of the large group of students whose hearing loss was caused by maternal rubella, will have left special education programs. Thus, the hypotheses depend on an assumption: that no major outbreaks of epidemics emerge to shift the etiological loss distribution of hearing loss for those reported as under age 17 in the

Table 2–4. Distributions of Causes of Impairment for Hearing Impaired Students, 1972–1973 and 1982–1983 School Years

Cause of Impairment	Number		Percentage	
	1972–1973	1982–1983	1972–1973	1982–1983
Total, all causes	43,792	55,136	100.0	100.0
Cause unknown	21,301	21,759	48.6	39.5
Cause reported	22,491	33,377	51.4	60.5
Maternal rubella	7,718	9,001	17.6	16.3
Heredity	3,708	6,390	8.5	11.6
Meningitis	2,335	4,033	5.3	7.3
Otitis media	715	1,667	1.6	3.0
Other, at birth				
Prematurity	2,259	2,225	5.2	4.0
Pregnancy complications	1,415	1,854	3.2	3.4
Trauma	1,001	1,350	2.3	2.4
Rh incompatibility	1,369	792	3.1	1.4
Other, after birth				
High fever	1,012	1,734	2.3	3.1
Infection	653	1,467	1.5	2.7
Trauma	403	438	0.9	0.8
Measles	899	419	2.1	0.8
Mumps	269	126	0.6	0.2
Other causes	1,085	4,406	2.5	8.0

Note: Due to multiple causes, totals for reported causes will not sum.

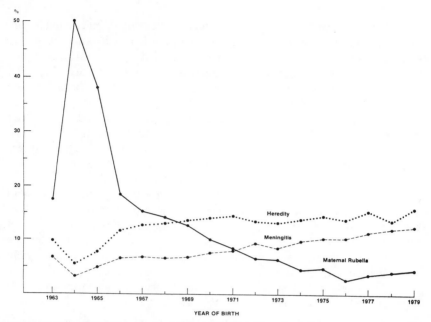

Figure 2-2. Percentages of children with hearing losses caused by maternal rubella, heredity, and meningitis, by year of birth.

1982–1983 Annual Survey. If that assumption is correct, then the characteristics of those students reported as age 16 and under may be representative of the handicap-related attributes of hearing impaired children and youth in the 1990s.

Examination of the distribution of cause of hearing impairments by age in the 1982–1983 Annual Survey indicates that those born in 1964 and 1965 who were in special education programs had distributions extremely different from those of other students. In fact, no other group by age had such a different cause distribution from the norm as these older students. Figure 2-2 shows that these differences by age are consistent with the changes that occurred in the distribution of causes over the past 10 years. The most extreme trend has been the decline in the percentage of hearing loss caused by maternal rubella among those born after 1966.

The departure from special education programs of those born prior to 1966 contributes to a rise in the percentage of students with heredity and meningitis reported as cause among hearing impaired students. The ongoing decline in the incidence of CRS will continue to contribute to increasing percentages of students for whom heredity and meningitis are reported as the cause of hearing loss, even if the numbers with these two causes do not grow.

Thus, maternal rubella should not cause hearing impairments to any great extent in the future. The percentage of students with this cause may drop by almost one half. Such a drop is implied by comparing the percentage with rubella as the cause of hearing loss for those born after 1965 (Table 2-5) with the corresponding 1982-1983 percentage for all hearing impaired students (Table 2-4).

The drop in CRS implies that the percentages accounted for by other causes will increase. Heredity and meningitis would continue their previous gains in percentages, but not necessarily in numbers. The percentages imply that otitis media could also increase as a cause of hearing loss, but not quite to the extent that it increased over the past 10 years. Continuing to rise may be pregnancy complications, trauma at birth, high fever, and infections. Trauma after birth, measles, and mumps should continue their declines. That the *other* cause category might continue to rise is somewhat disturbing. Perhaps more important is the probability that the *unknown* group also will increase. Design of future surveys may yield improvements in the specificity of these two categories.

How likely are these possible trends? Stuckless and Hinman (1983) have argued that because of the rubella vaccine

> . . . the most important implication for tomorrow's children in this country is that almost none will be physically or mentally impaired because of rubella. Among the consequences should be the reduction by 10 to 20 percent in the incidence of childhood deafness from what we have known in the past, assuming the current birthrate and maintenance of the present immunization program nationally. (p.9)

Thus, the percentage of hearing impaired students with hearing losses caused by maternal rubella has already declined and will continue to do so for the immediate future.

The future of hearing impairments attributable to the other causes is less certain at this time. As noted earlier, universal introduction of a vaccine against *Hemophilus influenzae* type B would reduce the number of students with hearing losses due to meningitis. Such a reduction in number could reduce the percentage of hearing impaired students with losses caused by meningitis. Conversely, medical improvements that save the lives of babies who might otherwise die could add to the hearing impaired population. If so, the causes of prematurity, pregnancy complications, and trauma at birth, whatever the exact meaning of these causes, could assume greater importance in the future.

The declining role of maternal rubella in causing hearing loss implies a slight decline in the severity of hearing loss and declines in the percentages of hearing impaired students with maternal rubella–related additional handicaps, such as visual problems and heart disorders. If additional handicaps and severity of hearing loss are indeed on the decline, such changes

Table 2–5. Distributions of Causes of Impairment by Years of Birth for Hearing Impaired Students

Cause of Impairment	Years of Birth			
	Number		*Percentage*	
	1961 to 1965	*1966 to 1982*	*1961 to 1965*	*1966 to 1982*
Total, all causes	13,982	40,347	100.0	100.0
Cause unknown	4,154	17,132	29.7	42.5
Cause reported	9,828	23,215	70.3	57.5
Maternal rubella	5,392	3,527	38.6	8.7
Heredity	940	5,391	6.7	13.4
Meningitis	602	3,395	4.3	8.4
Otitis media	232	1,407	1.7	3.5
Other, at birth				
Prematurity	515	1,691	3.7	4.2
Pregnancy complications	376	1,459	2.7	3.6
Trauma	285	1,051	2.0	2.6
Rh incompatibility	205	581	1.5	1.4
Other, after birth				
High fever	373	1,349	2.7	3.3
Infection	219	1,228	1.6	3.0
Trauma	135	298	1.0	0.7
Measles	180	236	1.3	0.6
Mumps	43	82	0.3	0.2
Other causes	932	3,428	6.7	8.5

Note: Due to multiple causes, totals for reported causes will not sum. Because the years of birth for some students are unknown, the sums of the two birth groups shown in this table will not add up to the corresponding sums shown in Table 2–4.

will complement another trend: the overall decline in the number of hearing impaired children and youth. All of these trends appear to be direct results of the dissemination of the rubella vaccine in the United States.

SUMMARY AND CONCLUSIONS

According to Vernon (1984), "The cause of a person's deafness can have major effects on that individual's life" (p. 6). Most studies on etiology of hearing loss since Gentile and Rambin (1973) have demonstrated this fact. Moreover, these studies have reported similar associations between etiology and the demographic and handicap-related phenomena. Time does not appear to alter these relations. However, the etiology of hearing loss does change over time. Thus, a review of the associations and changes over time by specific cause may be appropriate.

Maternal Rubella: The most striking relations and trends concern the students with hearing impairments caused by maternal rubella. Maternal rubella resulted in a disproportionate amount of hearing loss among those born between 1964 and 1966, particularly among females. This cause has been the most devastating cause of hearing loss in terms of the number of students affected, severity of hearing loss, and additional handicapping condition. The handicaps associated with this cause have been visual problems, heart disorders, mental retardation, and emotional and behavioral problems. However, immunization against rubella throughout the United States means that this cause is not likely to add large numbers to the hearing impaired population in the future.

Heredity: Those with genetic hearing loss are probably the most internally varied group. As a group, they have tended to resemble hearing impaired students as a whole in characteristics. These children and youth usually have high percentages of females and whites. The amount of additional handicapping conditions has been relatively low for this group. The percentage of students with hereditary hearing losses may be on the increase.

Meningitis: Although the percentage of students with hearing losses caused by meningitis has also risen, this percentage may decline in the future because of a successful introduction of a vaccine against *Hemophilus influenzae* type B. In the past, meningitis has caused hearing loss in the South, attacking blacks and males disproportionately. Roughly one quarter of the students with meningitis-caused hearing losses were reported as being less than 7 years of age. They generally have profound losses of hearing and are unlikely to have an additional handicapping condition when compared to other hearing impaired children and youth.

Otitis Media: Otitis media probably caused hearing losses in some colder areas of the United States, especially among whites and males. More than 4 of every 10 of such students were reported as being 7 to 12 years of age. This group has less-than-severe hearing losses but also tends to have retardation or learning disabilities. The future importance of this group is extremely hard to predict.

Since the relationships between these major causes of hearing losses and demographic and handicap-related phenomena have remained relatively constant over time, future research should probably focus on identifying causes of hearing loss that may not have been explored thoroughly in the past. For example, as maternal rubella declines as an important cause of hearing loss, it is likely that there will be increased interest in those losses attributable to hereditary causes. As mentioned previously, these students form an extremely heterogeneous group. In the future it would be helpful to obtain greater specificity for those whose loss is linked to genetic causes. For example, it would be interesting to know whether loss is greater for those who had deaf or hard-of-hearing parents than for those who inherited their hearing loss through a recessive gene in their parents.

The search for greater specificity in hereditary causes should be accompanied by attempts to obtain greater specificity in other categories. There are other important causes (e.g., congenital cytomegalovirus infections) that have not been reported to the Annual Survey. Greater specificity would increase our knowledge of hearing loss due to cytomegalovirus, heredity, and other causes, as well as our understanding of hearing impairment in general.

REFERENCES

Bergstrom, L. (1977). Viruses that deafen. In F. H. Bess (Ed.), *Childhood deafness: Causation, assessment and management*. New York: Grune & Stratton.

Calvert, D. R. (1969). *Report on rubella and handicapped children*. Washington, DC: Project Centers Branch, Division of Educational Services, Bureau of Education for the Handicapped, HEW.

Cochi, S. L., Broome, C. V., and Hightower, A. W. (1985). Immunization of US children with *Hemophilus influenzae* type B polysaccharide vaccine. *Journal of the American Medical Association, 253,* 521–529.

Davis, H. (1965). Guide for the classification and evaluation of hearing handicap in relation to the international audiometric zero. *Transactions of the American Academy of Ophthalmology and Otolaryngology, 69,* 740–751.

Gentile, A., and Rambin, J. B. (1973). *Reported causes of hearing loss for hearing impaired students, United States: 1970–71* (Series D, No. 12). Washington, DC: Gallaudet College, Office of Demographic Studies.

Gregg, N. M. (1941). Congenital cataract following german measles in the mother. *Transactions of the Ophthalmological Society of Australia, 3,* 35–46.

Horstmann, D. M. (1971). Mumps. In P. B. Beeson and W. McDermott (Eds.), *Textbook of medicine* (Vol. 1). Philadelphia: W. B. Saunders.

Jensema, C. (1974). Post-rubella children in special education programs for the hearing impaired. *Volta Review, 76,* 466–473.

Jensema, C. (1975). Children in educational programs for the hearing impaired whose impairment was caused by mumps. *Journal of Speech and Hearing Disorders, 40,* 164–169.

Lepow, M. L., Samuelson, J. S., and Gordon, L. K. (1984). Safety and immunogenicity of *Haemophilus influenzae* type B polysaccharide-diphtheria toxoid conjugate vaccine in adults. *Journal of Infectious Disease, 150,* 402–406.

Lim, D. J. (1977). Infectious and inflammatory auditory disorder. In F. H. Bess (Ed.), *Childhood deafness: Causation, assessment and management.* New York: Grune & Stratton.

McEldowney, D., and Kessner, D. M. (1972). Review of the literature: Epidemiology of otitis media. In A. Glorig and K. S. Gernin (Eds.), *Otitis media.* Springfield, IL: Charles C. Thomas.

Masland, R. L. (1968). Rubella can rob children of their hearing. *Volta Review, 70,* 304–307.

Nance, W. E., and Sweeney, A. (1975). Genetic factors in deafness in early life. *Otolaryngologic Clinics of North America, 8,* 19–48.

Paparella, M. M. (1977). Labyrinthitis. In F. H. Bess (Ed.), *Childhood deafness: Causation, assessment and management.* New York: Grune and Stratton.

Ries, P. W., and Voneiff, P. (1974). Demographic profile of hearing impaired students. *P R W A D Deafness Annual, 4,* 17–42.

Rose, S. P., Conneally, P. M., and Nance, W. E. (1977). Genetic analysis of childhood deafness. In F. H. Bess (Ed.), *Childhood deafness: Causation, assessment and management.* New York: Grune & Stratton.

Schein, J. D. (1981). Hearing impairments and deafness. In W. C. Stolov and M. R. Clovers (Eds.), *Handbook of Severe Disability.* Seattle: University of Washington, Department of Rehabilitation Medicine.

Schlech, W. F., Ward, J. I., Band, J. D., Hightower, A. W., Fraser, D. W., and Broome, C. V. (1985). Bacterial meningitis in the United States, 1978 through 1981. *Journal of the American Medical Association, 253,* 1749–1754.

Shaver, K. A., Boughman, J. A., Kenyon, N., Mohanakumar, T., and Nance, W. E. (1984). HLA antigens in the congenital rubella syndrome. *Disease Markers, 2,* 381–391.

Singer, J. T., Tomberlin, J., Smith, J. M., and Schrier, A. J. (1982). *Analysis of noise-related auditory and associated health problems in the United States adult population 1971–75* (Vols 1 and 2). Washington, DC: U.S. Government Printing Office.

Stuckless, E. R., and Hinman, A. R. (1983). Elimination of rubella as a cause of disability in children. Unpublished paper, National Technical Institute for the Deaf, Rochester, NY.

Vernon, M. (1967). Characteristics associated with post-rubella deaf children: Psychological, educational and physical. *Volta Review, 69,* 176–185.

Vernon, M. (1984). Editorial in *American Annals of the Deaf, 129,* 6.

Wolff, A. B., and Brown, S. C. (in preparation). Demographics of meningitis-induced hearing impairment: Implications for immunization of children against *Hemophilus influenzae* type B.

Chapter 3

Multihandicapped Students

Anthony B. Wolff
Judith E. Harkins

Between 10 percent and 11 percent of all school children in the United States have educationally significant handicaps (U.S. Department of Education, 1983). Among hearing impaired children the prevalence of handicaps in addition to hearing impairment is, according to the Annual Survey of Hearing Impaired Children and Youth, approximately three times as large or 30.2 percent.

The implications for the U.S. educational system are obvious. Given the disproportionate effort and resources that must be mobilized to provide special education and related services for these children, it is reasonable to suppose that they account for well over a third of the resources devoted to deaf education. It is also likely that these students pose some of the greatest difficulties in educational settings for deaf students. When problems associated with mental retardation, severe visual impairment, learning disabilities, emotional disorders, and other conditions are superimposed on hearing impairment, the educational challenge increases immensely.

Like the other variables explored in this book, the variable of additional handicapping condition (AHC) is in turn related to several other variables. In some instances, such as the relationship between AHC and cause of hearing impairment, the link appears to be pathophysiologically related: The same virus, trauma, genetic syndrome, or other cause of deafness also causes other disabilities. In other instances, such as the relationship between AHC and ethnic background, there may be social factors that explain the relationship. This chapter explores these relationships and makes some attempt to interpret them. However, definitive judgments of cause and effect cannot be determined through the analyses used here because the data are descriptive and essentially correlational.

The chapter also examines the definitions and methods used in the Annual Survey to explore how these factors can affect interpretation of the data. Of the information collected in the Annual Survey, the material on AHC has long been considered by researchers to be among the most susceptible to error. The discussion explores the reasons for exercising caution in examining this variable.

DEFINITIONS OF ADDITIONAL HANDICAPPING CONDITIONS AND THEIR IMPLICATIONS

There are many ways to define AHCs, but for the purposes of the Annual Survey only those additional handicapping conditions judged to be "educationally significant" have been included. In the field of education the criterion of educational significance is also used in identifying students eligible for special education and related services, and it is thus more meaningful, from a practical standpoint, than more inclusive criteria would be. This criterion, however, excludes individuals with less severe conditions (e.g., certain kinds of heart murmur or minor orthopedic problems traditionally counted in more medically oriented studies) that are not thought to affect educational performance significantly. Therefore, the actual prevalence of all types of handicaps and other conditions, including those without major functional educational significance, is likely to be underestimated in the Annual Survey.

To avoid overidentification of AHCs, the instructions in the survey call for respondents to check only those conditions documented by appropriate medical, psychological, or other diagnostic criteria. Table 3–1 displays the list of AHCs as defined in the Annual Survey. Despite these clear operational definitions, however, the standards are almost certainly not applied uniformly by the programs reporting data to the Annual Survey. Although awareness of handicapping conditions has been enhanced by U.S. Public Law 94-142 and other legislation, variability in classifying disabilities remains a potential source of ambiguity and error in Annual Survey data (as well as in other efforts to categorize individual students or groups of students).

It is probably impossible for any set of definitions in the area of AHCs to be both exhaustive and mutually exclusive; the material in Table 3–1 is no exception. The definitions are designed to be clear and specific enough to generate reasonably valid and reliable ratings. Nevertheless, some limitations exist, and the following critique of categories is therefore intended

Table 3–1. Additional Handicapping Conditions: Categories and Definitions

Condition	Definition or Explanation
Legal blindness	Condition in which corrected vision in the better eye is less than 20/200 and/or a specialist designates legal blindness.
Uncorrected visual problem (but not legally blind)	Uncorrected or uncorrectable visual problem, including blindness in one eye, muscular imbalance or paralysis, and retinitis pigmentosa.
Brain damage or injury	Condition verified by abnormal EEG or physician's neurological findings.
Epilepsy (convulsive disorder)	Condition in which the student is subject to uncontrollable seizure behavior.
Orthopedic (other than cerebral palsy)	Condition which restricts use of extremities as a result of permanent injury, paralysis, or polio.
Cerebral palsy	Check if this condition has been medically diagnosed.
Heart disorder	Malfunction of the heart which restricts physical functioning and requires monitoring by a physician.
Other health impaired	Any other physical condition which restricts functional ability, such as asthma, diabetes, kidney defects.
Mental retardation	Condition that is documented by scores within defective limits from individually administered scale(s) of intelligence (a measured IQ at least two standard deviations below the mean). Degree of hearing impairment and communication level should determine whether verbal or performance scale scores would be appropriate.
Emotional/behavioral problem	Condition in which inappropriate behaviors interfere with normal academic progress. These behaviors include passive/withdrawn; aggressive/abusive; rapid mood changes/sudden outbursts; bizarre, unexplainable actions; and chronic, unfounded physical complaints and symptoms.
Specific learning disability	Condition in which normal general intelligence is present, but specific learning deficits restrict accomplishments. These restrictions may be attributable to difficulty in visual/auditory perception, perceptual-motor functioning, as well as to a lack of control of attention, impulse, or motor function.
Other	This category would include any other observed condition which would restrict functioning, such as nutritional deficits, educational deprivation, neglect.

Source: 1982–1983 Annual Survey of Hearing Impaired Children and Youth.

to inject some caution into readers' interpretations of information on additional handicaps.

Uncorrected visual problem may include conditions that could respond readily to treatment but have not been treated. The confounding influence of socioeconomic status or other variables may affect membership in this particular group, thus weakening its generality.

The category of *brain damage* is questionable on several grounds. Most obviously it is rendered somewhat redundant because impairments stemming from damage to the central nervous system could be noted under one or more of the other categories, such as cerebral palsy, epilepsy, mental retardation, or specific learning disabilities. *Brain damage* is a highly nonspecific term that does not necessarily imply the existence of a functional impairment. This is the only category of AHC in the Annual Survey for which no particular set of functional characteristics can be cited. Many individuals with brain abnormalities produce normal electroencephalograms (EEGs), and neurological evaluations frequently fail to detect more subtle or covert brain damage (Solomon, Holden, and Denhoff, 1963). Many children whose brain damage is detected during surgical exploration, for example, nevertheless show no abnormalities upon neurological examination (Rutter and Chadwick, 1980). Children such as these probably are not included in the brain damage group in the Annual Survey. On the whole, this category is not very descriptive of functional ability, especially when considered by itself. Most likely, the category functions as a residual classification for those youngsters who are thought to have neurological involvement but who do not fit into any of the other groups. Historically, both learning disability and attention deficit disorder (ADD) have been associated in the literature with brain damage, which was thought to be the cause of these impairments. Although it is now believed that not all cases of learning disabilities or ADD are attributable to brain damage, children with these problems are still classified by some practitioners as brain damaged, even in the absence of any supportive neurological findings. In addition, this category may include a small number of children who have experienced head trauma with related injury to the central nervous system.

The definition of *epilepsy* has certain limitations as well, as it includes only those individuals whose seizures are uncontrollable. While these may be the most severe cases, problems such as cognitive impairment and psychosocial difficulties (which may or may not be classified under another handicapping condition in the survey) can accompany even well-controlled seizures (Lezak, 1983).

The area of *mental retardation* is particularly difficult and is discussed in more detail later. It suffices at this point to acknowledge the reliance on intelligence testing of uneven quality, sometimes administered by professionals who have little experience evaluating deaf individuals and who lack the necessary communication skills (Spragins, Karchmer, and Schildroth, 1981). Since mental retardation is frequently defined in terms of IQ score, it is likely that, based upon such testing, some deaf children are inappropriately classified as mentally retarded.

The category of *emotional or behavioral problem* is subject to varied interpretation. Although diagnostic reliability of emotional problems is said to have improved with the introduction of the third edition of the *Diagnostic and Statistical Manual of Mental Disorders* (DSM III) by the Task Force on Nomenclature and Statistics in 1980, situational factors related to hearing impairment are likely to affect this category of handicap. Some investigators argue that many so-called additional handicaps among deaf persons are simply results of inappropriate conditions imposed by a hearing world (Moores, 1982; Stewart 1971; Vernon, 1977). The number of hearing impaired children categorized as emotionally or behaviorally disturbed who would be considered well adjusted in a different environment cannot be determined from the Annual Survey data.

The definition of *learning disability* is controversial in special education, and the condition is even more difficult to diagnose when hearing impairment is present. The category of specific learning disability may also be affected by situational factors, such as educational programs not matched to needs.

In summary, problems of diagnosis combined with problems of definition cloud, to some extent, the understanding of additional handicapping conditions, as is the case in many efforts to examine aggregate, demographic, or epidemiological data.

ADDITIONAL HANDICAPS AND THE ANNUAL SURVEY POPULATION

In general, estimates of AHCs in the Annual Survey tend to be conservative because the survey requests that only adequately documented handicaps be included for each child. Moreover, as has been mentioned elsewhere in this book, the Annual Survey does not include every hearing impaired youngster in the United States, but rather covers approximately 70 percent of the deaf population in special education. With respect to the multiply handicapped, it is also likely that both ends of the severity distribution are to some extent underrepresented. The most severely handicapped, for whom hearing impairment may be thought of as a secondary handicapping condition, are frequently placed in programs designed to address the child's primary handicap (e.g., profound mental retardation or severe cerebral palsy). Youngsters with very mild hearing impairments are, on the other hand, more likely to be mainstreamed or unreported or both.

A high rate of hearing impairment has frequently been observed in institutions for the mentally retarded (Moores, 1982), but because such programs do not generally participate in the Annual Survey, these children are undercounted. Although the extent of this undercount is unknown, one data source suggests that the extent of the Annual Survey's underestimate of severely handicapped children is very considerable. For several years, the New York State Office of Mental Retardation and Developmental Disabilities has conducted a Developmental Disability Information Survey (DDIS) (Janicki and Jacobson, 1982). This survey attempts to document and describe the individuals served by mental retardation/developmental disabilities (MR/DD) programs operated or licensed by the state of New York. It does not include children served in educational settings only, and it is therefore considered to undercount children.

After accounting for this and other limitations in data collection, New York state officials estimated that the DDIS covers approximately 42 percent of the substantially, functionally disabled MR/DD population of New York State. It is therefore of great interest to note that the DDIS data base, as of September 1984, included 1012 children of school age, ages 5 to 20 years, who were hearing impaired. Correction for 42 percent coverage yields an estimated 2409 children served in New York State MR/DD programs who manifest hearing impairment. In contrast, the Annual Survey identifies only 409 New York children in the Annual Survey who are classified as mentally retarded (584 after correction for incomplete coverage). Moreover, because children in the Annual Survey are drawn from educational settings and children in the DDIS are not, the two groups overlap minimally, suggesting that the total number of hearing impaired mentally retarded children in New York State is equal to at least the sum of these two surveys. Among the hearing impaired group in the DDIS (without respect to age), 15 percent are categorized as mildly retarded, 19 percent as moderately retarded, 22 percent as severely retarded, and 36 percent as profoundly retarded. This example thus reinforces the assertion that the Annual Survey misses a considerable number of significantly handicapped children who have a hearing impairment.

Also underrepresented in the Annual Survey are those mildly hearing impaired children, mainstreamed with hearing children, who do not receive any special services, but who may nevertheless experience some disadvantage in school. What the Annual Survey does include is the vast majority of educational programs identified as primarily serving hearing impaired children and youth. In summary, it may be advisable to consult the literature dealing with various other disorders if one wishes to develop an exhaustive picture of all multiply handicapped children with hearing impairment. However, the Annual Survey does provide a good representation of deaf children served by educational programs for the hearing impaired, and the multiply handicapped youngsters within such programs are well documented through the survey.

Previous Research
on Additional Handicapping Conditions

Throughout the history of the Annual Survey, the proportion of students reported as having additional handicapping conditions has remained rather constant. Reports by Rawlings and Gentile (1970), Ries (1973), Gentile and McCarthy (1973), and Karchmer (1985) indicate that slightly more than 30 percent of the students covered by this survey in the past have had at least one handicapping condition in addition to hearing impairment. When similar survey methods and definitions were used in a survey in Canada, once again the prevalence of AHCs was 30 percent (Karchmer, Allen, Petersen, and Quaynor, 1982). The lowest percentage reported from survey data was 30.5 percent and the highest, 32.4 percent (Gentile and McCarthy, 1973).

Over the years the definitions and instructions for indicating an AHC in the Annual Survey have changed somewhat. For example, in 1968 (Rawlings and Gentile, 1970), the survey form listed the following choices: (a) cleft lip or palate, (b) severe visual, (c) mental retardation, (d) emotional problems, (e) behavioral problems, (f) perceptual-motor disorders, (g) cerebral palsy, and (h) other. In the 1971 survey, emotional problems and behavioral problems were combined into one category, and several handicapping conditions—brain damage, epilepsy, heart disorders, and learning disabilities—were added. More recent reports use a still different combination of conditions. In the data described in this chapter, as well as in the data described by two previous reports (Karchmer et al., 1982; Karchmer, 1985), *legally blind* and *uncorrected visual problems* have been differentiated (from the single *severe visual* category in earlier surveys), the category *other health impairments* has been added, and *cleft lip or palate* has been deleted.

Given that categories of handicapping conditions have changed over the years, it is somewhat surprising that the percentage of children identified as having AHCs (i.e., approximately 30 percent) has remained so stable. The common thread has been the stipulation that the AHC must be educationally significant. Perhaps school personnel have identified children with notable problems and then checked the conditions closest to the children's disabilities, the result being little fluctuation in overall reporting of AHCs despite changing definitions.

Other investigators using different samples have found different prevalences of AHCs among hearing impaired children (see Table 3-2). Conrad (1979), in a study of 468 hearing impaired 15- to 16-year-old children in England and Wales, asked teachers to report any educationally significant handicaps in addition to hearing loss. The question was open-ended; Conrad reviewed each answer and judged the acceptability of the teachers' decisions. He found that, after excluding mental retardation and visual defects from consideration, AHCs were present in only 11 percent of the hearing impaired children in his sample. As Conrad points out (1979, p. 61), the exclusion of mental retardation and visual defects may account for a large part of the discrepancy between his data and Annual Survey data. In fact, data from the 1982–1983 Annual Survey indicate that 12.5 percent of the children for whom AHCs were reported were visually impaired, mentally retarded, or both. Adding this 12.5 percent to Conrad's 11 percent yields a total of 23.5 percent with one or more AHCs—a 7 percent discrepancy.

Conrad points to the categories of emotional or behavioral problems and brain damage as possible reasons for the high prevalence of AHCs in the Annual Survey data. Others (Meadow and Trybus, 1979; Moores, 1982) have also challenged these categories as prone to error. Another source of discrepancy may be the presence of a large proportion (approximately 16 percent) of rubella-deafened children in the Annual Survey population, as opposed to less than 6 percent in Conrad's sample. Children deafened as a result of rubella have more AHCs than do children deafened from other causes (Trybus, Karchmer, Kerstetter, and Hicks, 1980).

Vernon (1969) collected data on 1468 children evaluated for admission by a residential school for deaf students. He examined 418 of these cases on whom relevant data were available to determine the relationship between cause of deafness and AHC. Vernon's data showed that 49.0 percent of his sample had one or more additional handicapping conditions. This higher prevalence probably relates to the nature of Vernon's sample, which included students who had been declared ineligible for residential school education because of insufficient academic potential. Among ineligible students, the prevalence of additional handicapping conditions would likely be much greater than among those attending school. In addition, the data were presented only on those students for whom cause of deafness could be determined. Many students whose cause of deafness cannot be determined from medical records are believed to be deafened as a result of heredity; and among genetically deafened students the prevalence of additional handicapping conditions is much lower than among students with other causes of deafness. Thus, the sample may have been biased toward overinclusion of children with multiple handicaps.

Table 3–2. Studies of the Prevalence of Additional Handicapping Conditions in Hearing Impaired Children

Author (Date)	Sample	Comments on Methods and Definitions	Percentage of Sample with One or More AHCs
Vernon (1969)	418 residential school students (one school)	School records, teachers' ratings, and psychological tests	49.0
Rawlings and Gentile (1970)	21,130 hearing impaired students enrolled in U.S. schools and programs (Annual Survey, 1968–1969)	School personnel checked conditions affecting educational potential. Categories differed from later surveys.	30.5
England's Department of Education and Science, 1972 (as cited in Conrad, 1979)	Hearing impaired students in schools for the deaf in England and Wales (aged 15–16 years)	Interviews with children (conducted by medical personnel) and school reports	54.0
Gentile and McCarthy (1973)	Annual Surveys from 1969 through 1972	Definitions varied over the years	Ranged from 30.5 to 32.4
Conrad (1979)	468 partially hearing and deaf students aged 15–16 years, enrolled in English and Welsh schools and programs	Interviews with teachers; excluded mentally retarded and visually impaired from categories of AHCs	11.0
Karchmer et al. (1982)	3683 hearing impaired students in Canadian schools and programs (Canadian Survey, 1979)	See Table 3–1 for definitions	29.2
Karchmer (1985)	51,962 hearing impaired students in U.S. schools and programs (Annual Survey, 1981–1982)	See Table 3–1 for definitions	30.5

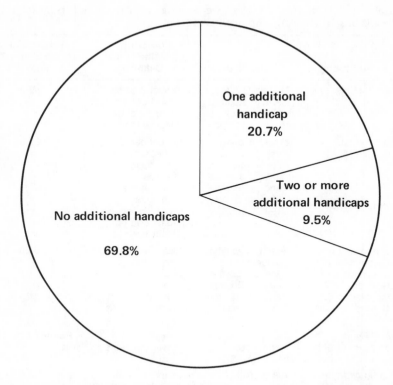

Figure 3-1. Additional handicapping conditions among 53,899 hearing impaired students. [Note: Information on additional handicapping conditions was not available for 1237 students, 2.2% of the 55,136 total reported to the 1982–1983 Annual Survey of Hearing Impaired Children and Youth.]

Prevalence of Additional Handicapping Conditions in the 1982–1983 Annual Survey

Figure 3-1 displays the 1983 Annual Survey percentages of students with no AHC, with one AHC, and with more than one AHC. Nearly 10 percent of hearing impaired children reported to the survey had more than one AHC.

Table 3-3 shows the percentages of hearing impaired students with various additional handicapping conditions. The three most common conditions were mental retardation (8.5 percent), specific learning disability (8.1 percent), and emotional or behavioral problem (5.6 percent). None of the physical disabilities approached these three cognitive-behavioral disabilities in prevalence. The most common physical disability, uncorrected visual problem (not including blindness), was present in only 4.0 percent of children in the survey.

Table 3–3. Percentage of Hearing Impaired Children Manifesting Various Additional Handicaps, 1982–1983

Handicapping Condition	Percentage of 1982–1983 Annual Survey Population[*]
No additional handicaps	69.8
Mental retardation	8.5
Learning disability	8.1
Emotional or behavioral problem	5.6
Uncorrected visual problem	4.0
Other health impairment	3.8
Cerebral palsy	2.9
Orthopedic problem	2.6
Other	2.2
Brain damage	2.1
Heart disorder	2.0
Legal blindness	2.0
Epilepsy	1.3

[*]Column totals more than 100% because approximately 10% of the children had more than one AHC.

Within the various categories of AHC considered here, certain clusters of disabilities are apparent in the Annual Survey data. In other words, certain handicapping conditions were not independent of each other. For example, 24 percent of children with severe visual impairment and approximately 55 percent of legally blind children were also categorized as mentally retarded, related, for the most part, to backgrounds of maternal rubella and other organic insults. Over 30 percent of children with cerebral palsy were also diagnosed as mentally retarded, presumably related to underlying neurological pathology. Children categorized as brain damaged had an almost 25 percent chance of being rated as emotionally disturbed, and nearly one half of them were also considered to be mentally retarded. Of children with orthopedic problems, 27 percent were reported as having severe visual problems or legal blindness.

As these clusters frequently derive from one cause, generally an organic insult with multiple symptomatic expressions, it may be best to think of some of these more prevalent clusters as coherent groupings in their own right. One of these groups in particular has been the subject of much attention in recent times: the large group of deaf youth who were victims of the rubella epidemic of 1964 to 1965. These youngsters, now approaching early adulthood, are still reflected to a considerable extent in these survey data. They bring with them a high prevalence rate of mental retardation, visual impairment, orthopedic impairment, and cardiac problems. The composition of hearing impaired youth is shifting markedly as this large cohort exits the secondary educational system (Karchmer, 1985).

COMPARISONS WITH THE GENERAL POPULATION

How do these prevalence rates compare with estimates of disability among school-aged children in the general population? For the answer to this question, data from the federal government were examined. Each year the states and territories of the United States are required to report to the U.S. Department of Education the numbers of handicapped children served under Public Laws 89-313 and 94-142. In reporting, the states must identify the child's primary handicap; for those with severe multiple disabilities, a category of multihandicapped is included. Thus, despite certain methodological weaknesses, the figures represent an unduplicated headcount of handicapped children receiving special education and related services under these federal entitlements.

Among the reports produced by the U.S. Department of Education is a breakdown by state of the percentage of total enrollments identified as handicapped under Public Laws 94-142 and 89-313. Table 3–4 summarizes information from this reporting procedure.

In 1982 the total percentage of children served under these laws was 10.64 percent. As stated before, AHCs were about three times more prevalent among hearing impaired children and youth than were handicapping conditions among all children and youth. Moreover, each of the specific handicaps listed by the U.S. Department of Education was more common in hearing impaired children reported to the Annual Survey than in the general population. Cognitive-behavioral handicaps (mental retardation, learning disability, and severe emotional disturbance) were much more common in the general population than were physical disabilities, a finding that parallels those of the Annual Survey.

In general, patterns identified in the Annual Survey are paralleled in special education, as reported in the states' head counts, but the prevalences are much higher for all conditions among hearing impaired children.

ADDITIONAL HANDICAPS AND EDUCATIONALLY RELATED CHARACTERISTICS

Cause of Hearing Loss

The relationship between cause of deafness and the presence or absence of AHCs is treated in detail in Chapter 2. Generally, certain causes of hearing impairment (e.g., rubella, trauma at birth, Rh factor incompatibility, and prematurity) tend to be associated with multiple disabilities; other causes of hearing impairment (e.g., heredity) tend to cause fewer additional handicaps. Genetically caused deafness results in the lowest prevalence of additional handicaps.

Table 3–4. Percentage of Total School Enrollment with Handicapping Condition, United States and U.S. Territories, 1982–1983

Handicapping Condition	Percentage of Total Enrollment
Total	10.64
Speech impaired	2.81
Learning disabled	4.32
Mentally retarded	1.98
Emotionally disturbed	0.88
Other health impaired	0.13
Orthopedically impaired	0.14
Multihandicapped	0.16
Deaf and hard of hearing	0.19
Visually handicapped	0.08
Deaf and blind	0.01

Source: U.S. Department of Education, Office of Special Education Data Analysis System (DANS), June 29, 1983 (TIA 33B05).

Ethnic Background

For a number of years the relationship between ethnic background and the existence of handicaps has caused controversy in education. Annual Survey data also indicate this relationship. Data from the 1982–1983 Annual Survey show that black hearing impaired students were more likely than others to be reported as having an AHC: 37.1 percent of black students had one or more handicaps in addition to hearing impairment. The bulk of this difference is found in the disproportionate number of blacks reported as mentally retarded. Blacks constituted less than 18 percent of students in the Annual Survey, but they accounted for more than 28 percent of the students reported as mentally retarded. In contrast, whites made up 66.5 percent of the total survey population but only 59.3 percent of the mentally retarded students. Blacks were also overrepresented in the emotional/behavioral category, but to a lesser extent.

These findings concerning ethnicity parallel those observed in the general population. To monitor suspected racial bias in the identification of cognitive or behavioral problems, the U.S. Department of Education's Office for Civil Rights (OCR) regularly surveys a sample of school districts to determine the racial composition of certain handicap groups. Data from the OCR 1982 survey (U.S. Department of Education, 1984) showed that in the general population black students were twice as likely as others to be categorized as mentally retarded. More than 51 percent of mentally retarded students in the OCR survey were black, compared to a 26 percent prevalence of mental retardation among all students in the OCR sample. Black students in the general population were also more likely to be reported as being seriously emotionally disturbed, but the overrepresentation was not nearly as dramatic: 20 percent higher prevalence than would be expected in the general population. In both the Annual Survey and the OCR survey, Hispanic children were distributed similarly to white children in relation to cognitive-behavioral handicapping conditions, including mental retardation.

The relationship between ethnic background and physical AHCs was weaker. There was a tendency for more black students than others to be identified as being legally blind or visually impaired or as having a heart disorder. White students were slightly more likely than others to have cerebral palsy. Generally, however, physical AHCs were more evenly distributed across ethnic background than were mental retardation or emotional disturbance. (Comparison with the OCR survey is not possible, as OCR does not collect data on these physical disabilities.)

These findings suggest that bias in evaluation procedures is still a problem. Although it is reasonable to suppose that certain factors, socioeconomic status, for example, may affect the cognitive and emotional development of some minority children, it is probable that being both black and deaf constitutes a double cultural jeopardy with respect to standardized testing and subsequent labeling.

Sex

Male students were more likely to have an AHC than were female students (see Table 3–5). Thirty-three percent of males were reported to have at least one AHC; only 27.4 percent of females were so reported. This pattern held true across all handicaps except heart disorder, in which females constituted a majority. The finding that males exhibit more AHCs than females parallels consistent reports for the general population, in which males exhibit a higher prevalence of most impairments, including hearing impairment, than do females.

In the category of emotional/behavioral problems, approximately 70 percent of the 1982 Annual Survey students were male. In the OCR survey on the general population, nearly four fifths (78.2 percent) of emotionally disturbed students were male. The reported emotional disturbance of hearing impaired students, therefore, was somewhat more evenly distributed by sex than was the case in the general population. This difference may be attributable to the relative sex neutrality of most of the causes of deafness that contribute to central nervous system pathology.

Similarly, among learning disabled hearing impaired students, 64 percent were male and 36 percent female. In the general population (OCR data), the proportions were 72 percent and 28 percent, respectively. Again, the distributions in the Annual Survey, although uneven, are not as skewed as the distributions in the general population, as sampled by OCR.

Table 3-5. Sex Distribution and Additional Handicapping Conditions, 1982-1983*

Sex	No AHC	One or More AHC	Total
Male	19,371 (67.0%)	9,541 (33.0%)	28,912
Female	17,954 (72.6%)	6,791 (27.4%)	24,745

*Information on sex is missing for 404 of the 54,022 students about whom information was reported on AHCs (0.7%).

Degree of Hearing Loss

Mild degrees of hearing loss (hearing threshold of less than 41 dB in the better ear) are much more common than profound hearing loss in the general population. In the Annual Survey the opposite is the case: severe and profound losses are more common. Because the Annual Survey mainly covers hearing impaired students who are receiving special educational services, it does not give a true picture of students who have the milder degrees of hearing loss.

This characteristic of Annual Survey data is shown clearly when the relationship between degree of loss and AHC is examined. In the 1982-1983 Annual Survey, students with mild to moderate degrees of loss were more likely to have AHCs than were students with more severe hearing loss (Table 3-6). One interpretation of this finding stems from the observation that mildly hearing impaired students tend to be underrepresented in the Annual Survey because a significant number of these youngsters receive no special educational services. Those mildly hearing impaired youngsters included in the Annual Survey would tend to have a greater probability of special education placement because of an interaction of two or more handicaps. Thus, the higher rate of additional handicaps in mildly hearing impaired children may be, in part, a consequence of the Annual Survey's coverage.

Generally, mildly hearing impaired students had higher percentages of mental retardation, learning disability, and other health impairments than did severely and profoundly deaf students. Severely to profoundly deaf students had higher percentages of cerebral palsy, heart disorders, uncorrected visual problems, and emotional/behavioral problems. Certain types of AHCs, including legal blindness, orthopedic impairments, brain damage, and epilepsy, did not vary significantly across various degrees of loss.

Age

Figure 3-2 shows the total number of individuals in the 1982-1983 Annual Survey with one or more AHCs as a function of age. There are

Table 3–6. Degree of Hearing Loss and Additional Handicapping Conditions, 1982–1983*

Degree of Hearing Loss (Better-Ear Average in Decibels)	N	Percent with No AHC	Percent with One or More AHCs
Normal (<27 dB)	3,423	60.0	40.0
Mild (27–40 dB)	3,677	63.5	36.5
Moderate (41–55 dB)	4,975	66.0	34.0
Moderately severe (56–70 dB)	6,151	69.4	30.6
Severe (71–90 dB)	11,304	71.5	28.5
Profound (≥91 dB)	23,211	72.4	27.6

*Information on degree of hearing loss is missing for 1158 of the 53,899 students about whom information was reported on AHCs (2.1%).

two prominent features of this figure. One is the obvious "rubella bulge" for birth years 1964 and 1965, representing the rubella epidemic of that period. As mentioned previously, this group is aging out of the educational system. Because the rubella cohort is so large and because AHCs are more prevalent among these individuals, they will continue to require many services in the future. However, these will tend to be vocational, health, mental health, rehabilitation, and social services rather than educational services.

Beyond the 1964 to 1965 rubella cohort, it is also clear that with increasing age the raw number and percentage of hearing impaired children manifesting AHCs increase. The only significant exceptions to this trend, on the aggregate level, are those children who were less than 3 years of age. These data can, to a great extent, be explained in terms of detection. For example, hearing impaired infants may be more likely to receive special services if they have multiple handicaps, thus inflating representation of AHCs for this age group. There is no evidence of any significant increase in specific causes of deafness that would otherwise account for these data. Similarly, it is assumed that as children progress through the educational system and, indeed, as they age, AHCs continue to be discovered, accounting at least in part for the general increase in AHCs as a function of age.

It is also apparent that beyond age 18 years there is a large increase in reported AHCs in the Annual Survey. This is attributable to the aging out, by leaving or graduating from school, of the Annual Survey population. Presumably, youth with more severe AHCs are less likely to leave school at age 18, thus inflating prevalence estimates for the 19-and-older age group.

Figure 3–3 shows the percentages of specific AHCs as a function of age. Examination of the graphs shows that most of the age-related increases

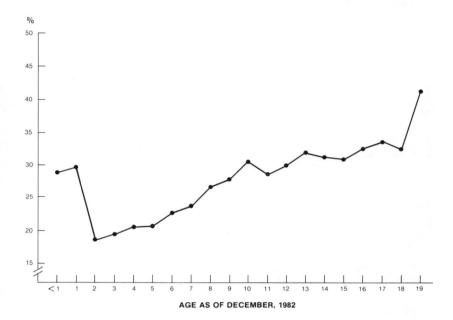

Figure 3-2 Percentage of students with one or more additional handicapping conditions, by age. From Annual Survey of Hearing Impaired Children and Youth, 1982–1983.

in AHCs can be attributed to mental retardation and emotional or behavioral problems. Learning disabilities also contribute to the general trend, increasing until age 13, although the percentage of learning disabilities unaccountably decreases after that. The other major AHCs are relatively stable by age of student, again with the exception of the rubella bulge and, for certain handicaps, those children younger than 3 years of age.

Variation by State

Generally, one would expect the prevalence of handicapping conditions to be fairly constant across the 50 states. However, two possible reasons for variation by state include (a) differences in state level policy in identifying and classifying handicaps and (b) demographic differences in covariates of handicapping conditions, such as ethnic background.

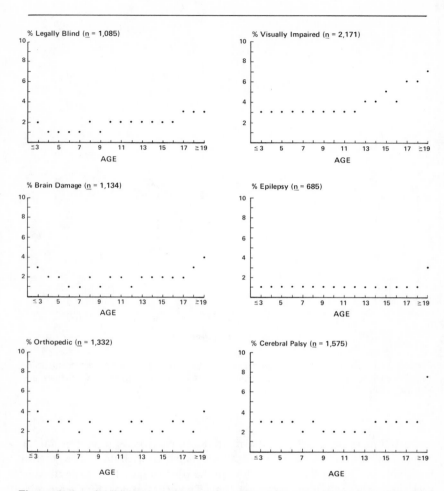

Figure 3-3. Additional handicapping conditions, by age. From Annual Survey of Hearing Impaired Children and Youth, 1982–1983.

In fact, there was considerable variation in the prevalence of certain handicapping conditions by state, both in the general population and in the Annual Survey. The largest variation was found in the learning disability category. In the state with the lowest reported proportion of learning disabled students for the general school population, these students constituted 1.8 percent of the total school enrollment; in the state with the highest proportion, they accounted for 8.5 percent of the total school enrollment. The proportion of hearing impaired students reported to the Annual Survey as learning disabled varied even more by state: from 3.7 percent to 14.8 percent.

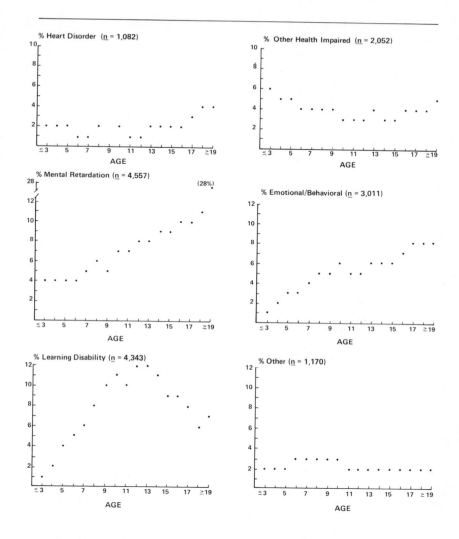

The diagnosis of mental retardation also appeared to vary by state in the general population, although to a less dramatic extent: from a low of 0.7 percent to a high of 4.7 percent of total school enrollment. Among hearing impaired students, the range was 4.6 percent to 15.3 percent, nearly as wide a range as in the learning disability category.

Children reported as emotionally disturbed made up 0.1 percent to 3.2 percent of total school enrollment, depending on the state. Among hearing impaired children in the Annual Survey, the prevalence of emotional disturbance was much higher and more varied: from 1.1 percent to 13.5 percent, depending on the state.

It is probable that this great variation is attributable, for the most part, to differences among states in policies and procedures regarding the identification and reporting of these conditions. In particular, both the fiscal climate and the organization of human service agencies tend to affect the process of identification and labeling.

Other disability types were distributed more evenly by state, both in the general population and among the hearing impaired. Among the physical disabilities reported in the general population (orthopedic impairment, other health impaired, deaf and hard of hearing, visually handicapped, and deaf-blind), the estimated prevalence of each varied across states by less than 1 percent. In the Annual Survey hearing impaired student population, the variation was generally somewhat greater across states—as much as 6.8 percent. Some of this variability may be associated with genetic factors such as selective migration, restricted gene pool, and inbreeding, because many of the approximately 150 genetic deafness syndromes also involve additional handicaps. For example, 6 percent of the hearing impaired children in Louisiana were reported to the Annual Survey as legally blind, a prevalence three times greater than in the general Annual Survey hearing impaired population. This effect in Louisiana is attributable to the migration during the eighteenth century of a small number of French Canadians to Louisiana, some of whom carried recessive genes for Usher's syndrome. Inbreeding has subsequently led to the phenotypic expression of what would otherwise have tended to remain a hidden, recessive genotype.

However, even after accounting for such subgroups, the variation in physical conditions among states was still much smaller than was the case with the cognitive-behavioral disabilities (learning disability, mental retardation, and emotionally disturbed). Unlike difficulties that are not obvious on visual inspection, the physical conditions are more readily detected and are less influenced by policy considerations. For example, a child who manifests uncontrollable behavior can either be considered to have an emotional problem (i.e., a handicap) or simply to have a discipline problem, but not to be handicapped. In contrast, such ambivalence is unlikely to apply to a child who cannot walk.

DISCUSSION

Mental Retardation

It is striking that hearing impaired students with all categories of AHCs manifest lower academic achievement scores than do hearing impaired students without AHCs (Jensema, 1975). As expected, students labeled as mentally retarded have the lowest attainment of any subgroup.

Retardation is especially prevalent in children whose hearing impairment is associated with maternal rubella, birth trauma, pregnancy complications, and prematurity, and it is particularly uncommon among those with hereditary deafness. It is thus likely that as methods for preserving the lives of progressively earlier premature infants become more successful the incidence of mental retardation among deaf youth may increase.

The presence of a disproportionate number of black students in the mentally retarded category suggests the existence of a significant group of deaf youth whose retardation may be functional or environmentally induced. It is unsettling to think that significant numbers of children are categorized and subsequently treated as mentally retarded partially as a result of social deprivation, testing biases, and policies governing educational placement. Yet this conclusion is suggested, although not proven, by the data. Clearly, many hearing impaired children categorized as mentally retarded have severe cognitive limitations. These youngsters are presumably best served by traditional programs for mentally retarded hearing impaired children, which emphasize communication skills, social competence, skills of daily living, prevocational training, and other concrete tasks (Naiman, 1982), although these programs are not without problems (Gruenewald, Schroeder, and Yoder, 1982). However, other children, specifically those who are black, who come from lower socioeconomic backgrounds, and who test poorly, may be seriously underserved by being relegated to programs not commensurate with their abilities.

Learning Disabilities

In the Annual Survey the category of learning disability is second in prevalence to mental retardation and also occurs heavily among blacks. Since Public Law 94-142, learning disabilities in school settings have tended to be defined consistently according to the federal regulatory definition, in which a specific academic skill (e.g., reading) must lag at least 2 years behind the child's ability. This comparison is generally based on standardized test scores, and the objections regarding biased tests, cited previously with respect to mental retardation, are again relevant.

Nevertheless, several causes of hearing impairment are also potential causes of subtle and severe neurological impairments that can produce various disorders, including specific learning disabilities. The Annual Survey data show that a diagnosis of learning disability is much more likely for cases of trauma at birth, pregnancy complications, and serious infections than for other causes (except otitis media, which is a special case, as discussed in Chapter 2). Neurological damage resulting from these organic insults can in turn lead to specific disturbances of cognitive functioning. Vernon (1968) has discussed the presence of aphasoid disorders among deaf individuals; Auxter (1971) has explored difficulties in motor control; Shroyer (1982) and Goetsch (1981) have discussed visuospatial and other perceptual difficulties in deaf children. Such conditions, involving impaired perceptual, motor, and cognitive processes, are particularly problematic for the hearing impaired child who is already laboring under conditions of reduced sensory experience and exposure to language. Many investigators have also studied cognitive style among deaf children (Belmont, Karchmer, and Bourg, 1985; Conrad and Rush,1965; MacDougall, 1979; McDaniel, 1980), and various differences from hearing subjects have emerged. What is unclear is the extent to which the diagnosis of learning disability may at times represent not a true disability, but rather a case of pronounced difference from the hearing norm in cognitive style.

Ultimately, in the case of both mentally retarded and learning disabled students, the question of the legitimacy of the diagnosis may be secondary. If a child is seen as handicapped by the adults in the child's environment, then that child is indeed handicapped, whether there is or is not anything intrinsically wrong. Indeed, Moores (1982) has suggested that the greatest handicap facing hearing impaired children is the education they receive; it can be added that the specific educational placement may also be a handicap, particularly if it is based on a misdiagnosis.

Emotional and Behavioral Problems

The same organic insults implicated as causes in learning disabilities are also known causative factors in some childhood behavioral syndromes, most notably attention deficit disorder, both with and without hyperactivity. This may, to some extent, explain the comparatively high prevalence of behavioral problems among deaf students, reported not only by the Annual Survey but also by others (Meadow and Trybus, 1979). Jensema and Trybus (1975) documented from analysis of previous Annual Survey data that higher rates of emotional or behavioral problems occur in children whose deafness was caused by conditions potentially injurious to the central nervous system. The most recent Annual Survey data confirm this pattern for rubella, birth trauma, pregnancy complications, and prematurity; the findings of Chess and Fernandez (1980) also demonstrated that, as a group, children with rubella-related deafness display a high rate of emotional and behavioral difficulties. The prognosis is, therefore, that the incidence and prevalence of childhood emotional and behavioral problems should be diminishing somewhat as the rubella cohort leaves school.

In addition to physiological causes, the social difficulties that often accompany hearing impairment, including strained family and peer relations, communication difficulties, and residential placement, may also contribute to emotional and behavioral difficulties. Unfortunately, there are relatively few mental health professionals who are trained to work with deaf individuals (Spragins et al., 1981), and the special needs of this group are often unattended (Edelstein, 1977).

Visual Impairment and Blindness

Students with visual handicaps in addition to hearing impairments present special problems because both major senses for symbolic and social communication are involved. Jensema (1980) and McInnes and Treffry (1982) have described in detail the educational methods used with this population. Fortunately, in some cases such as those with retinitis pigmentosa, loss of vision is progressive, and the child frequently has the opportunity to become communicatively proficient before loss of sight is severe. Likewise, blind children whose hearing loss is adventitious have a reasonable prognosis for adjustment. In general, however, this dual sensory loss is associated with considerable cognitive and other developmental impairments. Jensema (1979a, 1979b) reported that 60 percent of the deaf-blind children in her study functioned in the severe-to-profound range of mental retardation; the work of Stein, Palmer, and Weinberg (1980) tends to confirm this finding.

A considerable proportion of today's deaf-blind youth is a product of the 1964 to 1965 rubella epidemic. The declining incidence of rubella in the United States thus creates a downward pressure on the number of individuals afflicted with this multiple handicap. However, severe visual impairments are also associated with heredity, as well as with birth trauma, pregnancy complications, and prematurity, which are not declining and may in fact be increasing in incidence (Budetti and McManus, 1982).

SUMMARY

As reported to the Annual Survey, the percentage of hearing impaired children identified as having one or more additional handicapping conditions is about 30 percent (i.e., nearly one hearing impaired child in three has one or more handicaps in addition to hearing impairment).

Because of limitations in survey research techniques, these findings need to be qualified somewhat. The definitions used in the Annual Survey are functional but imperfect; some of them overlap, and most are open to interpretation. The problems of identifying additional handicaps among hearing impaired students in the absence of fair tests need to be acknowledged. There is evidence that many severely or profoundly handicapped hearing impaired children and youth are placed outside the educational system and therefore are not reported.

Despite these drawbacks, the Annual Survey data do appear reliable in most respects. They present consistent trends over time, with the overall proportion of students with AHCs remaining stable over the history of the survey. They describe only conditions that are of interest in planning and implementing educational programs (i.e., educationally significant AHCs). They also reflect demographic trends in special education in general. When Annual Survey data are compared with data on the general population (as extracted from U.S. government reports), the demographic characteristics of hearing impaired students with AHCs are comparable to the characteristics of other handicapped students.

For example, the Annual Survey suggests that males have a greater tendency to be identified as having AHCs, especially emotional disturbance, learning disability, and mental retardation. In the general school population, males also are disproportionately represented in these areas. Blacks are overrepresented in the mentally retarded, emotionally disturbed, and learning disabled categories both among hearing impaired students and in the general school population. In the general population and in the Annual Survey population there is a great deal of variability by state in the percentage of students identified as having handicaps. Generally, the distributions by sex, ethnic background, and state are skewed in the cases of mental retardation, learning disability, and emotional disturbance. Physical handicaps, on the other hand, are less subject to variability by ethnic background and by state. These data suggest that bias in evaluation procedures may still be a problem in the areas of cognitive and behavioral handicaps.

This problem, in turn, has implications for the overall prevalence of AHCs among the Annual Survey population. Mental retardation, learning disability, and emotional disturbance—the three handicaps that appear most vulnerable to bias in evaluation procedures—are also the three most prevalent AHCs in the Annual Survey.

The relationship between AHC and cause of deafness, discussed at greater length in Chapter 2, is a relatively strong one; the profile of AHCs throughout the history of the survey is affected to some degree by the presence of the large rubella cohort born in 1964 and 1965. These students are more likely than the general survey population to have AHCs. As they exit the educational system, there may be a reduction in the prevalence of AHCs in the Annual Survey.

Whatever the future trends in prevalence of AHCs, this variable will continue to be one of major importance to educators and other professionals. The challenge to improve methods of evaluation, instruction, and habilitation for these students will remain.

REFERENCES

Auxter, D. (1971). Learning disabilities among deaf populations. *Exceptional Children, 37,* 573–577.

Belmont, J. M., Karchmer, M. A., and Bourg, J. W. (1985). Structural influences on deaf and hearing children's recall of temporal/spatial incongruent letter strings. *Educational Psychology, 3,* 259–274.

Budetti, P. P., and McManus, P. (1982). Assessing the effectiveness of neonatal intensive care. *Medical Care, 10,* 1027–1039.

Chess, S., and Fernandez, P. (1980). Do deaf children have a typical personality? *Journal of the American Academy of Child Psychiatry, 19,* 654–664.

Conrad, R. (1979). *The deaf schoolchild.* London: Harper & Row.

Conrad, R., and Rush, M. L. (1965). On the nature of short-term memory encoding by the deaf. *Journal of Speech and Hearing Disorders, 30,* 336–343.

Edelstein, T. J. (1977). Educational treatment programs for emotionally disturbed deaf children. In *Mental health in deafness* (Publication No. ADM 77–524). Washington, DC: U.S. Department of Health, Education and Welfare.

Gentile, A., and McCarthy, B. (1973). *Additional handicapping conditions among hearing impaired students—United States: 1971–1972 (Series D, No. 14).* Washington, DC: Gallaudet College, Office of Demographic Studies.

Goetsch, E. A. (1981 November/December). *Does your deaf child have learning disabilities? The Endeavor.* (Newsletter, available from International Association of Parents of the Deaf, 814 Thayer Ave., Silver Spring, MD 20910).

Gruenewald, L., Schroeder, J., and Yoder, D. (1982). Considerations for curriculum development and implementations. In B. Campbell and V. Baldwin (Eds.), *Severely handicapped hearing impaired students* (pp. 163–179). Baltimore: Paul H. Brookes Publishing Co.

Janicki, M. P., and Jacobson, J. W. (1982). The character of developmental disabilities in New York State: Preliminary observations. *International Journal of Rehabilitation Research, 5,* 191–202.

Jensema, C. (1975). *The relationship between academic achievement and the demographic characteristics of hearing impaired children and youth* (Series R, No. 2). Washington, DC: Gallaudet College, Office of Demographic Studies.

Jensema, C. K. (1979a). A review of communication systems used by deaf-blind people: Part 1. *American Annals of the Deaf, 124,* 720–725.

Jensema, C. K. (1979b). A review of communication systems used by deaf-blind people: Part 2. *American Annals of the Deaf, 124,* 808–809.

Jensema, C. K. (1980). *Methods of communication used by and with deaf-blind children and youth in classroom settings.* Unpublished doctoral dissertation, Gallaudet College, Washington, DC.

Jensema, C., and Trybus, R. (1975). *Reported emotional/behavioral problems among hearing impaired children in special education programs: United States, 1972–1973* (Series R, No. 1). Washington, DC: Gallaudet College, Office of Demographic Studies.

Karchmer, M. A. (1985). A demographic perspective. In E. Cherow, N. P. Watkin, and R. J. Trybus (Eds.), *Hearing impaired children and youth with developmental disabilities* (pp. 36–56). Washington, DC: Gallaudet College Press.

Karchmer, M. A., Allen, T. E., Petersen, L. M., and Quaynor, A. (1982). Hearing-impaired children and youth in Canada: Student characteristics in relation to manual communication patterns in four special education settings. *American Annals of the Deaf, 127,* 89–104.

Lezak, M. D. (1983). *Neuropsychological assessment* (2nd ed.). Oxford: Oxford University Press.

MacDougall, J. C. (1979). The development of visual processing and short-term memory in deaf and hearing children. *American Annals of the Deaf, 124,* 16–22.

McDaniel, E. (1980). Visual memory in the deaf. *American Annals of the Deaf, 125,* 17–20.

McInnes, J., and Treffry, J. (1982). *Deaf-blind infants and children.* Toronto: University of Toronto Press.

Meadow, K., and Trybus, R. (1979). Behavioral and emotional problems of deaf children: An overview. In L. J. Bradford and W. G. Hardy (Eds.), *Hearing and hearing impairment* (pp. 395–403). New York: Grune and Stratton.

Moores, D. F. (1982). *Educating the deaf: Psychology, principles, and practices* (2nd ed.). Boston: Houghton Mifflin.

Naiman, D. (1982). Educational programming for hearing-impaired mentally retarded adolescents. In D. Tweedie and C. Shroyer (Eds.), *The multihandicapped hearing impaired: Identification and instruction* (pp. 148–161). Washington, DC: Gallaudet College Press.

Rawlings, B., and Gentile, A. (1970). *Additional handicapping conditions, age at onset of hearing loss, and other characteristics of hearing impaired students—United States: 1968–1969* (Series D, No. 3). Washington, DC: Gallaudet College, Office of Demographic Studies.

Rutter, M., and Chadwick, O. (1980). *Neuro-behavioral associations and syndromes of minimal brain dysfunction.* In F. C. Rose (Ed.), *Clinical neuroepidemiology.* Tunbridge Wells, England: Pitman Medical Publishing.

Shroyer, C. (1982). Assessing and remedying perceptual problems in the deaf. In D. Tweedie and C. Shroyer (Eds.), *The multihandicapped hearing impaired: Identification and instruction* (pp. 135–147). Washington, DC: Gallaudet College Press.

Solomon, G., Holden, R. H., and Denhoff, E. (1963). The changing picture of cerebral dysfunction in early childhood. *Journal of Pediatrics, 63,* 113–120.

Spragins, A. B., Karchmer, M. A., and Schildroth, A. N. (1981). Profile of psychological service providers to hearing impaired students. *American Annals of the Deaf, 126,* 94–105.

Stein, L., Palmer, P., and Weinberg, B. (1980). Characteristics of a young deaf-blind population. *The Siegel Report* (No. 10). Chicago: The David T. Siegel Institute for Communicative Disorders, Michael Reese Hospital and Medical Center.

Stewart, L. (1971). Problems of severely handicapped deaf: Implications for educational programs. *American Annals of the Deaf, 116,* 362–368.

Task Force on Nomenclature and Statistics. (1980). *Diagnostic and Statistical Manual of Mental Disorders* (3rd ed.). Washington, DC: American Psychiatric Association.

Trybus, R. J., Karchmer, M. A., Kerstetter, P. P., and Hicks, W. (1980). The demographics of deafness resulting from maternal rubella. *American Annals of the Deaf, 125,* 977–984.

U.S. Department of Education, Office for Civil Rights. (1984, February). *1982 Elementary and Secondary Schools Civil Rights Survey, National Summaries,* Washington, DC.

U.S. Department of Education/Office of Special Education Data Analysis System (DANS), June 29, 1983 (TIA 33B05).

Vernon, M. (1968). Current etiological factors in deafness. *American Annals of the Deaf, 113,* 106–115.

Vernon, M. (1969). *Multiply handicapped deaf children: Medical, educational and psychological considerations* (Monograph). Washington, DC: Council for Exceptional Children.

Vernon, M. (1977). Mental health needs of deaf children and their parents. *Mental Health in Deafness, 1,* 85–87.

Chapter 4

Residential Schools for Deaf Students: A Decade in Review

Arthur N. Schildroth

In 1884 J. Noyes, superintendent of the school then known as the Minnesota Institute for the Deaf and Dumb and the Blind, reported to the governor of that state on a National Teachers' Association meeting held in Madison, Wisconsin:

> It was then and there claimed that [local] departments connected with our public schools should be opened for the education of the deaf, articulation the sole medium of instruction, and the deaf made to mingle freely with other children, and also share the care and comforts of home, thus discarding State schools and the sign system teaching entirely. (p. 23)

One hundred years later the bitter controversy over "articulation" and the "sign system" may have abated, but the debate over the place and purpose, the costs and educational benefits of residential schools has again surfaced. Noyes could dismiss local education of deaf students as "impracticable" and a "failure" in its European counterparts (1884, p. 23). But his successors in their current struggle to maintain and revitalize the residential schools are confronted with the stringent realities of demographics, economics, and public law: declining enrollment, spiraling energy and operating costs, and the integration of hearing impaired children in schools with hearing students, symbolized for many in the "least restrictive environment" requirement of U.S. Public Law 94-142. Additional questions have been raised about the suitability of a segregated, sheltered environment for children and their need to reside in a family home (Evans, 1975), a concern also raised in the 1884 Noyes report.

In light of these demographic, economic, and legal issues, the original nineteenth century rationale for the existence of centralized, state-supported residential schools—the need for children with a low-incidence handicap to receive specialized training in a land with large distances between communities and a fledgling transportation system—has appeared to become less and less cogent.

This chapter uses data collected in the Annual Survey of Hearing Impaired Children and Youth to examine national and regional enrollment patterns and educationally related characteristics of students in 60 public residential schools in the United States. It also describes some of the changes occurring in these schools over the past decade, and, in light of these changes, makes some cautious projections about the future of the residential schools.

Of the 15,298 students reported to the Annual Survey by these schools during the 1982–1983 school year, 91 percent had severe to profound hearing impairments (i.e., hearing levels of 71 dB or greater in the better ear). Almost 97 percent incurred their hearing loss before the age of 3 years. These percentages have changed only minimally since 1973; in both cases they have risen slightly.

The 60 schools included in this study have consistently participated in the Annual Survey since 1968. They represent more than 90 percent of the public residential schools educating deaf children in the United States; they enrolled almost 40 percent of the severely and profoundly hearing impaired students reported to the 1982–1983 Annual Survey. For purposes of this analysis, the 60 schools have been grouped into the four regions of the country established by the U.S. Bureau of the Census:

Northeast: Connecticut, Maine, Massachusetts, New Hampshire, New Jersey, New York, Pennsylvania, Rhode Island, Vermont

Midwest: Illinois, Indiana, Iowa, Kansas, Michigan, Minnesota, Missouri, Nebraska, North Dakota, Ohio, South Dakota, Wisconsin

South: Alabama, Arkansas, Delaware, District of Columbia, Florida, Georgia, Kentucky, Louisiana, Maryland, Mississippi, North Carolina, Oklahoma, South Carolina, Tennessee, Texas, Virginia, West Virginia

West: Alaska, Arizona, California, Colorado, Hawaii, Idaho, Montana, Nevada, New Mexico, Oregon, Utah, Washington, Wyoming

The study does not include private residential schools. These schools have held and will continue to hold an important place in the education of many deaf children, though their enrollments are generally smaller than the public residential schools. Although there are some semantic and legal difficulties in describing exactly what constitutes a "public" residential school for deaf students, this chapter adopts the generally accepted meaning when educators speak of state residential schools for deaf students (i.e., separate schools supported by public funds).

A similar problem exists with the term *residential*. One of the schools included in this study reported itself as a "day school" ("Tabular Summary," 1984) and listed no students living at the school. This school has traditionally been included among the public residential schools, and the characteristics of its students parallel those of the residential schools (e.g., age, degree of hearing loss, age at onset of loss, additional handicapping conditions). It has, therefore, been included in this study—though its self-designated change in classification is an indication of what is happening in a number of states across the country.

A final preliminary remark should be made. The Annual Survey data are collected in the second semester of a school year, unlike, for example, the information reported each year to the Reference Issue of the *American Annals of the Deaf*, which reflects student population during the first semester of a school year. Thus, this chapter generally uses a single date to indicate a school year (e.g., 1978 to refer to the 1977–1978 school year).

ENROLLMENT

Citing data from the Annual Survey of Hearing Impaired Children and Youth, Schildroth (1980) described enrollment changes in 62 public residential schools for deaf students between 1971 and 1979. The overall drop in enrollment for these schools over the 8 years was 9.8 percent; the largest losses were registered in the Northeast (22.8 percent) and Midwest (18.9 percent). Even in the South, where enrollment was up 4.2 percent for this period, a decline began to appear in the 1977–1978 school year. In the West the loss was 9.1 percent between 1971 and 1979, but a period of stable pupil enrollment began in 1975–1976 and continued through the 1978–1979 school year.

Data from the 1983 Annual Survey revealed that the overall declining enrollment pattern observed in these schools between 1971 and 1979 continued through 1983. Table 4–1 shows enrollment figures for the *same*

Table 4–1.   Enrollment in Public Residential Schools for Deaf Students, 1979 and 1983

Region	Number of Schools	Enrollment		Percent Change 1978–1979 to 1982–1983
		1978–1979*	*1982–1983†*	
Total	60	16,504	15,481	− 6.2
Northeast	16	3,661	3,135	− 14.4
Midwest	12	3,052	2,852	− 6.6
South	20	6,994	6,748	− 3.5
West	12	2,797	2,746	− 1.8

*Enrollment data for two schools were obtained from the Reference Issue of the 1979 *American Annals of the Deaf*.

†Enrollment data for one school were obtained from the Reference Issue of the 1983 *American Annals of the Deaf*.

60 residental schools for deaf students for the 1978–1979 and 1982–1983 school years. (Since publication of Schildroth's 1980 article, 1 residential school has closed, and 2 schools in one state have merged.)

Nationally, enrollment in these 60 schools declined 6.2 percent over the 4 years between 1979 and 1983. As in the previous 8 years, the Northeast and Midwest regions sustained the largest losses: 14.4 percent in the Northeast and 6.6 percent in the Midwest. Thus, between 1971 and 1983 enrollment in the 16 northeastern schools declined by one third, and in the 12 midwestern schools by almost one quarter. The enrollment stability noted earlier in the West between 1975 and 1978 continued through 1983; a decline of less than 2 percent was reported to the Annual Survey between 1979 and 1983. The South experienced a moderate loss of 3.5 percent over this 4-year period. Figure 4–1 depicts the enrollment decline in these schools between 1974 and 1983.

This overall enrollment drop came in spite of the fact that 41 of the 60 schools expanded their age range for attendance at the schools, either lowering the minimum entrance age or extending the maximum enrollment age—or both—in the decade preceding the 1982–1983 school year.

Some of the enrollment decline in residential schools merely reflected the enrollment decrease in regular schools across the United States in the late 1970s and early 1980s. During that period (between October 1978 and October 1982) school enrollment for the general population 3 through 17

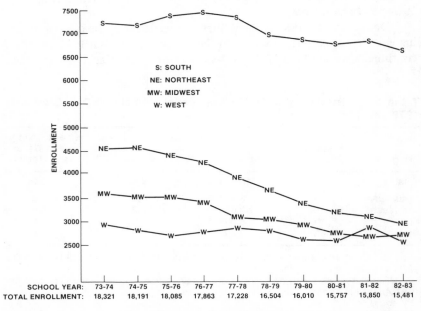

Figure 4–1.   Enrollment changes in public residential schools, 1974–1983.

years of age dropped by almost 2 million students, approximately 4 percent (U.S. Bureau of the Census, 1979, 1984a). Here, too, the Northeast and Midwest experienced the heaviest losses: 12.2 percent and 8.7 percent, respectively. Enrollment in regular schools declined a modest 1.5 percent in the South and actually rose in the West by a very small amount: 0.2 percent.

A combination of factors influenced enrollment in the general U.S. school system during the 1970s and early 1980s, among them the end of the baby boom period (1946 through 1964) and migratory patterns both within and from outside the borders of the United States. These same elements also undoubtedly affected enrollment in residential schools for deaf students during this period. However, there were also special factors that influenced enrollment in these schools, including the departure from the residential schools of students born during the 1964–1965 maternal rubella epidemic and the trend toward integrating handicapped children into regular schools fostered by U.S. Public Law 94-142.

The sex ratio (i.e., the number of males for every 100 females) was higher in these 60 residential schools (126.2) than it was in the 1982–1983 Annual Survey as a whole (116.9). It was considerably higher than the 104.2 figure in the 1982 general population for the 3- to 17-year-old age group (U.S. Bureau of Census, 1984a), a fact due largely to the higher prevalence of hearing impairment among males than among females.

The preponderance of males in these residential schools has implications for curriculum and staffing because deaf male students generally have a much higher rate of handicaps in addition to their hearing impairment than do females, especially emotional and behavioral problems (Gentile and McCarthy, 1973; Rawlings and Gentile, 1970). For example, during the 1982–1983 school year, 95 of each 1000 males in the 60 residential schools were reported to have emotional or behavioral problems, in contrast to the 58 in every 1000 females reported with this additional handicap. A similar reporting pattern was found in regard to learning disabilities: 92 for each 1000 males were reported to the survey as having this additional problem; the rate for female students with learning disabilities was 57 for each 1000. (The rates for severe visual problems and mental retardation were similar for males and females: slightly more females were reported with visual problems and slightly more males with mental retardation.)

AGE

One important difference in the residential schools between the 1978 and 1983 survey years involves age of the students enrolled. Table 4–2 is a comparison of various age categories for the two school years.

Table 4–2.   Percentage Distribution of Hearing Impaired Students in 60 Public Residential Schools, by Age and Region of the United States, 1978 and 1983

				Age				
	<6		6–13		14–17		≥18	
Region	1978	1983	1978	1983	1978	1983	1978	1983
Total	4.8	8.6	48.5	30.2	29.2	35.2	17.5	26.1
Northeast*	5.4	7.9	51.2	31.0	30.3	31.0	13.1	30.1
Midwest†	2.6	6.4	46.5	28.9	32.3	39.2	18.6	25.4
South	4.6	9.1	48.7	30.1	26.0	31.9	20.6	28.9
West	6.6	10.3	46.7	30.8	32.7	43.7	14.0	15.3

*One northeastern residential school closed between 1978 and 1983.
†Data from one midwestern school were from 1977 and 1984.

Nationally, during the 1977–1978 school year 53.3 percent of the students in these 60 schools were less than 14 years of age; by 1983 the percentage of youth less than 14 had dropped to 38.8 percent of total enrollment. Conversely, residential school population 18 years and older in 1978 accounted for only 17.5 percent of the total enrollment. In 1983 that group represented 26.1 percent of the total; and if the age bracket is lowered to "17 years of age and older," the 1983 figure jumps to 40.0 percent of total enrollment. Even granted the tendency for deaf students to remain in high school longer than hearing students, it is still obvious that a significant portion of the 1982–1983 residential school population had reached or was quickly approaching the age of departure from the residential secondary school system.

There were important differences in age distribution among the four regions of the country. Residential programs in the Northeast saw the percentage of their students age 18 years and older more than double between 1978 and 1983: from 13.1 percent to 30.1 percent. In the South 28.9 percent of the students were age 18 years or older in 1983. (If this age category is lowered to include 17-year-olds, then 40.3 percent of the southern residential school students were 17 years or older.) In the West the 18-year-old and above group increased only a very slight amount, rising from 14.0 percent in 1978 to 15.3 percent in 1983, a situation due largely to the rubella epidemic not reaching the west coast until 1965. (The West had the largest percentage of 17-year-olds in the 1982–1983 Annual Survey among the four regions: 19.7 percent.)

The difference in age distributions between 1978 and 1983 is largely the result of the movement through the school system of students deafened during the maternal rubella epidemic of 1964–1965. In 1978 these rubella children were included in the 6- to 13-year-old age group. In 1983, by far the largest number of the rubella residential school students—those

born in 1964 and numbering 1618—fell into the 18-years-and-older category. The 1964–1965 rubella students, 64 percent of the students age
18 years and older in the residential schools, have been the critical factor,
as far as enrollment goes, for the residential schools. They account for
the very large classes graduating from the residential schools in 1983, 1984,
and 1985. (White, Karchmer, Armstrong, and Bezozo, 1983). Their departure from state residential schools has been the principal reason for the
recent steep enrollment decline experienced by these schools.

One final reference to Table 4–2 is in order. Between 1978 and 1983
the number of students under the age of 6 years in these schools increased
by 61 percent, rising from 4.8 percent of the total residential school population in 1978 to 8.6 percent in 1983. This somewhat surprising increase
was observed in all regions of the country, but especially in the South and
West, and was due, in part, to a change in admissions policy by a large
number of the schools: 40 of these schools lowered their entrance age during the past decade. Also, residential schools for deaf students in many
areas have been cooperating closely with local school districts in the placement of hearing impaired youngsters, with the result that these schools
are being seen as a special resource in educational planning for children
at an early age (Williams, 1984). Finally, this increase in younger students
in the residential schools has been a result of the enrollment of a large
number of day students in preschool or parent-infant programs: Almost
one quarter of all the day students in the 60 residential schools for
1982–1983 were under 6 years of age.

DAY AND RESIDENT STUDENTS

All of the residential schools in this study enrolled day students (i.e., students living at home and commuting to school) as well as students who
resided at the school. Table 4–3, based on data reported to the Reference
Issue of the *American Annals of the Deaf* (1973, 1983), shows the changing pattern of enrollment of day students in these residential schools that
emerged in the decade preceding 1983.

Nationally, the ratio of resident to day students in these schools
between 1973 and 1983 dropped from 4 to 1 to a little over 2 to 1. Regional
differences in 1983 ranged from 4.2 resident students for every day student in the Midwest to 1.1 resident for each commuting student in the
Northeast. Almost one third of all day students in 1983 were enrolled in
the southern residential schools. (Day students outnumbered resident pupils
in 8 of the 16 northeastern schools.) Except for the South, where the number of day students almost doubled between 1973 and 1983, this substantial change in the ratio of resident to day students resulted more from a
large decline in the number of resident students at these schools than from

Table 4–3.   Resident and Day Students in 59 Public Residential Schools for Deaf Students, 1973 and 1983

	Resident		Day		Number of Residents for Each Day Student	
Region	1973	1983	1973	1983	1973	1983
Total	14,915	10,932	3,702	4,682	4.0	2.3
Northeast*	2,951	1,611	1,530	1,464	1.9	1.1
Midwest	3,320	2,305	529	553	6.3	4.2
South	6,598	5,351	817	1,515	8.1	3.5
West	2,046	1,665	826	1,150	2.5	1.5

Source: Tabular summary of schools and classes in the United States, October 1, 1972. (1973). *American Annals of the Deaf, 118*. Tabular summary of schools and classes in the United States, October 1, 1982. (1983). *American Annals of the Deaf, 128*.

*One school did not report data for 1972–1973 or 1982–1983 to the *American Annals of the Deaf*.

any numerical increase of day students. The number of day students in the Northeast actually declined between 1973 and 1983.

This new enrollment pattern has certain implications for the residential schools. Karchmer and Petersen (1980), basing their conclusions on two surveys of the mid-1970s, noted certain differences between resident and day hearing impaired students attending residential schools. Data from the 1983 Annual Survey confirm the Karchmer and Petersen findings that day students in the residential schools tend to be younger than their classmates residing at the school, have a higher percentage of white students, are reported to have proportionately fewer emotional and behavioral problems and less mental retardation, and wear hearing aids more frequently than do resident students in these schools. Karchmer and Petersen also found that day students generally were rated by their teachers as having more intelligible speech than resident students but that the achievement levels of the two groups were similar, findings noted by Quigley and Frisina (1961) two decades earlier.

The 1983 Annual Survey uncovered further differences between resident and day students that have program and curriculum implications for these schools. Day students in 1983 used sign language less frequently than the residents; they were also receiving regular classroom instruction with hearing students more frequently than their resident schoolmates: 14.2 percent of the commuters compared to 3.3 percent of the residents, a pattern of integrated instruction found in all four regions of the country. Although 1983 Annual Survey data do not permit a description of the exact nature of this instruction with hearing students, previous investigation has revealed a variety of classroom arrangements initiated by residential schools: satellite programs in which students are enrolled in the residential school but attend classes at other locations in a state, cooperative classroom arrangements with local school districts, and reverse main-streaming in which hearing students attend classes on the residential school campus (Brill, 1978; Craig and Salem, 1975).

Geographic location undoubtedly has played and will continue to play a part in the enrollment of day students in residential schools. For example, although 5 of the 12 midwestern residential schools are located outside a metropolitan statistical area (MSA)— a U.S. government designation for an area of concentrated population, including a city of 50,000 or more—only two northeastern schools, both with very small enrollments, are located outside an MSA. Schools situated within such comparatively large population reservoirs have greater opportunities for enrolling day students in their classrooms than schools not so situated.

ETHNIC BACKGROUND

During the mid-1970s the percentage of minority students in the 60 residential schools climbed steadily, rising from 19.9 percent of the residential school population in 1972 to 25.4 percent in 1978. This increase was due chiefly to two factors: (a) the steep decline in the number of white students in these schools (a loss of more than 1700 students), and (b) the large increase in black students, especially in the South, over this 6-year period (Schildroth, 1980).

As Table 4–4 shows, the trend of an increasing minority percentage in the residential schools between 1972 and 1978 continued through the 1982–1983 school year. Numerically, the overall minority population remained stable between 1978 and 1983, increasing by only 78 pupils. The percentage, however, of minority students rose from 25.4 percent of total enrollment in 1978 to 28.5 percent in 1983, a result due almost entirely to the ongoing decline in the number of white students within these schools.

Between 1978 and 1983 white enrollment in the 60 schools declined by more than 1600 students, a drop of 13.0 percent. (Thus, between 1972

Table 4–4. Percentage Distribution of Students in 60 Public Residential Schools for Deaf Students, by Ethnic Background and Region of the United States, 1978 and 1983

	White		Black		Hispanic		Other	
	1978	*1983*	*1978*	*1983*	*1978*	*1983*	*1978*	*1983*
Total	74.6	71.5	18.4	19.6	4.8	6.0	2.2	2.8
Northeast	84.2	77.9	8.5	11.1	5.9	9.1	1.4	1.9
Midwest*	89.8	86.3	8.3	10.0	0.8	1.5	1.0	2.3
South	63.9	62.6	33.1	32.9	2.3	3.2	0.7	1.3
West	72.2	71.2	5.0	5.4	14.5	15.0	8.3	8.4

*Includes one school with data from 1977 and 1984.

and 1983 white enrollment in these residential schools decreased by 23.7 percent.) Regionally, the Northeast experienced the heaviest loss, where a drop of almost 900 white students between 1978 and 1983 translated into a percentage loss of 28.4 percent. Although white enrollment declined least in the South, numerically this represented a loss of 300 students.

Enrollment of black students in the residential schools took a somewhat surprising turn between 1978 and 1983. Their numbers had increased by 22 percent between 1972 and 1978. The 1983 Annual Survey data, however, reveal that black enrollment, though showing a slight percentage increase over 1978 because of the decline in white student enrollment, decreased nationally by 103 students between 1978 and 1983. The loss was due entirely to fewer black students in the southern schools in 1983 than in 1978; the other three regions of the country showed small numerical gains in black enrollment between 1978 and 1983.

Although Hispanic children and youth made up only 6 percent of students in the residential schools in 1983, their attendance in these schools has been steadily increasing. Comparison of the 1977–1978 and 1982–1983 Annual Surveys shows that enrollment of Hispanic children in the residential schools increased by 13.1 percent, an increase of 105 students. (In the 11-year period between 1972 and 1983 Hispanic enrollment in these 60 schools increased by 27.9 percent.) Slightly more than 4 of every 10 Hispanic students in the residential schools for 1983 attended schools in the West, although overall Hispanic enrollment in this region declined slightly between 1978 and 1983. At the state level, one quarter of the total Hispanic enrollment in the 60 residential schools attended the three schools in California and Texas.

Minority students from other ethnic backgrounds in the residential schools for the 1982–1983 school year were Asian/Pacific (the majority within this *other* group), Native American, or children from multi-ethnic backgrounds. Their numbers were relatively small (a total of 426 in 1983), but like the Hispanic group, they too have been growing steadily. Slightly over one half of these students from other ethnic backgrounds were enrolled in the western residential schools, undoubtedly reflecting recent immigration patterns in the western part of the United States.

Thus, the 1983 ethnic composition of students in these 60 schools differed considerably by region of the country. Black students were heavily concentrated in the South. A plurality (42.5 percent) of all Hispanic students in these programs were enrolled in the 12 western schools, although the Northeast also had a relatively large Hispanic group (29.1 percent). A majority of the students from other ethnic backgrounds, chiefly Asian/Pacific children, attended schools in the western region. Minority enrollment was lowest in the 12 midwestern schools (13.7 percent).

ADDITIONAL HANDICAPPING CONDITIONS

From its national origin in 1968 the Annual Survey has collected information on handicaps other than hearing impairment of the students
reported to the survey. According to the instructions accompanying the
survey form, the criterion for deciding to report an additional handicap
should be whether or not it is "educationally significant," that is, whether
the handicap is one that places "additional demands or requirements upon
instructional arrangements, causes modification of teaching methods, or
alters or restricts the student's activities in ways additive to those occa-
sioned by hearing loss alone." Schools are encouraged to report only those
additional handicaps that have been documented by medical or other
appropriate assessment personnel.

Qualifications of the Annual Survey information on additional handicaps are described more fully in Chapter 3. Although survey participants
are asked to base their responses in this area, as much as possible, on tests
and clinical results, a certain subjective element, as well as state legal
requirements or local school policies, may affect the reporting of these
data. In addition, the schools are asked to list only the presence of additional handicaps according to the criterion quoted previously. They are
not asked to list the severity of the handicap, the basis of the report, or
the qualifications of the person making the diagnosis or completing the
question on the survey form.

A final limitation involves missing or unusable data. During the
1977–1978 school year information on additional handicaps was not
reported for 9.4 percent of the students in the 60 residential schools. In
1982–1983 only 4.0 percent of the residential school students did not have
this question answered on their survey forms. In both school years these
missing data have been excluded from the percentage calculations, on the
assumption that the distribution of the unknown information is similar
to that of the known.

Throughout the 1970s the public residential schools consistently
reported an enrollment of multiply handicapped children and youth in
the 25 percent to 29 percent range (i.e., slightly lower than the 30 percent
to 33 percent level reported by other types of programs to the survey).
Schildroth (1980) noted an overall increase of 3.3 percent in multiply handicapped students in the residential schools between 1971 and 1978, an
increase particularly evident in the Midwest, where the 12 residential
schools reported an 8 percent increase of multiply handicapped students
over the 7 years. The pressure on residential school superintendents to
enroll more multiply handicapped youngsters, especially those "with low
intelligence," noted by Anderson, Stevens, and Stuckless in 1966 (p. 81),
seemed to be having an effect. Because such a population shift would have

important implications for the character, the staffing, and the curriculum of the residential schools, the question may be asked: Has this 1971 through 1978 trend of increasing enrollment of multiply handicapped students continued through 1983?

Residential school data on multiply handicapped students from the 1982–1983 Annual Survey in comparison to the data from 1977–1978 are presented in Table 4–5. Approximately 30 of every 100 students in these 60 residential schools for 1983 were reported to have one or more educationally significant handicaps in addition to their hearing impairment. As a percentage of total enrollment this represents a slight increase of 1.0 percent over the 1978 school year. Numerically, however, there were 62 fewer multiply handicapped students reported by these 60 schools in 1983 than in 1978. Thus, while the multiply handicapped population of these schools remained fairly stable over the 5 years, the number of non-multiply handicapped students was dropping.

Regionally, there were differences between 1978 and 1983. In 1978, 31 of every 100 students among the northeastern residential school students were reported to be multiply handicapped; by 1983, 35 of every 100 were counted in that category, even though this represented a numerical drop of more than 100 multiply handicapped students from 1978. (In 1971, 23 of every 100 northeastern residential school students had been reported as multiply handicapped.) In the South the number of multiply handicapped children between 1978 and 1983 rose by 280 students, reaching slightly more than 27 percent of total enrollment. In the Midwest the rate of multiply handicapped students dropped from 31 in every 100 students in 1978 to 26 in every 100 in 1983. Multiply handicapped students in the West remained relatively stable over these 5 years: 35 per 100 in 1978, compared to 34 per 100 in 1983.

Table 4–5 shows general national and regional data on the enroll-

Table 4–5. Students with One or More Additional Handicapping Conditions in 60 Public Residential Schools for Deaf Students, 1978 and 1983

Region	Number of Schools	Students with One or More Additional Handicapping Conditions			
		1978		1983	
		N	%	N	%
Total	60	4,487	28.7	4,425	29.7
Northeast	16	1,096	31.3	991	34.5
Midwest*	12	908	31.1	737	26.1
South	20	1,531	23.6	1,811	27.4
West	12	952	34.8	886	34.2

*Includes one school with data from 1976–1977 and 1983–1984 school years.

ment of multiply handicapped children and youth in the residential schools. How do these general numbers translate into specific categories of multiply handicapped students?

Table 4–6 is a comparison between the 1977–1978 and 1982–1983 school years of the four most frequent additional handicaps reported by the residential schools: specific learning disability, emotional or behavioral problem, mental retardation, and visual problem (including legal blindness). The most obvious feature of this table is that of the four handicaps, only learning disability showed an increase between 1978 and 1983 at the national level and also in each of the regions, an increase reported even more frequently among hearing students during this period (U.S. Department of Education, 1983). None of the other three handicaps displayed this consistency. Nationally, the number of students reported as learning disabled by these schools increased by 58 percent between 1978 and 1983. In the southern residential schools students reported with learning disabilities increased by 114 percent over the 5-year period. Approximately 10 percent of the students from the northeastern and western residential schools were reported as learning disabled.

Although emotional and behavioral problems were the most frequently reported additional handicap in 1978 and in 1983, students with this handicap declined both in numbers and as a percentage of total enrollment between 1978 and 1983. In spite of this overall decline, almost 11 percent of the student body in the northeastern and western residential schools were reported with emotional or behavioral problems in 1983, a rate considerably higher than that among hearing children (Meadow and Trybus, 1979.)

Because of earlier predictions that the public residential schools would be pressured to enroll more multiply handicapped students, especially those

Table 4–6. Percentage Distribution of Four Additional Handicapping Conditions in 60 Public Residential Schools for Deaf Students, by Region of the United States, 1978 and 1983

Region	Mental Retardation		Emotional or Behavioral Problems		Learning Disabilities*		Severe Visual Problems	
	1978	1983	1978	1983	1978	1983	1978	1983
Total	6.0	5.9	8.3	7.8	4.5	7.5	6.2	5.5
Northeast	4.1	4.6	7.5	10.9	5.2	9.6	7.5	6.4
Midwest†	6.6	5.0	9.4	6.4	3.6	7.3	5.0	3.4
South	6.7	6.9	5.4	5.9	2.6	5.4	5.6	6.0
West	6.4	6.1	14.8	10.9	9.2	10.8	7.4	5.4

*Includes perceptual-motor handicaps.
†Includes one school with data from the 1976–1977 and 1983–1984 school years.

with mental retardation as an additional handicap, another feature of Table 4–6 should be noted: The percentage of mentally retarded youth in these residential schools remained relatively stable between 1978 and 1983.

Black (34.0 percent) and Hispanic (33.9 percent) students were more likely to be reported as having additional handicaps than white students (28.8 percent) in 1983. The 294 students from the *other* ethnic group for whom no specific background was reported had an especially large percentage of additional handicaps: 40.2 percent.

For the specific handicap categories, mental retardation was reported for 10 of every 100 black students in these schools in 1983, for 6 of every 100 Hispanic children, and for 5 of every 100 white students. Of the students with specific ethnic backgrounds reported, emotional and behavioral problems were reported more often among white (8.1 percent) and Hispanic (8.8 percent) children than among black children (6.3 percent). The highest percentage of learning disabilities was reported among Hispanic students: 10.7 percent.

SUMMARY AND DISCUSSION

In light of the data examined in this chapter, what stable features and what changes can be cautiously predicted for the residential schools in the near future? This section summarizes some of the major findings documented earlier from the Annual Survey and briefly discusses these findings and some factors that may affect them. (Findings are indicated in italics.)

Students' Hearing Loss

The residential schools continue to enroll over 90 percent of their student body from students in the severe-to-profound hearing loss range whose impairment occurred before the age of 3 years.

It is unlikely that the residential schools will enroll substantial numbers of students with less-than-severe hearing losses or students with postlingual losses. These students are candidates for mainstreaming and, given the present emphasis on "least restrictive environment," the large majority of these students will undoubtedly be integrated in some fashion with hearing students. The pool from which the residential schools are able to enroll students will continue to be the severe-to-profound loss students with prelingual hearing impairment.

However, as mentioned earlier, in some areas of the country residential schools are establishing themselves as resource centers for parents and local school districts, regardless of the students' degree of hearing loss.

They are conducting audiological assessments of infants and adolescents, using campus facilities and staff for classes in adult education of graduates and other hearing impaired individuals, establishing summer sessions, parent-child programs, and extension courses, both on and off campus—in general, becoming a source of information and services in the field of hearing impairment for the whole state or the immediately surrounding area (Patterson and Baud, 1985). These nontraditional activities reflect a broader role for the residential schools in the field of information dissemination and in education of both hearing and hearing impaired individuals, even though these programs and services may not be directly reflected in the student enrollment of the residential schools.

Enrollment

Overall enrollment at these schools has been declining since the early 1970s. This decline reflected the decreasing enrollment in regular schools across the United States during this period but was magnified in the residential schools by the departure of students deafened during the rubella epidemic of 1964–1965 and by implementation of U. S. Public Law 94-142. Regionally, the enrollment losses have been particularly heavy in the Northeast and Midwest regions of the country. In the western residential schools enrollment appeared to stabilize in the late 1970s and early 1980s. (For more recent data, see the "Postscript" to this chapter.)

The influence of the departure of rubella-deafened children from these schools is discussed in the next section.

Barring unforeseen events (e.g., epidemics or medical breakthroughs) the number of hearing impaired children varies as the general birth rate of the population increases or decreases, with school enrollment naturally following in the wake of the birth rate. (As noted, the decline in residential school enrollment during the 1970s corresponded almost exactly to the declining regular school enrollment during this period.) The National Center for Education Statistics (Gerald, 1985) projects a continuing decline in regular public school enrollment for kindergarten through grade 12 into 1984, with an upturn in enrollment beginning in 1985. Between 1985 and 1992 it is estimated that the general public school enrollment in grades kindergarten through 12 will increase by more than 2 million students.

Thus, if the incidence of hearing impairment continues to vary with general population figures, beginning around 1985–1986 the residential schools will face a somewhat stable pool of potential students. This does not take into account, of course, the impact of Public Law 94-142 on residential school enrollment or of regional differences—influenced by immigration, for example—on this enrollment.

Chapter 2 on cause of hearing loss also has relevance for residential school enrollment. The introduction of the rubella vaccine in 1969 makes unlikely any large-scale epidemic due to this cause. Since more than 40 percent of the 9001 rubella-deafened students in the 1982–1983 Annual Survey attended residential schools, this potential source of students will no longer exist. For very different reasons, children whose hearing loss is caused by otitis media are not candidates for residential school placement; otitis media children, with their less severe hearing losses, do not attend residential schools in any significant numbers.

On the other hand, students with deafness caused by hereditary factors or by meningitis (of whom 31 percent in each group attended residential schools during the 1982–1983 Annual Survey) would appear to remain candidates for residential school placement. This assumes that no medical breakthroughs affecting these two causes will occur in the near future. (A recent vaccine for one type of meningitis may offer such a breakthrough: see Chapter 2.)

Two other cause groups supplied large numbers of students to the residential schools in 1982–1983: the unspecified *other* cause group, of whom 32 percent attended residential schools, and the *undetermined cause* category, from which 30 percent enrolled in these schools. Since these causes remain unspecified, there is no way of predicting how the number of students deafened by these causes may change in the future. For the present, it would seem that these two groups, substantially affected by severe or profound hearing losses, will continue as potential sources of students for the residential schools.

Regionally, whichever set of population assumptions one chooses from those offered by the U.S. Bureau of the Census, the South and West will continue to claim, at the expense of the Northeast and Midwest, larger shares of the total U.S. population well into the 1990s (U.S. Bureau of the Census, 1983). Thus, on the basis of population alone, and without attempting to use regional age projections too freely, the residential schools in the South and West appear to have the greatest opportunities for recruiting students because of the population pool accessible to them.

Age

The enrollment decline in the residential schools is exacerbated by the presence of a large number of students in these schools who are about to leave the secondary school system (i.e., students 17 years of age and older). This troubling side of the enrollment picture in 1983 was somewhat balanced by the increase in enrollment of hearing impaired children less than 6 years of age in the residential schools of all four regions of the country.

As indicated earlier, the large number of older students in the residential schools was chiefly due to the rubella-deafened children born in 1964 and 1965. Because these older students were still enrolled in large numbers during the 1982–1983 school year, their imminent departure in subsequent years will undoubtedly reduce enrollment in these schools still further. (The rubella-deafened students appear to be remaining in high school longer than other students.) The increase of children less than 6 years old, first noted in the South in 1978, reflects the establishment of preschool programs, various kinds of parent-child services, and other curriculum innovations that may help to stabilize enrollment in these schools.

Day Students

The traditional preponderance of resident students in these schools has been altered over the past decade, dwindling from four residents for every day student in the early 1970s to a little more than two to one in 1983. The change is significant because day students generally differ from resident students in several ways: They are younger, have fewer additional handicaps and better speech intelligibility, are more likely to come from a white ethnic background, use sign less frequently, and are integrated with hearing students more than resident students. Their achievement level, however, is similar to that of resident students.

The trend toward increasing enrollment of day students in the residential schools would appear to be fostered by the present mainstreaming climate and by certain curriculum innovations on the part of the residential schools (e.g., reverse mainstreaming: hearing students attending residential school classes). Schools located within large metropolitan areas, which afford greater job opportunities for parents, and those offering specialized services have more opportunities to recruit day students into their programs. In effect, some of the residential schools are becoming large day programs.

It is difficult to estimate what effect the increased presence of day students will have on the residential schools. Staffing patterns (e.g., dormitory and weekend staff) will certainly be modified. However, fundamental similarities between the resident and day students—their concentration in the severe and profound hearing loss range and their achievement levels—make less likely any radical changes in school curriculum or services.

Minority Enrollment

The percentage of minority students has been climbing steadily in the residential schools, rising from 19.9 percent of total enrollment in 1972 to 28.5 percent in 1983. The increase has been largely due to the decline in white, non-Hispanic enrollment. Regionally, 75.0 percent of the black students were concentrated in the southern schools during the 1982–1983 school year; 42.6 percent of the Hispanic students were enrolled in the West.

It is difficult to determine why there has been such a precipitous decline in the number of white, non-Hispanic students in these residential schools. Whether their families have more incentives or better resources for mainstreaming or for enrolling these students in private schools is conjectural.

At present the black population of the United States is growing at a much more rapid rate than the white population (6.7 percent as compared to 3.2 percent), due largely to higher fertility (U.S. Bureau of the Census, 1985). At the same time, nonblack minority groups, including Hispanics, Asians, and Pacific Islanders, are also growing rapidly, due both to a higher birth rate and to immigration factors (U.S. Bureau of the Census, 1984b). There are also regional differences within these minority demographics. For example, people of Spanish origin made up 19 percent of the population of California in 1980, but accounted for 32 percent of the birth-through-age-4 group; in Texas, Hispanics totaled 21 percent of the population in 1980, but 30 percent of the birth-through-age-4 group (Dolman and Kaufman, 1984a, 1984b).

Whatever factors have influenced the departure of white students from the residential schools between 1972 and 1983, the increasing minority population within the United States, especially in some sections of the southern and western regions of the country, argues for continuing enrollment opportunities among these students for the residential schools.

Multiply Handicapped Students

Although the number of multiply handicapped students rose from 25.4 percent of total enrollment in these schools in 1971 to 29.7 percent in 1983, this increase occurred largely in the 1971 through 1978 period. Regionally, more than one third of the students in both the northeastern and western residential schools were reported as multiply handicapped in 1983. Emotional or behavioral problems and learning disabilities were the two additional handicaps most frequently reported by these 60 schools in 1983. In both the Northeast and West in 1983, 11 percent of the students were reported with emotional or behavioral problems; 10 percent of the students in these two regions were reported as having learning disabilities.

Residential schools have traditionally served a variety of multiply handicapped students. Although the southern schools were the only ones to report an overall numerical increase in multiply handicapped students between 1978 and 1983, all four regions of the country reported an increase of learning disabled students. In addition, increasing minority enrollment in these schools may well increase the numbers of multiply handicapped students because black and Hispanic students are more likely to be reported as having a handicap in addition to their hearing impairment. These factors, along with the pressure of an ongoing enrollment decline, may encourage residential schools to modify their entrance requirements and curricula to accommodate multiply handicapped students even more so than in the past.

CONCLUSION

It is somewhat ironic that the future of the residential schools for deaf students may depend, in great measure, on the success or failure of mainstream programs educating these students within local school districts. In Chapter 5, Moores and Kluwin note the gap between the rhetoric and the reality of mainstreaming at the present time. There is some evidence to indicate this gap will be difficult to close, at least within a short space of time. The evidence includes (a) a shortage of special education teachers and staff generally and in the field of hearing impairment specifically (Smith-Davis, Burke, and Noel, 1984; Spragins, Karchmer, and Schildroth, 1981); (b) certain administrative practices, such as temporary or provisional certification of teachers in areas of special education for which they have not been trained; and (c) federal and local funding restrictions that will undoubtedly affect the provision of specialized services critical for many mainstreamed hearing impaired students (e.g., interpreting and tutoring services).

Perhaps of even more concern in the integrated setting is the establishment of a workable communication climate for hearing impaired students, both within and outside the classroom—between teachers and deaf students and between deaf students and hearing students. Johnson, Johnson, and Maryuma (1983) investigated the ideal conditions for constructive classroom interaction of ethnically diverse students and of handicapped with nonhandicapped students. They found that interaction based on cooperative and interpersonal collaboration and communication rather than individualistic learning experiences based on competition fostered constructive relationships and ultimately better achievement. This is a challenge presented to all types of schools serving hearing impaired children, of course, but one that is perhaps more problematical in the integrated classroom setting, especially if very few deaf students are enrolled in a particular local school. The more this type of communication environment can be established and specialized services provided in mainstream programs, the more these programs will be seen as alternative school placements for hearing impaired children and youth. However, the magnitude of the task of providing this type of environment should not be underestimated.

In any case, the decade of the 1980s will undoubtedly continue to be a difficult period for the residential schools. It is questionable that the slight upturn in the general school enrollment mentioned earlier in this chapter will benefit the residential schools to any great extent. It will almost certainly not offset the consequences of three serious threats to their well-being: the enrollment decline being experienced by these schools, the present educational and legal climate encouraged by Public Law 94-142, and the fiscal austerity being enacted at all levels of government. The future of these schools may well depend upon their ability to react vigorously and imaginatively to these forces.

POSTSCRIPT

As this chapter was nearing completion, preliminary results from the 1984–1985 Annual Survey became available. The 1984–1985 data reported by the 60 residential schools examined here reveal a continuing steep enrollment decline: Between 1983 and 1985 enrollment in these schools dropped by 2691 students (17.4 percent). The Midwest and Northeast again sustained the largest losses, 22.1 percent and 18.4 percent respectively, although the South and West did not lag far behind with declines of 13.9 percent and 16.3 percent.

Nationally, the enrollment of children less than 6 years old in these schools inched above 10 percent of total enrollment, and the group of students 18 years of age and older dropped to 24.2 percent, almost two percentage points lower than in 1983. Although there were 459 fewer minority children in these schools in 1985 than in 1983, their percentage of the total enrollment rose to 30.1 percent, due (as noted for the earlier period) to the large ongoing decline in the number of white students. One third of the students in 1985 were day students, a 3 percent increase over 1983. Almost 6 percent of the students from these residential schools were partially integrated in classes with hearing students.

Multiply handicapped students, as a percentage of total enrollment, rose slightly, from 29.7 percent in 1983 to 30.6 percent in 1985. Students reported as mentally retarded were 6.8 percent of the enrollment in 1985, as compared to 5.9 percent in 1983. Learning disability was the only other additional handicap reported for a higher percentage of students in 1985 (8.2 percent) than in 1983 (7.5 percent).

Thus, all of the earlier trends noted in the "Summary and Discussion" section of this chapter appear to be continuing into the second half of the 1980s.

REFERENCES

Anderson, R., Stevens, G., and Stuckless, R. (1966). *Provisions for education of mentally retarded deaf children in residential schools for the deaf* (Report No. BR-5-0977, Grant OEG-32-48-1110-5008). Pittsburgh University, Pennsylvania School of Education.

Brill, R. (1978). *Mainstreaming the prelingually deaf child.* Washington, DC: Gallaudet College Press.

Craig, W., and Salem, J. (1975). Partial mainstreaming of deaf with hearing students: Residential school perspectives. *American Annals of the Deaf, 120,* 28–36.

Dolman, G., and Kaufman, N. (1984a). *Minorities in higher education: The changing Southwest (California)* (No. 2A134b). Boulder, CO: Western Interstate Commission for Higher Education.

Dolman, G., and Kaufman, N. (1984b). *Minorities in higher education: The changing Southwest (Texas)* (No. 2A134e). Boulder, CO: Western Interstate Commission for Higher Education.

Evans, A. (1975). Experiential deprivation: Unresolved factor in the impoverished socialization of deaf school children in residence. *American Annals of the Deaf, 120,* 545–552.

Gentile, A., and McCarthy, B. (1973). *Additional handicapping conditions among hearing impaired students—United States: 1971–1972* (Series D, No. 14). Washington, DC: Gallaudet College, Office of Demographic Studies.

Gerald, D. (1985). *Projections of education statistics to 1992–93: Methodological report with detailed projection tables* (NCES 85-408). Washington, DC: National Center for Education Statistics.

Johnson, D., Johnson, R., and Maruyama, G., (1983). Interdependence and interpersonal attraction among heterogeneous and homogeneous individuals: A theoretical formulation and a meta-analysis of the research. *Review of Educational Research, 53*(1), 5–54.

Karchmer, M., and Petersen, L. (1980). *Commuter students at residential schools for the deaf* (Series R, No. 7). Washington, DC: Gallaudet College, Office of Demographic Studies.

Meadow, K., and Trybus, R. (1979). Behavioral and emotional problems of deaf children: An overview. In L. J. Bradford and W. G. Hardy (Eds.), *Hearing and hearing impairment* (pp. 395–403). New York: Grune and Stratton.

Noyes, J. (1884). *The third biennial report of the directors and officers of the Minnesota Institute for the Deaf and Dumb and the Blind and the School for Idiots and Imbeciles.* St. Paul, MN: The Pioneer Press Company.

Patterson, D., and Baud, H. (1985). *Are residential schools for the deaf meeting the challenge of the future?* Paper presented at the 52nd Biennial Convention of American Instructors of the Deaf, St. Augustine, FL, June 23–27, 1985.

Quigley, S., and Frisina, D. (1961). *Institutionalization and psychoeducational development of deaf children* (Monograph, Series A, No. 3). Washington, DC: Council for Exceptional Children.

Rawlings, B., and Gentile, A. (1970). *Additional handicapping conditions, age at onset of hearing loss, and other characteristics of hearing impaired students— United States: 1968–1969* (Series D, No. 3). Washington, DC: Gallaudet College, Office of Demographic Studies.

Schildroth, A. (1980). Public residential schools for deaf students in the United States, 1970–1978. *American Annals of the Deaf, 125,* 80–91.

Smith-Davis, J., Burke, P., and Noel, M. (1984). *Personnel to educate the handicapped in America: Supply and demand from a programmatic viewpoint.* College Park, MD: University of Maryland.

Spragins, A., Karchmer, M., and Schildroth, A. (1981). Profile of psychological service providers to hearing-impaired students. *American Annals of the Deaf, 126,* 94–105.

Tabular summary of schools and classes in the United States, October 1, 1972. (1973). *American Annals of the Deaf, 118.*

Tabular summary of schools and classes in the United States, October 1, 1978, (1979). *American Annals of the Deaf, 124.*

Tabular summary of schools and classes in the United States, October 1, 1982. (1983). *American Annals of the Deaf, 128.*

Tabular summary of schools and classes in the United States, October 1, 1983. (1984). *American Annals of the Deaf, 129.*

U.S. Bureau of the Census. (1979). *School enrollment—social and economic characteristics of students: October 1978* (Current Population Reports, Series P-25, No. 346). Washington, DC: Government Printing Office.

U.S. Bureau of the Census. (1983). *Provisional projections of the population of states, by age and sex: 1980 to 2000* (Current Population Reports, Series P-25, No. 937). Washington, DC: Government Printing Office.

U.S. Bureau of the Census. (1984a). *School enrollment—social and economic characteristics of students: October 1982 (Advance Report)* (Current Population Reports, Series P-20, No. 392). Washington, DC: Government Printing Office.

U.S. Bureau of the Census. (1984b). *Projections of the population of the United States, by age, sex, and race: 1983 to 2080* (Current Population Reports, Series P-25, No. 952). Washington, DC: Government Printing Office.

U.S. Bureau of the Census. (1985). *Estimates of the population of the United States, by age, sex, and race: 1980 to 1984* (Current Population Reports, Series P-25, No. 965). Washington DC: Government Printing Office.

U.S. Department of Education. (1983). *To assure the free appropriate public education of all handicapped children. Fifth annual report to Congress on the implementation of Public Law 94-142: The Education for All Handicapped Children Act.* Washington, DC: Government Printing Office.

White, C., Karchmer, M., Armstrong, D., and Bezozo, C. (1983). Current trends in high school graduation and college enrollment of hearing-impaired students attending residential schools. *American Annals of the Deaf, 128,* 125–131.

Williams, P. (1984). Admission policies and practices of state-operated schools for the deaf. *Exceptional Children, 50,* 550–551.

Chapter 5

Issues in School Placement

Donald F. Moores
Thomas N. Kluwin

Because of the recent development of the mainstreaming movement in the United States, many educators have assumed that there has been a steady progression from traditional separate residential schools toward the enrollment of hearing impaired children in local public schools. However, this has not been the case either historically or currently. There is a gap between the rhetoric of school placement for hearing impaired children and the reality of that placement. This gap can be explored historically as well as empirically.

HISTORICAL PERSPECTIVE

Placement in the Nineteenth and Early Twentieth Centuries

Educators have long been sensitive to the benefits of having deaf children living at home. It is not widely known that many of the first residential schools for the deaf in the United States were established originally as day schools, including the New York and Pennsylvania Schools for the Deaf, which in terms of antiquity represent the second and third oldest schools for the deaf in America (Moores, 1982).

During the first half-century of education of the deaf in America—up to the Civil War—deaf children were enrolled in residential schools located in metropolitan areas such as New York, Philadelphia, Hartford, and Pittsburgh. At that time, the United States was a rural agrarian economy. The majority of deaf children came to the schools as residential students from farms and villages. However, substantial numbers resided in the cities in which the schools were located.

Programs for deaf students, as well as for students with other handicapping conditions, that were developed in the early and middle parts of the nineteenth century reflected an essentially optimistic attitude towards the potential benefits of education and training for the handicapped. The great early special educators were influenced in this capacity by prevailing philosophies in France. Education of the deaf in America was based on a French model, and the first teacher of the deaf in America was a deaf man from France, Laurent Clerc. Not coincidentally, the basis for education of the retarded in America was established by another Frenchman, Edouard Seguin, who immigrated to the United States around 1850. Thus, programs for the handicapped in America for most of the nineteenth century were characterized by humane treatment, with an educational emphasis designed to prepare students to function in society at large (Kanner, 1967; Kauffman, 1980; Moores, 1982).

For a number of reasons, the situation began to change in the late nineteenth and early twentieth centuries. There was concern that the expansion of residential schools constituted a drain on state treasuries and a growing conviction that many handicapped individuals constituted a threat to society, Terman (1916), for example, claiming there was a relationship between mental subnormality and moral subnormality.

One result was that residential facilities for the handicapped became less educational and more custodial, with the expectation that many individuals would remain in them throughout their lives. There was also the tendency to locate any new residential facilities away from population centers. Although residential schools for deaf students did not become custodial institutions, they were influenced by the trends (Moores, 1982). Unlike the first schools, which were located in metropolitan areas, schools for the deaf constructed during this period were often placed away from large cities. It was not uncommon for a school for the deaf, for the retarded, and for the blind all to be constructed in the same small town 50 or 100 miles or more from the largest city in a state. In many ways, then, the late nineteenth century witnessed increasing isolation of deaf children from their families and from society at large.

Given the natural desires of parents to keep their children at home, it should not be surprising to learn of attempts to teach deaf and hearing children in integrated settings. Gordon (1885) reported on efforts to educate deaf children in public schools in Europe as early as 1815. An experimental school in which deaf children received special tutoring and were integrated with hearing children was established in Bavaria in 1821. It served as a model for other schools, and in 1828 the German Ministry of Education predicted that all deaf children in the kingdom would be educated in such schools by 1838. However, by 1854 there remained no common classes for deaf and hearing children (Gordon, 1885). There were similar developments in other parts of Europe. In 1855 the French Council of Public Education endorsed the system of integrated coeducation of deaf and hearing children that had been established in many schools in France. By 1882 only an estimated 30 pupils remained in the system (Gordon, 1885). Gordon also reported that 40 percent of deaf children in Prussia were educated in schools for hearing children in 1871 but that not one deaf child could be identified in such a placement by 1881.

In the United States of the nineteenth century, education of deaf children did not witness the extremes found in the placement of these children in Europe. The United States did not experience any nationwide mainstream movement. Overall, the evidence suggests that, on balance, American deaf people were better educated, more socially integrated, and more financially independent than their European counterparts (Moores, 1982).

Alexander Graham Bell was a major force in arguing against the existence of separate residential schools (1884) and was influential in his support of the establishment of integrated public school programs for deaf students. However, the largest integrated program in the nineteenth century was the private bilingual German/English Knapp Institute in Baltimore. The institute had a department for deaf children, who received special training in speech and speechreading (Knapp, 1893). The addition of German to the Baltimore Public School curriculum caused a rapid decrease in enrollment and the eventual closing of the school.

It should be clear from this brief description that enrollment trends for deaf children from the early nineteenth century up to the beginning of World War II were not consistent. There had been numerous false starts in Europe and America. There is little or no support for the idea that public schools became consistently more accepting over this period. In fact, there is evidence to suggest that, if anything, there were periods in which the public school became more exclusive and rejecting of deaf students.

Developments Since World War II

Since World War II there has been a clear trend toward increasing accommodation of deaf children in public school settings, a trend accelerated by the passage in 1975 of U.S. Public Law 94-142, The Education for All Handicapped Children Act. As in previous periods, trends in educational placement of deaf children have been influenced by developments in general and special education, as well as by changes specific to the education of deaf students.

Of a general nature, the country has become urbanized and much more populous. Because of an extended baby boom, extensive immigration, and increases in life expectancy, the U.S. population is nearly double that of 50 years ago. There are more people and they are more highly concentrated in urban metropolitan areas. At a time when the baby boom was ending in the early 1960s, education of deaf children was faced with the results of the largest known worldwide rubella epidemic, which greatly increased the number of deaf children (Moores, 1982).

The appearance of this unusually large number of deaf children from the middle of the 1960s presented unique problems to the field of education of the deaf. As in American society in general, the numbers of deaf children in the U.S. population and in U.S. schools had steadily increased over a generation. However, from 1965 the general preschool and elementary school age population was beginning to decline, but education of the deaf was faced with the problem of moving an unusually large block of children through the educational system. At each step in the preschool, elementary, secondary, and postsecondary school systems this block would present unprecedented challenges to the education of the deaf.

It is to their credit that educators responded quickly and effectively to the challenges presented by these children. One important outcome was that the presence of such numbers substantially altered the ways in which deaf children are educated from preschool through adulthood. In terms of placement, it speeded up the process of public school placement, which may be seen as the result of several interacting, often disparate, factors. Three of the more notable are the following:

1. Postwar increase in the American school age population up to 1965
2. Urbanization and suburbanization of the population, accompanied by efficient metropolitan highway systems
3. Rubella-related increase in deaf children from 1964 to 1965 concurrent with a decline in births in the general population

Although the issues are quite complex, some brief statements might clarify the impact of each of these factors. First, the post-World War II baby boom triggered an unprecedented construction of elementary and then secondary schools throughout the country. In many areas, construction of such facilities could not keep pace with the demand. The population increase was most evident in metropolitan areas, especially in the growth of suburbs. Suburbanization itself was related to aspects of the developing federal highway system, which involved construction of interstate routes through and around the cities in the form of beltways. For the first time there were very large concentrations of people in many areas throughout the country with ready intrametropolitan highway access, thus mitigating the age-old problem of providing educational services to persons with a low incidence condition such as deafness.

With the appearance of children deafened through the rubella epidemic, some implicit decisions were immediately made regarding school placement. Of primary importance was the fact that the existing residential schools did not have the resources to handle such an influx of students at one age level. In most residential schools, preschool programs themselves were relatively recent phenomena, and there was a scarcity of teachers of the deaf trained to work at the preschool level. Also, many children deafened through rubella had secondary handicaps, and not all schools were equipped to deal with this type of student. In addition, except for a few states, little or no consideration was given by state legislatures to the construction of additional residential facilities. The children were seen as a one-time-only educational problem, and there was a reluctance to invest in construction that would be underused after they left.

The third factor, the contemporary birth rate decline, was of at least equal importance. For the first time, schools built to accommodate a burgeoning population had empty classrooms. It was clear that in many towns and cities elementary and secondary schools eventually would be closed. Thus, the presence of children deafened because of the rubella epidemic coincided with the appearance for the first time in decades of unused classroom space.

Public Law 94-142

Beginning in the 1960s, leaders in special education began to question the efficacy of residential or special class placement of handicapped children (Dunn, 1968). It was at this time that the term *mainstreaming* came into popular use. Several court cases regarding educational treatment and placement of handicapped individuals established precedents. The most well known of these were *Pennsylvania Association for Retarded Citizens (PARC) v. Commonwealth of Pennsylvania* (1972) and *Mills v. Board of Education of the District of Columbia* (1972). In both cases it was ruled that exclusion of retarded individuals from a free public education was illegal. In both cases regular classroom placement was judged to be preferable to special class placement, which in turn was preferable to placement in a residential school or institution. The implication was that, to be acceptable, placement in a residential school or institution should be demonstrably *superior* to placement in a special class or regular class for a particular child. The burden of proof was on the educator to justify enrollment of a child in a residential program.

In the fall of 1975 President Ford signed into law U.S. Public Law 94-142: The Education For All Handicapped Children Act. This legislation represented a shift toward direct federal involvement in special education. In fact, it fundamentally altered the relationship between the federal government and state and local agencies educating handicapped children. The basic thrust of the law was a mandate for a free appropriate public education for all handicapped children in the least restrictive environment (LRE) appropriate to an individual child's needs (Harvey and Siantz, 1979).

To ensure accommodation to individual needs, the law calls for non-discriminatory testing and assurance of an individualized education plan (IEP) to be developed for every child and to be reviewed at least annually in consultation with parents. The IEP should describe a child's present level of performance, educational objectives, and the procedures for evaluating progress.

Although Public Law 94-142 has been considered a mainstreaming law, that word was not used in the legislation. The law stipulates that handicapped children should be educated with nonhandicapped children to the greatest appropriate degree. Because many of the key terms in the law—including *least restrictive environment* and *free appropriate public education*—have not been operationally defined, differences of opinion remain in interpreting the meaning of the law, and there has been controversy regarding federal regulations written to implement Public Law 94-142. As a result the process has followed a sequence that is common with implementation of major laws, namely, legislation—regulation—litigation. Subsequent to the passing of the legislation and development of federal regulations to guide implementation, there have been numerous due process procedures and court cases to establish the parameters of the law. Concerning school placement, it appears that the mandate for least restrictive environment is subsumed under that of appropriate public education. This is interpreted as meaning that placement cannot be limited to one type of setting; alternatives may include instruction in regular classes, resource rooms, self-contained classes, and special schools and institutions. Bersoff and Veltman (1979), in a review of educational placement, summarized the impact of Public Law 94-142 as follows:

> Despite the preference for mainstreaming in Public Law 94-142, placement of handicapped children in regular classrooms may be inappropriate, as recent judicial decisions have held. In *Frederick L. v. Thomas* (1977) the court concluded that Pennsylvania had to identify all learning disabled students. These students were already receiving an education in regular classrooms but the court found that many such students should be placed in separate classes while others should be provided supplemental support services. Similarly, the court in *Howard S. v. Friendswood Independent School District* (1978) found that placement of the plaintiff in regular classes with a resource teacher was an inappropriate program considering the severity of his disability. From these examples it seems that although placement in regular classes is viewed as desirable under PL 94-142, such a placement will still be open to challenge as being inappropriate for a particular student's educational needs. (pp. 19–20)

In the field of education of the deaf, the most important case relative to Public Law 94-142 involved the provision of support services in the form of an interpreter for a deaf girl integrated into a regular elementary school class. The differences between the U.S. Supreme Court 1982 ruling and the 1979 decision of a lower court highlights the great diversity in interpreting the meaning of Public Law 94-142. In brief, as presented in a New York district court, the deaf parents of an integrated deaf child requested that a stipulation for provision of an interpreter be provided to facilitate their daughter's ability to function at the level of her academic and intellectual capacity. The school district refused, arguing that the child was achieving at grade level, thus indicating she was receiving adequate support. The conflict rested in the parents' argument that the child should receive support to enable her to function at maximum levels, whereas the school district maintained the position that Public Law 94-142 mandates the provision of adequate, not necessarily optimal, services. At the district court level (*Rowley v. the Hendrick Hudson Board of Education and the Commissioner of Education of the State of New York*, 1979), the ruling was in favor of the child; and the plaintiffs were upheld on the grounds that the educational needs of the child in question could best be met through the services of an interpreter in the regular classroom.

The school district and the state of New York appealed the decision, and the case was heard by the U.S. Supreme Court. The U.S. Supreme Court overturned the district court judgment and ruled that the school did not have to provide an interpreter. The particular decision itself may be of relatively minor importance in relation to the rationale presented to justify it (Rehnquist, 1982). The U.S Supreme Court decided that in its enactment of Public Law 94-142 the U.S. Congress did not impose on the states any greater substantive educational standard than would be necessary to make access to education meaningful, declaring that "the intent of the Act was more to open the door of public education to handicapped children on appropriate terms than to guarantee any particular level of education once inside" (p. 14). The U.S. Supreme Court further declared that Public Law 94-142 imposes no clear obligation upon recipient states beyond the requirement that handicapped children receive some form of specialized education: "to require . . . the furnishing of every specialized service necessary to maximize each handicapped child's potential is, we think, further than Congress intended to go" (p. 22).

One is faced, then, with the U.S. Supreme Court interpreting Public Law 94-142 as offering only a "floor of opportunity" for handicapped children, as opposed to maximizing the potential achievement of each handicapped child. The implication is that the legal mandate for extensive special services is, therefore, limited, and it will be necessary to study the provision of services throughout the country before a definite pattern can be identified.

It should be acknowledged, however, that the thrust of Public Law 94-142 and the educational philosophy behind it have not met with universal approval or support. In a paper entitled "The Education Crisis," Gardner (1983) presented strong criticisms of the goals and implementation of Public Law 94-142, claiming it has had a negative impact on American education in general: Such legislation "has directed funding, attention, and policy to the 'special' student. The evidence shows regrettably that such programs yield minimal positive results for that student, and generally damaging results for the normal student" (pp. 1–2). She continued:

> Laws for the education of the handicapped have drained resources from the normal school population, probably weakened the quality of teaching, and falsely labeled normal children. In a misguided effort to help a few, the many have been injured. . . . Public schools should not be required to educate those children who cannot, without damaging the main purpose of public education, function in a normal classroom setting. Additional expenditures for special schools or self-contained classroom placements should be the responsibility of the family and local community. Responsibility for oneself, one's family and one's neighbors is a fundamental aspect of American social history and a key to the success of American society. (pp. 12–13)

This chapter has constructed four points of argument so far to set the stage for a discussion of the reality of the mainstreaming experience for the hearing impaired child. Historically, the education of hearing impaired children has been a mixed system of residential and day programs, with the emphasis changing during different periods for various reasons. Traditionally, general education programs have responded to reductions in their conventional school populations by increasing services to other populations. Legally, the definition of appropriate placement under Public Law 94-142 has been defined very narrowly by the U.S. Supreme Court, with the result that the issue of appropriate placement, rather than being resolved, has in effect become more complex. Politically, there is a backlash to the cost of public education, with a specific attack on special education as an area of higher expense and of questionable value.

EMPIRICAL RESEARCH

Literature Review

In a treatment of data from the 1977–1978 Annual Survey of Hearing Impaired Children and Youth, Wolk, Karchmer, and Schildroth (1982) have pointed out that the type of educational program in which a hearing impaired student is enrolled is an important factor both in the amount of integration that the student will experience and in the type of experience it will be. Variation can be considerable.

An illustration of this point can be found in the work of Libbey and Pronovost (1980) who surveyed 557 hearing impaired adolescents "mainstreamed or partially mainstreamed" in 32 local school programs in 18 states. Because the average number of students per program was small (less than 18), it might be expected that academic integration with hearing students would be extensive. However, the Libbey and Pronovost findings do not support those expectations. Twenty-seven percent of their sample were not *academically* integrated at all, and an additional 18 percent were integrated only in a single academic class. Such figures fall between the numbers in the national study of Wolk and coworkers (1982), in which 6.2 percent of students in part-time special education programs and 62 percent of students in full-time special education programs had no academic integration. Frequency and type of mainstreaming vary considerably from program type to program type.

Because of the programmatic differences and the complex interaction between individual characteristics and type of integration, each hearing impaired child has unique needs. However, some commonalities can be identified, based on Libbey and Pronovost's figures, in regard to the type of integration that is occurring. Examination of their figures indicates that nonacademic integration is the most frequent, followed by vocational education. Academic integration is much less frequent. Of the academic subjects, mathematics and science courses are the most likely integrated courses for deaf students, followed by social studies; English is the least likely.

The increasing placement of hearing impaired children in public school settings with a small and specialized trend toward integration with hearing students prompts two questions: First, who are the most appropriate candidates for integration? Second, are all of the appropriate candidates being integrated on an equitable basis? The decision to integrate a deaf child into a regular classroom is conditioned by two primary considerations: the characteristics of the child and the nature of the situation into which the child will be placed. The characteristics of the child that influence the decision fall generally into three broad categories: academic achievement or ability, communication skill, and personal or social adjustment (Bishop, 1979; Kindred, 1980). Academic considerations include both the child's previous achievement and an estimation of the child's ability to learn in a new situation. Communication factors involve the degree of hearing loss of the child, the child's speech expression and reception skills, knowledge of English, and use of simultaneous communication. Personal and social adjustment includes issues of social adjustment or maturity, as revealed by ratings of maturation, responsibility, self-confidence, and initiative.

In addition to the child's abilities and potential, there are issues involving the nature of the classroom into which the child will be placed and the availability of support services. Factors such as the experience of the teacher, type of subject matter, curriculum, and the other students in the class must be considered. In addition, the quantity and quality of support that can be provided to the child by specialists such as audiologists, interpreters, and resource room teachers must be weighed in the decision to place the child.

Previous research has investigated some of these factors influencing integration. For example, three separate studies showed that degree of hearing loss is directly related to the decision to integrate, the degree of integration, and the nature of the integration. Karchmer and Trybus (1977) reported differences of degree of hearing loss on the basis of the type of placement, but the Allen and Osborn study (1984) indicated that even within school programs that have relatively high degrees of integration, students who are actually integrated have less severe hearing losses. Wolk and coworkers (1982) examined the extent of hearing loss across several different types of programs and found that the degree of integration, as measured by the number of hours during the week that the child was integrated, predicted the degree of hearing loss of the child, that is, the less severe the hearing loss, the greater the number of hours of integration for the child. Degree of hearing loss also interacts with subject matter assignment. In social studies and English classes, less severe hearing loss is a strong predictor of placement, but in mathematics classes it is a weaker predictor.

Age at onset of hearing loss is also related to placement. Allen and Osborn (1984) reported that a greater percentage of integrated children are postlingually deafened, thus suggesting that greater English knowledge and better speech intelligibility are factors in the decision to integrate deaf children. They also reported that the reading ability of integrated children, more of whom are postlingually deafened, is significantly higher than the reading ability of nonintegrated children.

From the available literature, therefore, it is apparent that communication ability, as influenced by degree of hearing loss and age at onset of loss, is an important factor in the decision to integrate deaf children into regular classes.

Unfortunately, there are no comparable reported studies of the social or emotional development of integrated versus nonintegrated deaf children, although the work of Allen and Osborn (1984) indirectly addressed the question of social adjustment. In their consideration of various demographic factors they included the presence of additional handicaps, one of which was the reported frequency of behavioral problems. They found that there were no differences between integrated and nonintegrated students on the basis of physical handicaps other than deafness but that the integrated students had fewer reported behavioral adjustment problems. This, of course, is to be expected. Many school programs have separate class placements for hearing children categorized as having behavior problems. It is logical to assume that few deaf children classified as having behavior problems would be identified as candidates for integration. For the moment it can only be assumed that the social maturity, initiative, and motivation of the children are factors in consideration for placement. The bulk of the previous research has focused on academic achievement or communication variables and not on these factors.

It must be acknowledged that there may be factors extraneous to academic ability, communication skill, and social development that may reduce the probability of a particular child being assigned to a regular classroom. Such factors include the race, sex, or economic status of the child. One study previously cited (Wolk et al., 1982) reported that ethnic status is a factor; black or Hispanic students are less likely to be integrated than Anglo students. Allen and Osborn (1984), on the other hand, found a higher proportion of black students among the integrated group, a result they described as "perplexing," given previous research (p. 102).

Wolk and coworkers (1982) and Allen and Osborn (1984) reported no statistically significant differences for sex of the child as influencing integration. Karchmer and Trybus (1977) reported no inferential statistics, but their data suggest parental income may be related to the type of program in which a child is placed.

Based on the review of the literature, it would be expected that integrated hearing impaired students would be academically more accomplished than nonintegrated students; that the integrated students would have better communication skills than nonintegrated students; and that the social maturity of the integrated students, including attitudes toward schooling, would be more developed. Although previous research results are mixed, it might also be expected that these integrated students would come from families with specific ethnic or economic characteristics. There is now a basis for a partial answer to the first question: Who is the most appropriate candidate for integration? The second question regarding the fairness of the process can be answered by first looking at who is integrated versus who might be eligible for integration. Following that the question of the fairness of the process can be addressed by examining additional characteristics of the students who might be integrated but are not, particularly considering the ethnicity and socioeconomic status of those children.

Integration in Three Urban Settings

The data for this study represent the first year's effort of a multiyear study of the placement of hearing impaired students in large urban public school systems. Programs in three of the largest city systems in the United States were examined. Because of the number of subjects (205), the results are reported as pooled, although in fact they are drawn from three separate locales.

Description of Sites

Site 1 was physically divided between two schools. Nonintegrated students received services at a core school for deaf children from preschool through high school. Integrated students were placed in a comprehensive high school of 1300 hearing students in two resource rooms with teachers of the deaf, an aide, and an interpreter for the integrated classes. The coordinator for the high school program at the self-contained site also functioned as liaison for the integrated site. Thirty-six students were in the self-contained site; 12 were in the integrated site. The program employed a total communication instructional system.

Site 2 was a comprehensive high school with an enrollment from grades 9 through 12 of approximately 1550 students, including 110 deaf students and 25 multiply handicapped students. The day-to-day functioning of the hearing impaired program was the responsibility of a supervisor of the high school program for the hearing impaired. The program followed a total communication philosophy, and sign interpretation was provided to students in the integrated classes through a trained staff of interpreters.

Site 3 was located in a comprehensive high school with more than 2000 students. The high school was divided into two facilities located across the street from each other; one housed freshman, sophomores, and the hearing impaired program, and the other housed juniors and seniors. Integration was in both locations. Responsibility for the functioning of the program for the deaf rested with supervisory staff located elsewhere. Day-to-day liaison was provided by a counselor for the deaf students.

Data Collection

Data for this aspect of the study came from student questionnaires, school records, the Annual Survey of Hearing Impaired Children and Youth of the Center for Assessment and Demographic Studies at Gallaudet College, and the Meadow/Kendall Social-Emotional Assessment Inventory for Deaf and Hearing Impaired Students.

At the start of the school year, a hearing researcher accompanied by a deaf research assistant and one or more school staff members who were either trained interpreters or teachers of the deaf administered a questionnaire to small groups of students. The instructions were signed and spoken simultaneously. Students were allowed to complete the questionnaire on their own. Any students who were having difficulty completing the questionnaire were taken through it individually item by item and their responses recorded. The questionnaire elicited personal information, family information, class schedules, attitudes toward the school program, and information about communication patterns.

School records were examined for current demographic and achievement data. In addition, the Center for Assessment and Demographic Studies at Gallaudet College, with the permission of the three school districts, provided demographic and achievement data from its Annual Survey of Hearing Impaired Children and Youth and from its record of data on the Stanford Achievement Test (sixth edition).

The Meadow/Kendall Social-Emotional Assessment Inventory for

Deaf and Hearing Impaired Students is intended to be an observational checklist of school-age deaf children's social and emotional behavior. It consists of 59 items divided into three subscales: social adjustment, self-image, and emotional adjustment. Each item in the inventory is intended to represent a critical type of behavior that is indicative of the emotional development of the child. Teachers of the deaf at these schools were asked to complete the inventories of the students they were most familiar with.

Results

A variety of data was available on 205 students from these sites. Before the question of appropriateness of placement could be answered, the issues of the actual numbers of integrated students and the type of placement of the students needed to be determined. Table 5–1 presents data on the type of instructional program for 185 students for whom class schedule information was available.

The type of academic integration reported by students in this sample fits the trends reported by Libbey and Pronovost (1980). The largest percentage of students was integrated into mathematics classes, followed by physical education and vocational education classes.

As is apparent from Table 5–1, it would be difficult to use students integrated in English, social studies, or science courses as an index of the criteria for integration because so few of them were integrated. Consequently, the study looks only at the students integrated into the mathematics classes.

At least four criteria could be used in the selection of a student for integration into a mathematics class: mathematics ability, reading ability, social adjustment, and hearing level. Based on the data available, the following variables were investigated:

1. Stanford Achievement Test: Hearing Impaired Version, Math Computation Subtest
2. Stanford Achievement Test: Hearing Impaired Version, Reading Comprehension Subtest
3. Social Adjustment scale on the Meadow/Kendall Social-Emotional Assessment Inventory for Deaf and Hearing Impaired Students
4. Better-ear average

The first three variables are self-explanatory. Better-ear average was selected because it has been repeatedly shown to correlate highly with speech intelligibility and with lipreading or other measures of audition.

For each of these four variables the mean and standard deviation of the group of students who were presently integrated into a mathematics class were computed. A limit of one half of a standard deviation from the mean in the negative direction was defined, thus creating a value range

Table 5–1. Class Placement of 185 Deaf Students by Subject Matter

	Class Placement (%)			
Subject	Self-Contained Class	Integrated Class	Total Taking Subject	Students Not Taking Subject
English	83.7	7.3	91.0	9.0
Mathematics	67.2	21.3	88.5	11.5
Social Studies	71.0	7.1	78.1	21.9
Science	65.7	8.9	74.6	25.4
Art	14.5	6.7	21.2	78.4
Vocational education	48.5	11.5	60.0	40.0
Physical education	38.3	13.2	51.5	48.5

for the index that covers approximately 66 percent of the integrated students. The 33 percent of the integrated students who were lowest on any variable therefore would not have been included in this measure. In the authors' judgment these set reasonable ranges for consideration of students as potential candidates for integration.

The criteria were applied in two stages. In the first stage, the 130 students who were taught in self-contained mathematics classes were divided on the basis of their mathematics ability. The cutoff was a Stanford Mathematics Computation Subtest scaled score of 160. Those at or above the score were considered potential candidates for integration with an interpreter. The cutoff score of 160 was computed on the basis of the mean mathematics computation scaled score for the integrated students less one half of the standard deviation. This produced two groups of mathematics students who were currently in self-contained classes. There were those students who were not candidates for integration ($n = 78$) and those students who were potential candidates for integration ($n = 52$); the former were below a Stanford mathematics computation scaled score of 160 and the latter were at or above 160.

The second stage was the application of three criteria concurrently: reading ability, social adjustment, and functional hearing ability. The criterion for reading ability was a scaled score in excess of 127 on the Stanford Reading Comprehension Subtest. The criterion for social adjustment was a score greater than 2.2 on the Meadow/Kendall Social-Emotional Assessment on the Social Adjustment subscale. The criterion for hearing was a hearing level of 99 dB or less in the better ear.

Only 22 of the original group of 52 students in self-contained mathematics classes scoring at or above 160 on math computation met all three criteria. When students who met two of the three criteria but had no data for the third were included, the number rose to 29. Allowing for success on two of the three secondary criteria, the number of possible candidates rose to 44.

In summary, on the basis of the mathematics ability criterion alone, 52 of 130 students in self-contained mathematics classes from a total of

205 students would be judged appropriate candidates for placement in an integrated mathematics class with an interpreter. By applying all four criteria, 22 out of 130 students in self-contained mathematics classes would be considered appropriate candidates for an integrated mathematics class.

It was pointed out in the review of literature that ethnicity, sex, and socioeconomic status might be factors influencing a student's placement in an integrated classroom setting. Therefore, the hypothesis that the students in self-contained classes who might be integrated were different from the integrated students on these variables was tested by using chi square statistics. Ethnicity was a factor in the distribution of students between the self-contained classrooms and the integrated classrooms. The chi square value for the 2 by 3 array of self-contained and integrated versus white, black, and Hispanic was 8.12, which has a p value of .017. Sex was not a factor in a 2 by 2 array of male and female versus self-contained and integrated. The chi square value for that comparison was .027. Socioeconomic status of the family also was not a factor. Socioeconomic status was defined on a five-point dichotomous scale consisting of the following points: nonworking parent or parents, semiskilled mother as the support of the family, semiskilled work, and either a father or both parents who have professional positions. The chi square value for that comparison was 6.06 for 4 degrees of freedom, which has a p value of .195.

Ethnicity was related to the assignment of students to integrated mathematics classes with interpreters. Based on the established criteria (mathematics achievement, reading ability, social adjustment, hearing level), the composition of deaf students in integrated mathematics classes with interpreters would have been 43 percent white, 34 percent black, and 23 percent Hispanic. The actual distribution in such classes was 58 percent white, 27 percent black, and 15 percent Hispanic. Assuming that the criteria used are valid for integration in mathematics classes, it appears that black and Hispanic students were underrepresented in integrated classes.

Discussion of Results

The first results of this study reflect three discrepancies between the rhetoric of integration and the reality. First, very few of the students in the study were integrated in academic classes. Other studies reporting large numbers of integrated students have used global indices of integration and have included placement for physical education and vocational education classes. This study was concerned with actual academic integration. Second, not all hearing impaired students who apparently possess the skills to be integrated are integrated. The study used more stringent criteria for its group of potential candidates for integration than the schools did and still found more than half as many additional candidates for integration into mathematics classes as were actually integrated. Third, ethnic background factors *may* be related to the failure to integrate some deaf children. The conclusion is that the integration of deaf children into public schools is not the unambiguous experience some might believe.

The increasing inclusion of deaf children in regular public school programs has raised great fears in some educators of the deaf and great expectations among others. There have been concerns that the mainstreaming movement would isolate children with severe and profound hearing losses from needed special education services and from interaction with other deaf children. On the other hand, there have been hopes that deaf children would become completely integrated in a "hearing world," with significantly higher levels of academic achievement over those demonstrated by deaf children in segregated settings.

From the evidence gathered in the first stages of the study reported here, neither the great fears nor the great expectations appear to be justified, at least in regard to the situation in large metropolitan areas. The most striking aspect of the data under consideration is the conservative manner in which the programs under study approach placement of deaf students in academic classes with hearing students. Even with the availability of sign interpreters, the only academic content area in which more than 10 percent of the deaf students were integrated was mathematics. It is apparent that in public school programs serving hearing impaired children in which there are large numbers with severe to profound losses, the term mainstreaming is a misnomer. Academic integration of the children, when it occurs, is highly selective. Possibly, the situation may be different in less populous areas, but in some large metropolitan districts the majority of deaf high school students are taught in self-contained academic classes, even when interpreters are available. Also, although much more information needs to be gathered, it appears that, at least in the integration of students into regular mathematics classes, socioeconomic status and sex are not factors influencing integration but ethnic status is.

CONCLUSION

Decisions regarding the educational placement of deaf children are influenced by complex interactions of a variety of factors. In addition to the unique characteristics of an individual child, consideration must be given to the appropriateness of resources and the qualifications of professional staff in different potential settings. Also, there has been little attention paid to the fact that the philosophy of education or goals of parents and educators may have an impact on where a child may be placed.

School placement decisions, then, are made within a socioeducational political framework. Therefore, changes in general value systems of the

American culture and in expectations for education can cause great shifts in the provision of educational services for the deaf.

There are two constraints, however, facing parents and educators of deaf children, constraints that have presented a dilemma since the establishment of schools for deaf students in the nineteenth century. First is the fact that deafness is a low incidence condition. With the exception of larger metropolitan areas, there will be relatively few deaf children in most locales. Even large comprehensive high schools with enrollments of 1500 to 2000 or more students probably would have few, if any, deaf students. Certainly the chances of having more than one student at any grade level in such a school would be small.

Interacting with the low incidence of deafness are the very special educational needs of deaf children. In many ways deaf children require qualitatively different services from hearing children and from children who have mental, behavioral, and physical handicaps. Hearing children begin school with a well-developed oral language system, which is used as the medium for their instruction and which is the basis for the development of reading and writing skills. For many deaf children a primary educational goal is to develop the English language skills that other children bring to the educational process. Deaf children, then, possess educationally relevant characteristics that most regular classroom teachers, reading specialists, and speech and language therapists rarely, if ever, encounter. A classroom teacher with 25 students a year probably would never have to teach a deaf child in a 10- or 15-year career. If called upon to do so, such a teacher would need extensive support services.

If a family with a deaf child lives within a heavily populated metropolitan area, they may have access to comprehensive services made feasible by the existence of a large population base. Such a base makes possible a concentration of resources and the provision of a range of options that, in terms of placement, range from self-contained classrooms, to a resource model, to provision of services to integrated children on an itinerant basis. Any comprehensive program should have all of these options available to meet the individual needs of deaf children. In the past only children with mild to moderate hearing losses or those with well-developed expressive and receptive oral communication skills were considered for placement in resource rooms or integrated classes.

The problem is much more complex in more sparsely populated areas. It is difficult for school districts of low or moderate density to provide the trained personnel and resources necessary for appropriate instruction, parent counseling, sound-treatment of rooms, speech therapy, and curriculum modification. This situation presents a dilemma that parents have faced since the beginnings of education of the deaf (Moores, 1982). The natural response of parents is to keep their children—especially when the children are young—as close to home as possible. On the other hand, it is often clear that local educational systems may not be able to meet the complex social and educational needs of a family's deaf child. Sending a child away to school can cause strains within the family, as can keeping the child at home if parents feel that this can retard academic and social development. There are no simple answers, and parents must consider both positive and negative implications of any educational placement. Frequently, the final decision represents an awareness of trade-offs or of relative benefits of differing placements.

REFERENCES

Allen, T., and Osborn, T. (1984). Academic integration of hearing impaired students. *American Annals of the Deaf, 127,* 100–113.

Bell, A. G. (1884). Fallacies concerning the deaf. *American Annals of the Deaf, 29,* 32–60.

Bersoff, D., and Veltman, E. (1979). Public Law 94-142: Legal implications for the education of handicapped children. *Journal of Research and Development in Education, 12(4),* 10–22.

Bishop, M. (1979). *Mainstreaming: Practical ideas for educating hearing impaired students.* Washington, DC: A. G. Bell Association.

Dunn, L. (1968). Special education for the mildly retarded: Is much of it justified? *Exceptional Children, 35,* 13–20.

Frederick L. v. Thomas, 419 F. Supp. 960 (E.D. Pa. 1976). Aff'd 557 F.2d 373 (3d Cir. 1977).

Gardner, H. (1983). Priorities in education: Handicapped and minority children. Working paper, Heritage Foundation, Washington, DC.

Gordon, J. (1885). Deaf mutes and the public schools from 1815 to the present day. *American Annals of the Deaf, 30,* 121–143.

Harvey, J., and Siantz, J. (1979). Public education and the handicapped. *Journal of Research and Development in Education, 12,* 1–9.

Howard S. v. Friendsworth Independent School District, 454 F. Supp. 634 (S.D. Tex. 1978).

Kanner, L. (1967). *A history of the care and study of the mentally retarded.* Springfield, IL: Charles C Thomas.

Karchmer, M., and Trybus, R. (1977). *Who are the deaf children in "mainstream" programs?* (Series R, No. 4). Washington, DC: Gallaudet College, Office of Demographic Studies.

Kauffman, J. (1980). Historical trends and contemporary issues in special education in the United States. In J. Kauffman and D. Hallahan (Eds.), *Handbook of special education* (pp. 3–23). New York: Prentice-Hall.

Kindred, E. (1980). Mainstreaming teenagers with care. *American Annals of the Deaf, 125,* 1053–1056.

Knapp, W. (1893). F. Knapp's Institute. In E. Fay (Ed.), *Histories of American schools for the deaf, 1817–1893: Volume 3. Denominational and private schools in the United States, schools in Canada and Mexico, schools which have discontinued* (pp. 1–13). Washington, DC: Volta Bureau.

Libbey, S., and Pronovost, W. (1980). Communication practices of mainstreamed hearing impaired adolescents. *Volta Review, 82,* 197–213.

Mills v. Board of Education of the District of Columbia, 348 F. Supp. 866, 868, 875 (D.D.C. 1972).

Moores, D. (1982). *Educating the deaf: Psychology, principles and practices.* Boston: Houghton Mifflin.

Pennsylvania Association for Retarded Citizens v. Commonwealth of Pennsylvania, 343 F. Supp. 279 (E.D. Pa. 1972).

Rehnquist, J. *Majority Opinion. Hendrick Hudson Board of Education v. Amy Rowley.* Case No. 80-1002, Washington, DC: Supreme Court of the United States, June 28, 1982.

Rowley v. The Hendrick Hudson Board of Education and the Commissioner of Education of the State of New York, 79 Civ. 2139 (VLB) (S.D.N.Y. 1979).

Terman, L. (1916). *The measurement of intelligence.* Boston: Houghton Mifflin.

Wolk, S., Karchmer, M., and Schildroth, A. (1982). *Patterns of academic and nonacademic integration among hearing impaired students in special education* (Series R, No. 9). Washington, DC: Gallaudet College, Center for Assessment and Demographic Studies.

Chapter 6

Patterns of Sign Use Among Hearing Impaired Students

I. King Jordan
Michael A. Karchmer

Over the past decade, there have been several studies on the extent of the use of signs. Jordan, Gustason, and Rosen (1976; 1979) documented the extent of the use of sign communication by schools and programs for hearing impaired students in two reports. The first described a trend toward increasing use of signs in American schools and classes and found that 64 percent of the programs surveyed used signs. A follow-up report 3 years later showed that the percentage of American programs then using signs was 65 percent.

Jensema and Trybus (1978) reported results from a 1974 study of a national sample of 657 hearing impaired students. Seventy-one percent were reported to use signs at least sometimes in communicating with their teachers. Approximately 31 percent of the parents of these students indicated they signed to their hearing impaired children.

This chapter summarizes patterns of sign use for more than 46,000 hearing impaired students reported to the 1982–1983 Annual Survey of Hearing Impaired Children and Youth, the first data collection on sign use for such a large number of hearing impaired students. In addition to examining the extent of signing among hearing impaired students and sign use within their instructional programs and family settings, the chapter also explores sign use in relation to other educationally relevant variables included in the Annual Survey. In what ways do signers differ from non-signers? What kinds of students are exposed to sign communication in their homes? By addressing questions such as these, the chapter attempts to provide a general picture for the early 1980s of the patterns of sign use among hearing impaired students in the United States.

It should be kept in mind that the collected information deals with whether or not sign communication of any kind was reported to be used by the student, by the student's school, and by the student's family. In the chapter, the terms *sign language, sign communication,* and *signing* are used synonymously. The terms are used here to refer to any kind of manual communication (e.g., American Sign Language, a specific system for manually coding English, simultaneous communication). No inferences regarding the nature or the quality of the sign communication are possible from the data. Indeed, it can be assumed that there is considerable variation in this regard in the schools and homes of deaf students. A recent study of about 1800 teachers of hearing impaired students by the Center for Assessment and Demographic Studies at Gallaudet College found many differences in sign usage according to characteristics of the teachers and of the educational programs (Woodward, Allen, and Schildroth, 1985). Initial analysis of the data collected in this study indicated that the vast majority of teachers sign in English word order, with their signs accompanied by speech or lip movements.

The nature of signing by families in the home also can be assumed to vary. For example, there can be no doubt that the kind of signing encountered in the homes of students with deaf parents is very different from the communications of hearing parents just learning to sign.

Two other limitations of the data discussed here should be noted. No questions were asked on the Annual Survey about speech use. It is therefore not possible to determine the extent that non-signing students use speech as their primary communication mode.

A final qualification concerns missing data. There is a relatively large amount of missing data about signing in the student's home. To the degree that these missing data are not random, distributions involving this variable can be misleading.

EXTENT OF SIGNING AT SCHOOL AND AT HOME

This brief section considers the overall results from the Annual Survey for three questions about the use of signs: (a) Does the student use sign language? (b) Does the student's instructional program incorporate the use of sign language? (c) Is sign language used by the student's family in the home?

Table 6–1 indicates that, of the students for whom information was reported, almost 65 percent were reported to sign. Sixty-six percent of the students were enrolled in educational programs in which sign communication was used for instruction. In comparison, far fewer students, only 35 percent of the total, were from homes in which the families signed.

Table 6–1.   Responses to Three Questions on Sign Use, Annual Survey of Hearing Impaired Children and Youth, 1982–1983

Question	Response		Total
	Yes	No	
Does the student use sign language?	28,876 (64.5%)	15,905 (35.5%)	44,781* (100.0%)
Does the student's instructional program incorporate the use of sign language?	30,622 (66.0%)	15,771 (34.0%)	46,393† (100.0%)
Is sign language used by the student's family in the home?	13,279 (35.3%)	24,335 (64.7%)	37,614‡ (100.0%)

*Of the 55,136 students reported to the 1982–1983 Annual Survey, information was left blank for 1413 students (2.6 percent); the question was not asked of 8942 students (16.2 percent).

†Information was left blank for 1497 students (2.7 percent); the question was not asked of 7246 students (13.1 percent).

‡Information was left blank or the data was not available for 15,615 students (28.3 percent); the question was not asked of 8943 students (16.2%).

Allowing for differences in sampling and methodology between this and previous studies, these data appear to show a striking consistency with other studies conducted over the past decade. This suggests that communication patterns have stabilized during the period.

A student's use of sign communication is closely related to whether that student attends an educational program where signing is used for instruction. Ninety-eight percent of the students who signed were also in educational programs in which signing was used. Of the non-signing students, 92 percent were enrolled in programs in which signing was not used. Thus, for the analyses that follow, understanding the patterns of student sign use is nearly equivalent to understanding when signs are used at school.

The patterns of reported signing can be summarized by looking at the three variables in combination. Eight patterns of responses to the three signing questions are possible. All eight actually occurred in the data. However, three patterns predominated:

1. Students who signed, who attended educational programs in which sign communication was used for instruction, and who had families who used signs in the home (34.2 percent of the reported total)
2. Students who signed and who attended educational programs in which sign communication was used for instruction but whose families did not use signs (24.0 percent)
3. Students who did not sign, who did not attend programs in which signs were used, and whose families did not sign (36.7 percent)

The other five patterns of sign use accounted for a total of only 5 percent of the reported data. Some caution must be exercised in interpreting this distribution. There was a large amount of missing data—particularly for the *signing in the home* variable. Levels of missing data for this variable were particularly high for students from minority backgrounds and for students residing at schools for the deaf.

FACTORS DIFFERENTIATING SIGNING FROM NON-SIGNING STUDENTS

Which characteristics differentiate hearing impaired students who sign from those who do not? To study the relative importance of major variables included in the Annual Survey, the proportion of students who signed was analyzed by using a Multiple Classification Analysis.* Whether or not students were reported to sign was analyzed according to (a) degree of hearing loss (less-than-severe, severe, or profound); (b) age at onset of hearing loss (before 3 years of age versus 3 years or later); (c) ethnic status (white versus minority); and (d) type of educational program (classroom instruction in special education settings only, classroom instruction in regular education settings only, classroom instruction in both regular and special education settings). Student age was covaried. The analysis included data on 41,795 students between 6 and 20 years of age for whom information was given for all of the variables.

The results of the analysis showed that age was associated with the extent of sign usage. With age held constant, the variables most strongly associated with student sign use were the degree of hearing loss and the type of classroom instruction received by the student. Ethnic status and age at onset of hearing loss were also statistically significant factors. In addition, each of the statistical interactions involving the type of classroom instruction was significant. Finally, degree of hearing loss and ethnic status interacted. These effects are described below.

---

*For this study, Multiple Classification Analysis (Andrews and Messenger, 1973) was used to measure the relative contribution of each variable (e.g., ethnic status) to variation in sign usage. The method also aids in determining whether differences in such communication between groups by ethnic status, degree of hearing loss, and other variables are statistically significant. In this manner, the relation of several variables with variance in sign usage can be explored, controlling for the effects of all of the other variables on sign communication. Such an exploration allows for an evaluation of the relative influence of each variable individually.

Student Characteristics and Sign Use

Age. The percentage of students who signed steadily increased by age (Figure 6–1). About half of the youngest group (6 to 8 years old) signed; the percentage who signed climbed to about 85 percent of the group 18 to 20 years old. This parallels Jensema and Trybus's (1978) finding of increasing sign use by age, at least for student to teacher communication. The finding of more signers among the older age groups is related to the fact that in the Annual Survey sample, the older groups have higher percentages of profoundly deaf students; older students also are more likely to be in full-time special education programs than younger students (e.g., Karchmer and Trybus, 1977; Wolk, Karchmer, and Schildroth, 1982).

Degree of Hearing Loss. A student's degree of hearing loss was highly predictive of whether or not he or she would sign. Only 26 percent of the students with less-than-severe hearing losses (unaided hearing level of 70 dB or less in the better ear) signed. For the group of students with severe

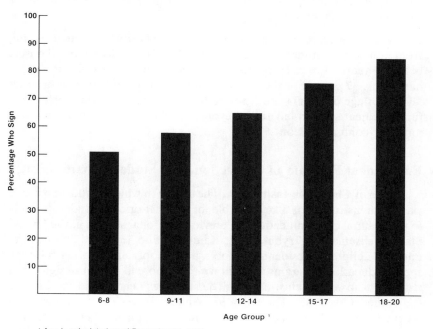

¹ Age is calculated as of December 31, 1982.

Figure 6–1. Percentage of hearing impaired students who sign, by age, 1982–1983 Annual Survey of Hearing Impaired Children and Youth.

hearing losses (71 to 90 dB), the percentage of signers increased to 74 percent. Finally, 87 percent of the students whose hearing losses were in the profound range (greater than 90 dB) were reported to sign. The finding of increasing sign use as a function of severity of loss is consistent with earlier national reports in the United States (Jensema and Trybus, 1978; Karchmer, Milone, and Wolk, 1979) as well as in Canada (Karchmer, Allen, Petersen, and Quaynor, 1982).

Ethnic Status. Taken as a group, minority students were more likely to sign than white students (73 percent as compared to 61 percent). These ethnic differences were mediated by degree of hearing loss. Differences in signing rate were small for profoundly deaf students (85 percent and 90 percent for whites and minorities, respectively). Only for students with severe (73 percent white versus 83 percent minority) and less-than-severe (23 percent white versus 35 percent minority) losses were differences sizeable. The ethnic differences partly may be a reflection of the fact that relatively fewer minority than white students were in mainstream settings. As will be described, educational setting is an important predictor of whether or not a student signs.

Age at Onset. Age at onset of hearing loss also differentiated signing from non-signing students. Of the group of students with reported onsets before 3 years of age, 66 percent were said to be signers. On the other hand, only 37 percent of the postlingually deafened students (age at onset 3 years of age or later) were reported to sign. Clearly, having the opportunity to hear spoken language beyond the age of 3 is a determinant of mode of communication.

Educational Program in Interaction with Student Characteristics

Type of Classroom Instruction. The setting in which a student receives classroom instruction is a key variable for whether or not a student is likely to use manual communication. In previous national studies in the United States (Jensema and Trybus, 1978; Karchmer and Trybus, 1977) hearing impaired children in residential schools, day schools, and in other full-time special education programs were shown to be more likely to use signs than students who were mainstreamed. The same has been found for Canada (Karchmer et al., 1982). The 1982–1983 Annual Survey did not collect data on the type of educational facility. Instead, the form solicited information on the nature of the classroom instruction: Did the child receive special education classroom instruction only, regular education with hearing students only, or some mixture of the two?

The results of the 1982–1983 Annual Survey on classroom instruction and sign use present a picture that extends the previously reported findings. In general, the group of students receiving only regular classroom services had relatively few among them who signed (10 percent of the total). At the other extreme, 86 percent of the hearing impaired students in full-time special education settings (day or residential schools or self-contained classrooms in local public schools) were signers. Forty-seven percent of the students receiving both regular and special education classroom instruction signed, approximately midway between the groups of regular education and special education only. Thus, the 1982–1983 Annual Survey data confirmed that the extent of signing is closely related to the amount of mainstreaming. Given that a majority of hearing impaired students only in regular education settings have less-than-severe hearing losses, these data suggest that most students in the mainstream are unlikely to use signs as a communication mode.

Interactions among Variables

The type of classroom instruction received by the student interacts with each of the other factors described previously. These interactions underscore the importance of type of classroom instruction for understanding which students sign and which do not. An example of how this variable mediates the others can be seen in Figure 6–2, which shows the percentage of students who signed according to degree of hearing loss and type of classroom instruction. As illustrated by the figure, the vast majority of students served in special education settings only were signers, regardless of degree of hearing loss. Analysis of the interactions of type of classroom instruction with age at onset and ethnic status showed similar patterns (Table 6–2); hearing impaired students receiving special education instruction only had similar percentages of signers, irrespective of their age at onset or ethnic status. In other words, significant variations in signing rate occur mainly in the groups of students who are partially or fully mainstreamed.

SIGN USE BY FAMILIES IN THE HOME

Overall, about 35 percent of the hearing impaired students for whom data were reported to the Annual Survey came from homes where signs were used. This percentage represents slightly more than half of the sample's hearing impaired students reported to sign or to be exposed to sign communication at school. However, the students whose families sign in the home were not evenly distributed within the Annual Survey sample. Sign use in the home is highly associated with specific student and educational

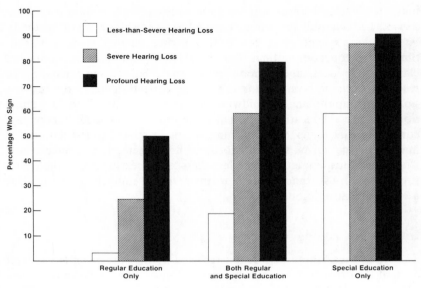

Figure 6-2. Percentage of hearing impaired students who sign, by type of classroom instruction and degree of hearing loss, 1982–1983 Annual Survey of Hearing Impaired Children and Youth.

program characteristics. The relative importance of the variables that predict the use of sign language in the home is described in this section. In interpreting these data, it is worth repeating that they do not address the issue of the type of signing that takes place or the quality of the communication. It is also not possible to state which family members were signing. The information merely deals with whether signing of any kind was used by the students' families in their homes. The proportion of students whose families signed in the home was analyzed by Multiple Classification Analysis. Four of the variables in the analysis were the same as in the analysis of student signing: degree of hearing loss, age at onset of hear-

Table 6-2. Percentage of Students Reported to Sign: Age at Onset of Hearing Loss and Ethnic Status by Type of Classroom Instruction

Type of Classroom Instruction Received	Age at Onset (%)		Ethnic Status (%)	
	Before 3 years	After 3 years	White	Minority
Regular education only	11	3	9	17
Both regular and special education	49	26	44	54
Special education only	86	81	85	87

ing loss, ethnic status, and type of classroom instruction. In addition, one new variable was added: whether or not the student's instructional program incorporated the use of sign language. Student age was used as a covariate. Altogether, information on 35,108 students between the ages of 6 and 20 years was included; this number reflects the large amount of missing information on the *signing in the home* variable.

The results of the analysis of sign use in the students' homes show clearly that sign use in the home is primarily a function of whether the student attends an educational program in which signs are used. A majority of students who attend such programs also are exposed to signing at home; students attending programs in which signs are not used have families who do not sign. A more complete description of this finding as well as the other significant results from this analysis follows.

Student Characteristics and Signing in the Home

Age. There were differences in sign use at home among the age groups studied. Unlike the analysis of sign use by the student, no constant increase by age was noted. The differences among the age groups were relatively small, with percentages varying only between 31 percent and 37 percent. The youngest and the oldest groups had the highest percentages for signing in the home; the age group in the middle (students 12 to 14 years old at time of study) had the lowest. Given the small size of the differences, it is probably unwise to interpret them.

Other Student Characteristics. Whether or not students' families use sign communication at home is associated with each of the student characteristics included in the analysis. Increases in home signing were noted according to the severity of the child's unaided hearing loss: 10 percent, 36 percent, and 56 percent for the groups of students with less-than-severe, severe, and profound losses, respectively. Only 13 percent of the students who lost their hearing postlingually had families who signed at home, in comparison with 37 percent of the students with prelingual hearing losses. Students from minority backgrounds (27 percent) were reported less likely to come from homes in which they were exposed to signing than white students (39 percent). This stands in contrast to other findings in this study, in which minority students were found *more* likely to sign and to be in educational programs that used sign. The difference strongly suggests that, from a communication point of view, there may be a larger mismatch for minority children between what happens at home and what happens at school than there is for white children.

Educational Program and Interactions
with Student Characteristics

Educational Program Considerations. Overall, a slight majority (56 percent) of hearing impaired students in educational programs using signs were exposed to signing in the home also. In contrast, very few (2 percent) of the students in non-signing programs were exposed to signing at home. Although cause-and-effect interpretations are unwarranted, it is tempting to speculate that school communication method greatly influences parental choice of communication mode in the home. Of course, it may equally be true that signing parents choose to send their children to educational programs in which sign communication is used.

Type of classroom instruction interacts with whether the student is in an instructional program in which sign communication is used. Table 6–3 shows that few students in non-signing programs signed at home, regardless of the type of classroom instruction received. On the other hand, considering only programs in which signs were used, percentages of families who signed at home differed according to type of classroom instruction; partly or fully mainstreamed students were less likely to encounter signing at home.

Interactions with Student Characteristics. Among the students enrolled in non-signing programs, few students used signs at home, regardless of their ethnic status, age at onset, or degree of hearing loss. On the other hand, strong differences were noted for these variables for the students enrolled in programs in which signs were used. Sign use at home increased with severity of hearing loss (Table 6–4); also, higher likelihood of home signing occurred for students whose onset of hearing loss occurred before the age of 3 years (Table 6–4) and for white students (Figure 6–3).

In summary, signing at home was reported to a significant extent only for the group of students who attended educational programs in which signing was incorporated as an instructional medium. For those students, systematic differences as to the extent of signing at home were related to ethnic status, age at onset, and to severity of hearing loss.

Table 6–3. Percentage of Students Whose Families Sign: Type of Classroom Instruction by Communication Mode of the Program

Type of Classroom Instruction Received	Program Uses Signs (%)	Program Does Not Use Signs (%)
Regular education only	33	0
Both regular and special education	41	3
Special education only	64	5

Table 6-4. Percentage of Students Whose Families Sign: Degree of Hearing Loss and Age at Onset by School Communication Mode

School Communication Mode	Degree of Hearing Loss (%)			Age at Onset (%)	
	Less-than-Severe	Severe	Profound	Before 3 Years	After 3 Years
Student in program where signs are used	33	49	64	37	56
Student not in program where signs are used	0	3	5	2	0

SUMMARY AND CONCLUSIONS

This chapter examines the extent and patterns of sign use of hearing impaired students at school and at home, based on the information provided by the 1982–1983 Annual Survey. Overall, two thirds of the students included in this data base were reported to sign and to attend schools in which signs were used for instruction. About 35 percent of the students' families used sign communication in the home. These overall results are similar to findings reported over the past decade, leading to the conclusion that a certain stability has evolved in the extent of sign use.

Whether a hearing impaired student signs, attends a school in which signing is used for instruction, or comes from a family in which signs are used are shown in this chapter to be related to demographic characteristics of the student, to characteristics related to the disability, and to the type of educational program in which the student is enrolled.

Student signing is most strongly associated with two factors: the severity of the hearing loss and the type of classroom instruction received. The type of classroom instruction received is a particularly important variable, and it interacts with each of the other variables studied. The vast majority of hearing impaired students who are receiving only special education instruction sign and are in programs that use sign, regardless of their ethnic status, age at onset, or degree of hearing loss. The proportion of partially or fully mainstreamed students who sign is lower, and clear differences in signing rate can be noted according to ethnic status, age at onset, and degree of hearing loss.

Student exposure to sign communication in the home is related most strongly to a single variable: whether or not the student attends a school in which signs are used. Very few students enrolled in non-signing programs see signs used by their families at home. For the students whose

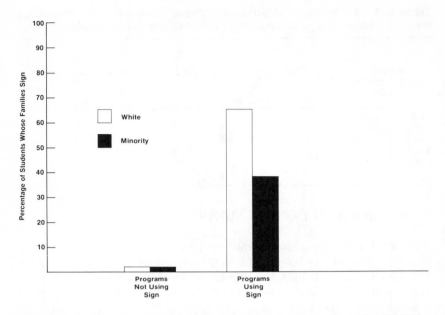

Figure 6–3. Percentage of hearing impaired students whose families sign in the home, by program's use of sign and ethnic status, 1982–1983 Annual Survey of Hearing Impaired Children and Youth.

schools use sign communication, differences in the other variables studied are evident. One of the most telling of these differences concerns the student's ethnic status. Black and Hispanic students are much less likely than white students to have sign communication used in their homes. This finding contrasts with the finding for student sign usage: minority students are more likely to sign and to be in schools in which signs are used. The large communication mismatch for these minority students between what happens at their schools and at their homes raises questions of psychoeducational importance.

The extent of sign use is related to variables not included in the 1982–1983 Annual Survey. Two factors that show important relationships to the extent of sign use are speech intelligibility and parental hearing status. The relationship between speech intelligibility and sign use is discussed in Chapter 7. Parental hearing status is known to be strongly related to sign use. Students with two deaf parents tend to use less speech and more signing than students with normally hearing parents. Students with one hearing parent, on the other hand, show the reverse trend—more speech and less signing (Jensema and Trybus, 1978; Karchmer, Trybus, and Paquin, 1978). Further, students with two deaf parents are more likely to attend non-mainstream educational programs, such as residential schools (Karchmer and Trybus, 1977). These, of course, are the kinds of programs in which students are likely to sign. The effects of differences in sign use according to parental hearing status on the overall patterns presented in this chapter would be minimal because the size of the group of students with deaf parents is so small. Only about 4 percent of the Annual Survey population have two deaf parents; an even smaller percentage have one hearing impaired and one normally hearing parent.*

Whether or not manual communication should be used in educating deaf children has long been one of the burning issues in the field. In the past, it has been commonplace for professionals and parents to choose one side of the issue or the other and energetically defend their choices. This chapter takes no position on the desirability of one communication mode or another for individual hearing impaired children. It does contribute to the informed discussion of this issue by showing that, from a demographic point of view, choice of communication method is not a random factor.

REFERENCES

Andrews, F.M., and Messenger, R.C. (1973). *Multivariate nominal scale analysis.* Ann Arbor: University of Michigan, Institute for Social Research.

Jensema, C., and Trybus, R. (1978). *Communication patterns and educational achievement of hearing impaired students* (Series T, No. 2). Washington, DC: Gallaudet College, Office of Demographic Studies.

Jordan, I.K., Gustason, G., and Rosen, R. (1976). Current communication trends at programs for the deaf. *American Annals of the Deaf, 121,* 527–532.

Jordan, I.K., Gustason, G., and Rosen, R. (1979). An update on communication trends at programs for the deaf. *American Annals of the Deaf, 124,* 350–357.

Karchmer, M.A., Allen, T.E., Petersen, L.M., and Quaynor, A. (1982). Hearing-impaired children and youth in Canada: Studant characteristics in relation to manual communication patterns in four special education settings. *American Annals of the Deaf. 127,* 89–104.

Karchmer, M.A., Milone, M.N., and Wolk, S. (1979). Educational significance of hearing loss at three levels of severity. *American Annals of the Deaf Directory of Programs and Services, 124,* 97–109.

Karchmer, M.A., and Trybus, R.J. (1977). *Who are the deaf children in "mainstream" programs?* (Series R, No. 4). Washington, DC: Gallaudet College, Office of Demographic Studies.

Karchmer, M.A., Trybus, R.J., and Paquin, M.M. (1978). *Early manual communication, parental hearing status, and the academic achievement of deaf students.* Toronto: American Educational Research Association.

Wolk, S., Karchmer, M., and Schildroth, A. (1982). *Patterns of academic and nonacademic integration among hearing impaired students in special education*

---

*These percentages are unpublished data that come from preliminary analysis of the 1984–1985 Annual Survey of Hearing Impaired Children and Youth.

(Series R, No. 9). Washington, DC: Gallaudet College, Center for Assessment and Demographic Studies.

Woodward, J., Allen, T., and Schildroth, A. (1985). Teachers and deaf students: An ethnography of classroom communication. In S. Delancey and R. Tomlin (Eds.), *Proceedings of the First Pacific Coast Conference on Linguistics*. Eugene, Oregon: University of Oregon Press.

Chapter 7

Deaf Children and Speech Intelligibility: A National Study

Steve Wolk
Arthur N. Schildroth

Speech and speech intelligibility are facets of that broader phenomenon occurring between persons, communication. Clearly they are an important part of this human experience. However, they remain a part, not the whole. Communication is possible without speech; the clenched fist and the raised eyebrows, unspoken though they may be, are powerful expressions of communication.

Granted the partial nature of speech intelligibility within the communication experience, it is still possible to examine its relationships to other facets of human life. The present effort attempts to do just that, taking into account the complexity of any such examination and the special difficulties encountered in assessing the speech of hearing impaired students.

Intelligibility of speech has long been a concern of a wide variety of individuals: parents, educators, professionals in the fields of speech production and pathology, and researchers. It has been a special concern to those teaching and interacting with hearing impaired children and youth. Yet, in spite of the obvious importance of this subject, there has been much disagreement and confusion, both in the areas of teaching speech to deaf children and, the primary interest of this chapter, in assessing the intelligibility of their speech (Moores, 1982). Ling (1976) noted the distressing fact that scant improvement in the speech production of deaf children has been realized in spite of the technical and educational advances in speech science and allied fields, a finding confirmed in a previous 1974 project of the Center for Assessment and Demographic Studies at Gallaudet College (Jensema, Karchmer, and Trybus, 1978). A longitudinal study of hearing impaired children in New York reached a similar conclusion (Smith, 1980). Although there is some evidence that speech intelligibility can be improved over time, this improvement is usually the result of intensive training with small numbers of deaf children (John and Howarth, 1965; Monsen, 1983; Moog and Geers, 1985).

Any study of speech intelligibility must address the basic question of how to define and then measure that intelligibility. In examining this issue, Conrad (1979) concluded that both objective and subjective measures of speech intelligibility have a place in research and that the purpose and nature of the research questions at hand should guide the selection of a specific, appropriate measure of speech intelligibility. He found in his own research that these two measures of speech intelligibility correlate in a moderately strong way, leading to very similar characterizations of the speech of deaf individuals when rated by teachers and when measured through an analysis of speech samples under standardized conditions. Although there is evidence to support the preference for a more standardized scale to measure speech intelligibility (Schiavetti, Metz, and Sitler, 1981), the present study has used a rating system by the teachers of hearing impaired students to measure student speech intelligibility. (See also the 1978 study by Geffner, Levitt, Freeman, and Gaffney, who found that classroom teachers of hearing impaired children tend to give more affirmative ratings of their students' speech than outside examiners do.)

Four basic issues have guided this investigation. The first is somewhat conceptual and concerns the relationship between speech intelligibility and degree of deafness: Is there variation in the speech intelligibility patterns of a large national sample of special education hearing impaired students that cannot be fully explained by the degree of hearing impairment of these students? Clearly, degree of hearing loss is a critical element in the lives of hearing impaired individuals, for example, affecting level of academic ability as measured by standardized achievement tests (Karchmer, Milone, and Wolk, 1979). The present study seeks to clarify the fundamental relationship between speech intelligibility and degree of hearing impairment within a large, national sample of hearing impaired students in special education programs.

A second and related issue involves the possible existence and nature of the relationships between speech intelligibility and nonauditory factors. Jensema and coworkers (1978) reported the existence of systematic relationships between rated speech intelligibility and demographic characteristics. Their study, however, left uncertain (a) whether these relationships existed independently of the effects of degree of hearing loss upon speech intelligibility and (b) whether these relationships were independent of one another. Thus, this second issue involves a clarification of the relation-ships between speech intelligibility and the demographic characteristics of the students in the sample.

This study addresses a third issue regarding educational placement and speech intelligibility. It is quite clear that the educational integration of hearing impaired children with hearing students is increasing. Comparison of Annual Survey data for the 1979–1980 and 1983–1984 school years reveals a sharp upsurge in this type of school placement. The mainstream educational setting is one in which hearing impaired students more and more find themselves, and the ability to communicate with hearing teachers and hearing classmates, both within and outside the classroom, becomes increasingly important. Thus, the level of speech intelligibility of these hearing impaired students appears crucial to the process of mainstreaming. Accordingly, building upon a previous investigation by Allen and Osborn (1984), this study asks: Is a hearing impaired student's level of speech intelligibility, over and above degree of hearing loss and other demographic characteristics, systematically related to the likelihood of being placed in an integrated academic school setting.

Finally, the present study attempts to analyze the relationship that exists between speech intelligibility and the primary communication method used by the student. Jensema and colleagues (1978) found that the frequency with which students used various communication methods (e.g., speech alone, signs with fingerspelling, or gesture) correlated with students' rated speech intelligibility. In that study the strongest positive relationship with speech intelligibility involved the communication method of speech alone. More recently, Brentari and Wolk (in press) found that the type of expressive mode used by profoundly deaf speakers related to the ability of hearing individuals to identify the words spoken by the deaf subjects. A fourth issue, therefore, addressed by the present investigation is whether the speech intelligibility of a large and representative sample of deaf students is systematically related to the mode of communication reported to be most used by those students. This relationship is examined for its independence: To what degree is method of communication systematically related to speech intelligibility after students' degree of hearing loss, ethnic background, and placement in an integrated classroom are taken into account?

No attempt has been made to determine how much cultural or dialect factors may have contributed to the ratings by teachers of their students' speech intelligibility (e.g., the intelligibility rating given by a white teacher to a black student's speech). This is an area that needs further study.

The present study has also ignored the role of internal, cognitive elements in the production of speech. For example, Conrad (1979) has examined the variation in speech intelligibility due to a child's ability to internally represent language (the use of "internal speech"). Except for the degree of loss factor, the analysis presented here should be viewed as a global analysis of external factors related to speech intelligibility. In this sense, this analysis may be accounting for a limited portion of the overall variance in the speech intelligibility of hearing impaired children and youth.

METHODOLOGY

Sample

Two data bases were the sources for this analysis. The first, the 1983 Annual Survey of Hearing Impaired Children and Youth, has been described in the introduction to this book and needs little further explication here. The demographic and audiological data from this 1983 survey provide central variables for the present study: degree of student hearing loss, ethnic background of student, age, academic integration with hearing students, and educationally significant handicaps in addition to hearing impairment. These variables are, for the most part, self-explanatory; Appendix 7-A, however, provides a further brief description and their derivation from the survey form. Limitations and qualifications associated with them are discussed in the introduction to this volume and in various chapters examining these variables more directly.

A second source of data for this study was the spring 1983 norming project of the Center for Assessment and Demographic Studies, in which the seventh edition of the Stanford Achievement Test was administered to a random sample of approximately 8500 hearing impaired students (Allen and Pugh, 1985). As a part of that norming project, a subsample of students from the larger group was selected for whom more detailed information regarding curriculum, teacher and family background, educational setting, and student communication was collected. Questionnaires for this special project were directed to the teachers of these students, and the communication section of the form included the following question on speech intelligibility:

> How do you, the teacher, think the average hearing person with whom this student might come in contact outside of school (i.e., bus driver, clerk in a store, etc.) would classify this student's speech?
> _____ 1. Very intelligible (very similar to the speech of a hearing person of the same age)
> _____ 2. Intelligible (somewhat difficult to understand)
> _____ 3. Barely intelligible (can only understand after repetition and use of other cues)

_____ 4. Not intelligible
_____ 5. Student would not ordinarily attempt to use speech.

The first two categories of this question were combined for the analysis into one category (speech intelligible); the last three categories of the question were also consolidated into one for the analysis (speech not intelligible). The rationale for reducing the original 5-point rating scale of intelligibility to a dichotomous measure was twofold: (a) to facilitate the log-linear analysis by reducing the number of categories that were necessary to crosstabulate with the other variables; and (b) to collapse adjoining categories of the original scale that may have been difficult for teachers to distinguish (e.g., barely intelligible and not intelligible).

Of the 8333 hearing impaired students included in the general norming project, approximately 3200 were selected for the subsample. Of these, forms on 2414 students were fully completed and returned by classroom teachers of the students. The information on speech intelligibility gathered from this subsample of students in the norming project and its relationship to other demographic and educationally related characteristics of these hearing impaired students is the focus of this study.

Design

One of the most frequently encountered tasks of educational researchers, as illustrated in the present paper, is the study of qualitative or categorical variables and their interrelationships. Traditional nonparametric techniques, such as the chi-square test, are suitable for the two-variable case but become both awkward and statistically questionable when the researcher either is studying more than two qualitative variables or is attempting to ascertain the degree of statistical independence among a set of relationships.

The statistical procedures of log-linear analysis, however, permit researchers to study the interrelationships or lack of independence of more than two qualitative variables. This technique is similar to analysis of variance in that main effects, simple interactions, and higher-order interactions among variables can be examined.

Any systematic relationship that might exist among the variables represented in a contingency table can be assessed by a statistical analysis of the _patterning_ of the frequency data. Basically, log-linear analysis examines whether the frequency data represented by the categories of one variable distribute themselves differently across the various subcategories of the remaining variables in the table (e.g., whether the ratio of intelligible to not intelligible speech in the total sample is reflected in the ratio of intelligible to not intelligible speech for white students compared to minority students). In this fashion the presence of one or more simple relationships between two variables, or complex relationships among three or more variables, can be identified.

The log-linear analysis used in this study is symmetrical. A symmetrical mode of inquiry, according to Kennedy (1983), is one in which the distinction between independent and dependent variables is not possible (as in the present case in which a child's speech intelligibility may be as much the cause as the result of educational placement or decisions).

RESULTS

This section analyzes the relationships between speech intelligibility and selected demographic, educational, and communication characteristics of hearing impaired students. The analysis examines the patterns within a contingency table comprised of the dimensions of speech intelligibility and six other characteristics of the student sample: degree of hearing loss, ethnic background, age, presence of an additional handicapping condition (AHC), academic integration with hearing students, and student communication method. (A prescreening of the data indicated that sex of the student was unrelated to speech intelligibility.) Any student with missing information on one or more of these variables was excluded from the analysis, resulting in a sample of 2414 students.

Table 7–1 presents the simple frequency distribution for each of the seven variables included in the analysis and for the sex variable. The most notable feature of Table 7–1 is that teachers reported that almost 55 percent of the students had either unintelligible or barely intelligible speech or would not use speech in the situation described in the survey question. Jensema and co-workers (1978) reported an almost identical figure of 55.2 percent for this category in their study of speech intelligibility. (The distribution for the five speech intelligibility categories in the latter study of 976 students paralleled the distribution found in the present analysis, with only the *very intelligible* category differing by as much as four percentage points.)

The complete 7-way contingency table—the two categories of speech intelligibility crosstabulated with the other six variables—was submitted to a log-linear analysis. A statistical screening of the data indicated that the highest order relationship in the data was a two-factor effect. Specifically, speech intelligibility related to each of the following variables at a statistically significant level ($p < .001$): degree of hearing loss, student communication method, academic integration with hearing students,

Table 7-1. Educational, Demographic, and Communication Characteristics of the Sample

Characteristic	Number (N = 2414)	Percentage
Speech Intelligibility		
Speech not intelligible	1,321	54.7
Speech intelligible	1,093	45.3
Sex		
Male	1,332	55.2
Female	1,082	44.8
Ethnic Background		
White	1,596	66.1
Minority	818	33.9
Additional Handicapping Conditions		
None	1,813	75.1
One or more	601	24.9
Academic Integration with Hearing Students		
None	1,431	59.3
Some	983	40.7
Degree of Hearing Loss		
Less-than-severe (≤ 70 dB hearing level)	476	19.7
Severe (71–90 dB hearing level)	597	24.7
Profound (≥ 91 dB hearing level)	1,341	55.6
Student Communication Method		
Speaks only	510	21.1
Signs only	403	16.7
Speaks and signs	1,501	62.2
Age (years)		
6–8	206	8.5
9–11	493	20.4
12–14	645	26.7
15–17	637	26.4
18–20	433	18.0

ethnic background, and AHC. (Age of the students did not relate statistically to speech intelligibility.) Additionally, degree of hearing loss related significantly to academic integration with hearing students, ethnic background, AHC, and student communication method. These relationships of degree of hearing loss with several of the educational and demographic variables confirm earlier results: the relationship of loss to level of academic integration by Wolk, Karchmer, and Schildroth (1982) and the relationship of loss to other handicapping conditions and demographic characteristics by Karchmer and colleagues (1979).

The hierarchical model that was fitted to the data included all of these effects and resulted in a highly acceptable statistical level of fit: $\chi^2 = 497.84$, $df\ 670$, $p = 1.00$. Table 7–2 presents each of the statistically significant effects involving speech intelligibility that were included in the

Table 7–2. Partial Association Values for Two-Factor Relationships Involving Speech Intelligibility

Relationship	df	Chi square	Significance
Speech intelligibility with degree of hearing loss	2	317.34	.001
Speech intelligibility with student communication method	2	246.05	.001
Speech intelligibility with academic integration	1	38.14	.001
Speech intelligibility with ethnic background	1	33.20	.001
Speech intelligibility with additional handicapping condition	1	30.20	.001

model, along with each effect's test of partial association, that is, the chi-square value when the effect is removed from the model. These values, and their levels of statistical significance, give the reader a relative measure of the importance of each speech intelligibility effect to the overall model.

In summary, then, the patterning of the frequency data in the seven-way contingency table can be accounted for by 10 two-variable relationships, 5 of which directly involve speech intelligibility. Each of these relationships, though discussed individually, is *statistically independent* from all other relationships: For example, the relationship of speech intelligibility with degree of hearing loss should be considered as independent of any other relationship involving *either* speech intelligibility *or* degree of hearing loss.

Table 7–3 presents the observed frequency crosstabulations involving the two categories of speech intelligibility and the related variables. These simple frequencies can be used to interpret the pattern of speech intelligibility for any subgroup within the demographic, educational, or communication variables.

As a first illustration, Table 7–3 presents the frequency data for the relationship of speech intelligibility to degree of hearing loss, statistically the strongest correlate of speech intelligibility. The subgroups within the degree of hearing loss variable display very different patterns of speech intelligibility, relative to one another and to the entire sample. Of the 476 students classified as less than severely impaired, 86.1 percent were rated by their teachers as having intelligible speech; only 13.9 percent were reported not to have intelligible speech. This pattern is essentially reversed for those 1341 students classified as profoundly deaf: 75.3 percent were rated as not having intelligible speech; only 24.7 percent were reported with intelligible speech. The group of students classified as severely hearing impaired reflected a speech intelligibility pattern intermediate to the

Table 7-3.   Observed Frequencies Corresponding to Significant Two-Factor Relationships Involving Speech Intelligibility

	Speech Intelligibility	
Relationship	Not Intelligible	Intelligible
Total sample	1321 (54.7%)	1093 (45.3%)
Degree of hearing loss		
Less-than-severe	66 (13.9%)	410 (86.1%)
Severe	245 (41.0%)	352 (59.0%)
Profound	1010 (75.3%)	331 (24.7%)
Student communication method		
Speaks only	49 (9.6%)	461 (90.4%)
Signs only	375 (93.1%)	28 (6.9%)
Speaks and signs	897 (59.8%)	604 (40.2%)
Academic integration with hearing students		
None	973 (68.9%)	458 (31.1%)
Some	348 (35.4%)	635 (64.6%)
Ethnic background		
White (non-Hispanic)	808 (50.6%)	788 (49.4%)
Minority	513 (62.7%)	305 (37.3%)
Additional handicapping conditions		
None	955 (52.7%)	858 (47.3%)
One or more	366 (60.9%)	235 (39.1%)

other two groups. This relationship between speech intelligibility and degree of hearing loss reflects the most basic and important correlate of speech intelligibility.

Table 7-3 also presents the frequency data corresponding to the relationship between speech intelligibility and student communication mode. A very systematic and strong pattern is evident in these data. Of all students reported by their teachers to rely upon speaking only in order to communicate, 90.4 percent were reported to have intelligible speech. Conversely, 93.1 percent of the students using sign only were reported not to have intelligible speech. The group of students reported as relying upon speaking and signing in the classroom had speech intelligibility ratings between the other two groups: 40.2 percent of these students were rated as having intelligible speech. Figure 7-1 illustrates this relationship: an increase of intelligibility as the dependence on speech increases, and a decline of speech intelligibility as the dependence on sign increases. (It may serve a purpose here to reemphasize that these data do not reflect a longitudinal analysis of the same students over time, that is, students progressing from signs to speech or from speech to signs.)

The purpose of Table 7-4 is to demonstrate the independent relationship between speech intelligibility and student communication mode. What

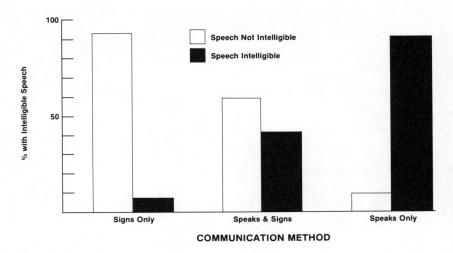

Figure 7-1. Speech intelligibility by communication method (*N* = 2414).

is most apparent is that mode of student communication demonstrates a *direct* and *independent* relationship to speech intelligibility regardless of degree of hearing loss. It has been shown previously that students who speak to communicate were very likely to be reported to have intelligible speech. As Table 7-4 indicates, this mode of communication correlates with higher than average rates of speech intelligibility across the three hearing loss groups. For example, Table 7-3 reveals that only 24.7 percent of all the students with a profound loss were reported to possess intelligible speech; however, as Table 7-4 indicates, the percentage rose sharply to 73.8 percent for those students with profound loss reported to rely primarily on speaking to communicate. Thus, even students with a 91+ dB average hearing level in the better ear had nearly a 3 in 4 probability of being rated as using intelligible speech when speaking was their primary mode of communication. The same basic trend held for students with severe and less-than-severe losses whose basic mode of communication was speaking only: These students were rated by their teachers as possessing intelligible speech well above the rates for the severe and less-than-severe groups in the *entire* sample.

In contrast, all three hearing loss groups who used signs only reflected much lower rates of intelligible speech than their averages across the entire sample irrespective of communication method. Finally, as might be expected, when the basic mode of communication was a combination of signing and speaking, all three hearing loss groups reflected levels of speech intelligibility intermediate to those for the speaks only and signs only stu-

Table 7–4. Speech Intelligibility Frequencies for Students Using Each Communication Method at Each Level of Hearing Loss

	Speech Intelligibility	
	Not Intelligible	*Intelligible*
Speaks only		
Less-than-severe	8 (2.9%)	266 (97.1%)
Severe	8 (7.3%)	102 (92.7%)
Profound	33 (26.2%)	93 (73.8%)
Total sample	49 (9.6%)	461 (90.4%)
Signs only		
Less-than-severe	15 (88.2%)	2 (11.8%)
Severe	62 (84.9%)	11 (15.1%)
Profound	298 (95.2%)	15 (4.8%)
Total sample	375 (93.1%)	28 (6.9%)
Speaks and signs		
Less-than-severe	43 (23.1%)	142 (76.9%)
Severe	175 (42.3%)	239 (57.7%)
Profound	679 (75.3%)	223 (24.7%)
Total sample	897 (59.8%)	604 (40.2%)

dents. Figure 7–2 highlights this systematic pattern of speech intelligibility ratings across the three modes of communication for each hearing loss subgroup of students.

A similar relationship was found involving ethnic background of the student. Table 7–3 indicates that 49.4 percent of the white, non-Hispanic students were rated as having intelligible speech, slightly above the population generally (45.3 percent), whereas only 37.3 percent of the minority students were reported to have intelligible speech. The ethnic background of students appears to be associated with teachers' ratings of students' speech intelligibility. Equally important, the type of relationship of ethnic background upon rated speech intelligibility holds up at each classification of hearing loss, as indicated in Table 7–5. For example, the overall likelihood of a profoundly deaf student's speech intelligibility being rated as intelligible rather than not intelligible is about 1 in 3, that is, 24.7 percent versus 75.3 percent (Table 7–3). However, as Table 7–5 shows, for minority students who are profoundly deaf that likelihood is a little more than 1 in 5.5 (i.e., 15.5 percent versus 84.5 percent). The ethnic background of students is related to speech intelligibility *over and above* the basic relationship between speech intelligibility and degree of hearing loss. The same general pattern appears in Table 7–5 for each of the three categories of degree of hearing loss: White students are consistently rated as possessing intelligible speech more often than minority students, especially in the severe loss range.

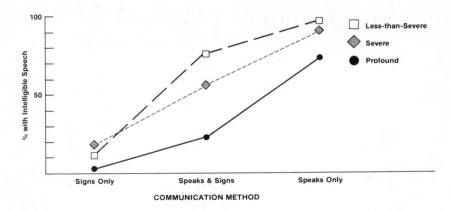

Figure 7–2. Speech intelligibility by communication method for each hearing loss group (*N* = 2414).

Equally compelling as evidence for the concept of statistical independence are the data corresponding to the association between speech intelligibility and academic integration. As shown in Table 7–3, students' rated speech intelligibility is strongly related to educational placement in an academically integrated classroom. The speech of students in integrated classrooms is nearly twice as likely to be rated as intelligible than as not intelligible (64.6 percent versus 35.4 percent); for students receiving no academic integration their speech is more than twice as likely to be rated as not intelligible (68.9 percent) than as intelligible (31.1 percent).

Table 7–6 shows that this relationship between speech intelligibility and academic integration is consistent at each level of hearing loss. As was true of student ethnic background, knowledge of a student's educational placement regarding academic integration contributes significantly to an understanding of rated speech intelligibility beyond the more fundamental influence of hearing loss. For example, across the entire sample approximately one fourth of the profoundly impaired students were rated as possessing intelligible speech (Table 7–3). However, for those profoundly deaf students in integrated classrooms, almost 40 percent were reported to have intelligible speech. Similarly, 86.1 percent of all less-than-severely-impaired students were rated as possessing intelligible speech; however, for those students whose loss was less-than-severe who were placed in nonintegrated situations, the percentage with intelligible speech fell to 76.6 percent. Students' enrollment or nonenrollment in an academically integrated classroom is related to teachers' rating of speech intelligibility beyond the basic influence that can be attributed to the students' hearing loss.

Table 7–3 also presents the relationship of speech intelligibility to the presence of handicapping conditions in addition to hearing impairment.

Table 7-5. Speech Intelligibility Frequencies for White and Minority Students at Each Level of Hearing Loss

	Speech Intelligibility	
	Not Intelligible	Intelligible
White		
Less-than-severe	30 (10.2%)	265 (89.8%)
Severe	116 (31.2%)	256 (68.8%)
Profound	662 (71.3%)	267 (28.7%)
Total Sample	808 (50.6%)	788 (49.4%)
Minority		
Less-than-severe	36 (19.9%)	145 (80.1%)
Severe	129 (57.3%)	96 (42.7%)
Profound	348 (84.5%)	64 (15.5%)
Total Sample	513 (62.7%)	305 (37.3%)

Compared to the first four relationships, this last relationship is not as strong statistically. Nevertheless, there is a systematic relationship between AHCs, and the ratings of students' speech intelligibility. Table 7-3 shows that those students without an AHC received speech intelligibility ratings very close to the rates for the sample as a whole: 52.7 percent had their speech rated as not intelligible and 47.3 percent had their speech rated as intelligible. However, when students were reported to have one or more AHCs, the rating of their speech as not intelligible increased to 60.9 percent, compared to 39.1 percent who received a rating of intelligible. Thus, teachers were more likely to rate a student as not having intelligible speech when that student had an AHC. Also, as in the case of the other relationships with speech intelligibility, the presence or not of an AHC related to speech intelligibility independently of degree of hearing loss. Table 7-7 presents data to support this conclusion.

Two points concerning these data should be noted. First, for students without an AHC, the rates of intelligible speech are somewhat higher than the average for each level of loss. For example, 86.1 percent of *all* students with a less-than-severe loss were rated as having intelligible speech (Table 7-3); however, 89.4 percent of the students without a handicapping condition at this same level of loss were reported as having intelligible speech (Table 7-7). Second, for students *with* an AHC, the rates of intelligible speech are lower at each level of hearing loss for these students than for the total sample. Specifically, Table 7-3 shows that the rates of intelligible speech across the entire sample for the less-than-severe, severe, and profound loss groups were 86.1 percent, 59.0 percent, and 24.7 percent. However, for students with an additional handicap these rates were 78.9 percent, 47.8 percent, and 14.3 percent. Speech intelligibility ratings are systematically related to the presence or absence of handicapping condi-

Table 7-6. Speech Intelligibility Frequencies for Integrated and Nonintegrated Students at Each Level of Hearing Loss

	Speech Intelligibility	
	Not Intelligible	*Intelligible*
Non–academically integrated		
Less-than-severe	34 (23.4%)	111 (76.6%)
Severe	188 (50.8%)	182 (49.2%)
Profound	751 (82.0%)	165 (18.0%)
Total sample	973 (68.0%)	458 (32.0%)
Academically integrated		
Less-than-severe	32 (9.7%)	299 (90.3%)
Severe	57 (25.1%)	170 (74.9%)
Profound	259 (60.9%)	166 (39.1%)
Total sample	348 (35.4%)	635 (64.6%)

tions over and above the very fundamental linkage to students' hearing loss.

Summary of Findings

In light of the results just reviewed, several conclusions may be drawn concerning the speech intelligibility of hearing impaired students examined in the present investigation.

1. A student's degree of hearing loss, when differentiated as less-than-severe, severe, and profound, is the strongest and most consistent correlate of speech intelligibility. None of the other demographic, educational, or communication characteristics of students can completely represent or subsume the relationship between hearing loss and speech intelligibility.
2. Student communication method relates very strongly to speech intelligibility. Again, the relationship is a direct one, independent of other relationships, particularly that involving degree of hearing loss. Intelligible speech was consistently reported for students who relied primarily on speaking as a communication mode. A nearly perfect opposite relationship exists for those students who relied upon signing to communicate: Nearly all were reported to have speech that was not intelligible. Students who used both speaking and signing to communicate were nearly as likely to be reported as having intelligible speech as they were to have speech that was not intelligible.

    In summary, three very primary dimensions of the overall process of communication for hearing impaired students are degree of loss, level of speech intelligibility, and mode of expressive commu-

Table 7-7. Speech Intelligibility Frequencies for Students with and without an Additional Handicapping Condition at Each Level of Hearing Loss

	Speech Intelligibility	
	Not Intelligible	Intelligible
No additional handicap		
Less-than-severe	35 (10.6%)	294 (89.4%)
Severe	161 (36.9%)	275 (63.1%)
Profound	759 (72.4%)	289 (27.6%)
Total sample	955 (52.3%)	858 (47.3%)
One or more additional handicaps		
Less-than-severe	31 (21.1%)	116 (78.9%)
Severe	84 (52.2%)	77 (47.8%)
Profound	251 (85.7%)	42 (14.3%)
Total sample	366 (60.9%)	235 (39.1%)

nication. Each of these dimensions has a direct bearing upon the expressive communication skills of these students. The highly significant relationships among these three variables within the present sample suggest that it would be conceptually incomplete to discuss the speech intelligibility of a hearing impaired student without a recognition of that student's degree of loss and communication method. These three variables and the characteristics they represent within the general population of hearing impaired students would appear intimately interrelated and anchored to the total process of communication.

3. A student's ethnic background and possession of an additional handicap also correlates significantly with speech intelligibility, independently of degree of hearing loss. White, non-Hispanic students and students without an additional handicap were more likely to be rated as possessing intelligible speech. Both of these relationships represent a consistent statistical effect that is independent of the manner in which degree of hearing loss correlates with speech intelligibility.

4. Students receiving some amount of academic integration with hearing students—as opposed to students not integrated—were more likely to be rated as having intelligible speech, independently of the students' degree of hearing loss, ethnic background, and additional handicap status. (Whether intelligible speech is the *cause* or the *result* of placement in an integrated setting cannot be determined by virtue of the research design represented in this paper.) Placement in an integrated academic setting with hearing students is a consistent correlate of intelligible speech, beyond whether the integrated student may happen to be profoundly deaf or mildly impaired.

5. Each of the five demographic or educational factors that have been found in the present study to relate to speech intelligibility represents a distinct element of the profile of the student with either intelligible or unintelligible speech. This is to say that a teacher's rating of intelligible speech for a given student must be understood in reference to that student's degree of hearing loss, communication mode, ethnic background, additional handicap status, and educational placement in an integrated or nonintegrated academic setting. Degree of hearing loss and primary communication mode do appear to be the strongest and most direct correlates of speech intelligibility. Nonetheless, each of the other educational or demographic factors analyzed in this study contributes an important component to any complete understanding of the phenomenon of the speech intelligibility of hearing impaired students.

DISCUSSION

Fifty-five percent of the random sample of 2414 children and youth selected in this study were reported by their teachers to have speech that was not intelligible (23 percent) or barely intelligible (22 percent) or, in their teachers' judgment, to be unwilling to use speech in a public situation (10 percent). These data do not represent a longitudinal study of the same students over time, nor do they provide information on the quality of the speech or auditory training routinely provided to approximately 85 percent of these students. However, as indicated earlier, the data are consistent with other studies that attest to the arduous work involved in hearing impaired children's acquisition of intelligible speech. The speech "not intelligible" category discussed here includes students at all age levels; 35 percent were more than 12 years old. In individualized, carefully planned, and long-term teaching intervention—as the Brentari and Wolk (in press) study shows—speech intelligibility can undoubtedly be improved; in general practice, it appears such improvement is difficult to achieve.

The student characteristics and program variables associated with poor speech intelligibility are undoubtedly various and complex; one, however, is especially prominent and pervasive. Profoundly deaf students are much more likely to produce less than intelligible speech; in general, the greater the degree of hearing loss, the less intelligible the speech. This relationship between hearing loss and speech intelligibility crosses age lines and ethnic differences, persists in the presence or absence of additional handicaps, and predominates among both academically integrated and nonintegrated students.

The one subgroup of profoundly deaf students in this analysis more likely to produce intelligible speech is those students whose primary means of communication is speech. Almost 75 percent of the 126 profoundly hearing impaired students in this sample who used speech only were reported to have intelligible speech. Since more than 90 percent of this group lost their hearing before age 3, the postlingual nature of their hearing loss had no impact on their acquisition and retention of speech intelligibility. What factors did affect the speech intelligibility of this group of profoundly hearing impaired students needs to be examined further.

Degree of hearing loss by itself, however, does not account for all the variation in the speech intelligibility ratings discussed in this chapter. Students who used speech as their primary mode of communication, who came from a white, non-Hispanic ethnic background, who were academically integrated with hearing students, or who were not multiply handicapped, tended to receive more positive speech intelligibility ratings than their signing, minority, nonintegrated or multiply handicapped peers. Furthermore, these relationships of communication method, ethnic background, integration, and handicap status to speech intelligibility proved to be statistically independent of degree of loss and of each other.

The results of this study have certain implications for programs educating hearing impaired children and youth. Although the analysis has stressed the independence of the relationship between the degree of loss and speech intelligibility from that of the relationship between integrated placement and speech intelligibility, the preponderance of profoundly hearing impaired children in separate schools indicates that these separate schools are faced with a formidable task in their efforts to achieve intelligible speech in their hearing impaired students.

The point to be made here is not to call attention to this formidable task encountered by residential and day schools for deaf students. They have long been aware, through experience, of the difficulties involved in fostering speech intelligibility in their students, as have many local schools educating hearing impaired students. However, with the decline in enrollment in the special schools and the growing trend to mainstream deaf children into local school programs, the need for speech and language professionals and for their special services will undoubtedly increase.

It will be a challenge complicated by two other findings of this study: the negative correlation of speech intelligibility with minority ethnic background and with the presence of an additional handicapping condition. (Minority enrollment, both of the hearing and the hearing impaired, is increasing in public schools [U.S. Bureau of the Census, 1984]; and multiply handicapped hearing impaired children make up approximately 30 percent of the hearing impaired children receiving special education.)

Minority deaf children, especially those exposed to a language other than English in the home (of whom there were 314 in the present study), are at risk in their attempts to acquire intelligible speech. Children with one or more handicaps in addition to their hearing impairment also are faced with special problems in acquiring speech intelligibility. Schools educating these children should be aware of such problems in their planning of support services for minority and multiply handicapped hearing impaired students. If intelligible speech is a characteristic considered desirable by educators and parents of hearing impaired children, then the establishment and development of support services to achieve intelligible speech become extremely important. A related issue to be confronted by researchers and professionals who work with hearing impaired students is whether speech intelligibility, as a major component of the communication process, can be significantly affected by factors within the school and home environments.

Appendix 7-A

The following list describes variables analyzed in this chapter and their derivation from the 1982–1983 Annual Survey form.

Degree of Hearing Loss: an average of the speech frequency audiometric data in the better ear or the student's functional hearing level estimated by the teacher and collapsed into three categories: *less-than-severe* (hearing level of 70 dB or less in the better ear), *severe* (71 to 90 dB level), and *profound* (level of 91 dB or greater in the better ear).

Ethnic Background: dichotomized into *white* and *minority*; the latter category includes black, Hispanic, Asian/Pacific, American Indian, and *other*.

Additional Handicapping Conditions: either *none* (no educationally significant handicaps in addition to hearing impairment) or *one or more* additional handicaps.

Academic Integration with Hearing Students: either *none* (student receives no regular classroom academic instruction with hearing students, either full- or part-time) or *some* (student receives regular classroom academic instruction with hearing students).

Student Communication Method: derived from the special subsample in the achievement test norm group, the responses to this question on the form were collapsed into three categories: *speaks only* (student is reported to use only speech when communicating with the teacher in the instructional context), *signs only* (student uses only signs when communicating in the classroom), *speaks and signs* (use of both methods of communication).

Age: computed from the birth year on the survey form and divided into five categories according to age in years: 6 to 8, 9 to 11, 12 to 14, 15 to 17, and 18 and over.

REFERENCES

Allen, T., and Osborn, T. (1984). Academic integration of hearing-impaired students: Demographic, handicapping, and achievement factors. *American Annals of the Deaf, 129,* 100–113.

Allen, T., and Pugh, G. (1985). *Speech and auditory training and the rated speech intelligibility of hearing-impaired students.* Manuscript submitted for publication.

Brentari, D., and Wolk, S. (in press). The relative effects of three expressive methods upon the speech intelligibility of profoundly deaf speakers. *Journal of Communication Disorders.*

Conrad, R. (1979). *The deaf schoolchild.* London: Harper & Row.

Geffner, D., Levitt, H., Freeman, L., and Gaffney, R. (1978). Speech and language assessment scales of deaf children. *Journal of Communication Disorders, 11,* 215–226.

Jensema, C., Karchmer, M., and Trybus, R. (1978). *The rated speech intelligibility of hearing impaired children: Basic relationships and a detailed analysis* (Series R, No. 6). Washington, DC: Gallaudet College, Office of Demographic Studies.

John, J., and Howarth, J. (1965). The effect of time distortions on the intelligibility of deaf children's speech. *Language and Speech, 8,* 127–134.

Karchmer, M., Milone, M., and Wolk, S. (1979). Educational significance of hearing loss at three levels of severity. *American Annals of the Deaf Directory of Programs and Services, 124,* 97–109.

Kennedy, J. (1983). *Analyzing qualitative data: Introductory log-linear analysis for behavioral research.* New York: Praeger.

Ling, D. (1976). *Speech and the hearing-impaired child: Theory and practice.* Washington, DC: Alexander Graham Bell Association for the Deaf.

Monsen, R. (1983). The oral speech intelligibility of hearing-impaired talkers. *Journal of Speech and Hearing Disorders, 48,* 286–296.

Moog, J., and Geers, A. (1985). EPIC: A program to accelerate academic progress in profoundly hearing-impaired children. *Volta Review, 87,* 259–277.

Moores, D. (1982). *Educating the deaf: Psychology, principles, and practices* (2nd ed.). Boston: Houghton Mifflin.

Schiavetti, N., Metz, D., and Sitler, R. (1981). Construct validity of direct magnitude estimation and interval scaling of speech intelligibility: Evidence from a study of the hearing impaired. *Journal of Speech and Hearing Research, 24,* 441–445.

Smith, C. (1980). Speech assessment at the elementary level: Interpretation relative to speech training. In J. Subtelny (Ed.), *Speech assessment and speech improvement for the hearing impaired* (pp. 18–29). Washington, DC: Alexander Graham Bell Association for the Deaf.

U.S. Bureau of the Census (1984). School enrollment—social and economic characteristics of students: October 1983. *Current Population Reports* (Series P-20, No. 394). Washington, DC: U.S. Government Printing Office.

Wolk, S., Karchmer, M., and Schildroth, A. (1982). *Patterns of academic and nonacademic integration among hearing-impaired students in special education,* (Series R, No. 9). Washington, DC: Gallaudet College, Office of Demographic Studies.

Chapter 8

Patterns of Academic Achievement Among Hearing Impaired Students: 1974 and 1983

Thomas E. Allen

Many studies of the achievement levels of hearing impaired students have been carried out over the last 10 years by the Center for Assessment and Demographic Studies (Allen and Karchmer, 1981; Allen and Osborn, 1984; Karchmer, Milone, and Wolk, 1979; Trybus and Karchmer, 1977). Much of the data for this research was collected during two major norming projects: the 1974 norming of the sixth edition of the Stanford Achievement Test (Madden, Gardner, Rudman, Karlsen, and Merwin, 1972) and the 1983 norming of the seventh edition (Gardner, Rudman, Karlsen, and Merwin, 1982) with representative samples of hearing impaired students from special education programs throughout the United States.

This chapter examines these two norming projects in depth. It addresses three major questions: (a) What are the average achievement levels attained by hearing impaired students throughout the United States? (b) Have the achievement levels of hearing impaired students changed over the last 10 years? and (c) What factors account for achievement among hearing impaired students? The chapter focuses on achievement in two academic areas: reading comprehension and mathematics computation.

The phrase *achievement levels of hearing impaired students* will be used throughout this chapter. It should be noted at the outset that in this chapter achievement level is determined by scaled score performance on either the Reading Comprehension or the Mathematics Computation subtest of the Stanford Achievement Test (sixth and seventh editions). The term should always be interpreted within that context. Its applicability to school achievement in general is limited to the domains of academic skill measured by these two Stanford subtests; generalizations are appropriate only to the extent that the subtests are reliable and valid. (See Allen, 1986, for a discussion of the technical properties of the seventh edition of the Stanford Achievement Test when used with hearing impaired students.)

The term *hearing impaired students* refers to those with hearing impairments between the ages of 8 and 18 years who receive special education services in schools throughout the United States. The population is defined by the Annual Survey of Hearing Impaired Children and Youth; detailed descriptions of this population appear elsewhere in this book. Briefly, the Annual Survey represents the population of hearing impaired students who receive special education services. Those with mild impairments who receive no special services from their schools are not included as part of the target population from which the norming samples were drawn. Part of this chapter describes how well the sample selected for norming the seventh edition of the Stanford Achievement Test represented the Annual Survey population.

The chapter begins by noting an empirical finding: Overall, hearing impaired students in the 1983 standardization sample for the seventh edition of the Stanford Achievement Test showed higher mathematics and reading achievement levels, as determined by their mean scaled score performance, than did the hearing impaired students in the 1974 standardization sample for the sixth edition of the test.

Table 8–1 shows the mean reading comprehension and mathematics computation scaled scores for each age group for the 1974 and 1983 norming samples. For all ages the means of the 1983 reading comprehension and mathematics computation scaled scores were higher than those of 1974. (It is important to note that the procedures used to scale the sixth and seventh editions of the Stanford test with hearing students were different. Therefore, in all tables reported in this chapter the sixth edition scaled scores have been converted to the seventh edition scales using conversion tables published by The Psychological Corporation.)

Figures 8–1 and 8–2 present graphs of these mean scaled scores for reading comprehension and mathematics computation. The median scaled score performance of hearing students at each grade level has also been indicated on Figures 8–1 and 8–2 by the dotted horizontal lines. On the assumption that the hearing students at the 3.0 grade level were 8 years old, that the 4.0 hearing standardization group was 9 years old, and so forth, the median age-by-age scaled scores in reading comprehension and mathematics computation for hearing students between the ages of 8 and 15 years have also been plotted on the figures. (Few hearing students beyond the age of 15 take the Stanford Achievement Test; thus, data for older students have not been plotted.)

The means shown in Table 8–1 and in Figures 8–1 and 8–2 suggest the following overall picture regarding the achievement levels of hearing

Table 8–1. Mean Scaled Score Comparisons of 1974* and 1983 Stanford Norming Samples, by Age

	Reading Comprehension						Mathematics Computation					
	1974			1983			1974			1983		
Age	N	Mean	SD	N	Mean	SD	N	Mean	SD	N	Mean	SD
8	517	467.0	42.6	349	506.8	58.5	486	503.0	53.8	356	545.9	65.7
9	1358	470.6	44.3	398	522.2	68.9	1246	513.6	51.9	399	569.5	69.8
10	509	492.6	58.3	435	538.6	65.3	495	543.6	55.8	422	589.6	69.3
11	429	505.6	59.9	575	543.9	61.6	419	561.1	56.4	572	608.5	65.0
12	477	521.7	64.8	584	558.0	61.0	468	582.4	57.2	578	622.2	67.8
13	489	523.2	68.5	616	569.7	64.5	479	595.9	56.5	616	640.1	67.3
14	573	533.2	70.3	658	580.7	64.8	563	607.0	62.2	649	651.0	61.8
15	797	542.3	72.6	622	586.7	63.8	787	614.0	60.5	616	662.7	60.0
16	491	556.3	73.3	648	586.1	67.7	487	627.6	63.1	643	661.9	66.0
17	394	567.5	71.8	904	584.8	64.8	391	641.2	63.5	893	664.6	61.4
18	318	571.8	73.4	262	578.8	59.6	319	642.9	66.5	1260	661.2	60.3

*Throughout this chapter, 1974 scaled scores have been converted from the scale of the sixth edition of the Stanford Achievement Test to the scale of the seventh edition by using conversion tables provided by the test publisher.

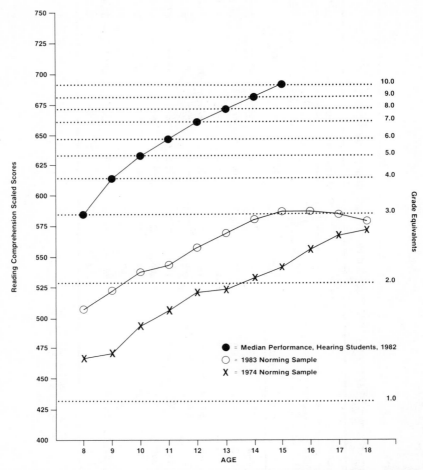

Figure 8–1.   Mean reading comprehension scaled scores for 1974 and 1983 hearing impaired norming samples, broken down by age (plotted with median performance of hearing students).

impaired students: (a) they lag behind their hearing counterparts in reading and math; (b) the deficit is more profound in reading comprehension than in mathematics computation; (c) there appears to be a "leveling off" in their reading comprehension achievement at about the third grade level; (d) a leveling off in mathematics computation is also apparent, but at about the sixth to seventh grade level; and (e) despite these low levels of achievement, hearing impaired students, as a group, appear to have achieved at higher levels in 1983 than in 1974.

The analyses presented in the remainder of this chapter clarify and, in some cases, challenge the conclusions that are suggested from this examination of the means alone. The analyses are divided into three sections.

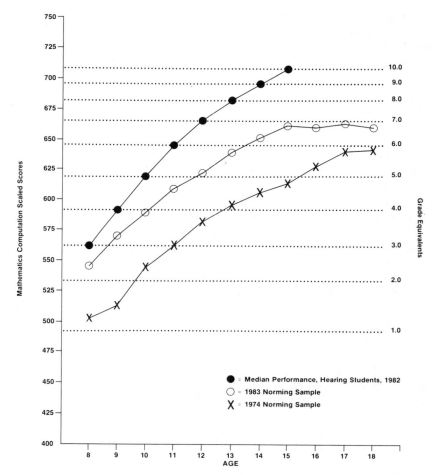

Figure 8–2. Mean mathematics computation scaled scores for 1974 and 1983 hearing impaired norming samples, broken down by age (plotted with median performance of hearing students).

The first section studies more carefully the score distributions of the sixth and seventh edition standardization samples of both hearing and hearing impaired students. This provides a clearer picture of achievement patterns than is possible from an examination of means and medians alone. The second section considers alternative explanations for the apparent gains in achievement among hearing impaired students from 1974 to 1983. This analysis explores differences in the norming sample characteristics and in the testing situations between the two norming projects that may explain the differences in mean achievement levels noted in Table 8–1. The relationship between characteristics of the 1983 norming sample and the 1983 Annual Survey population from which it was drawn are also examined.

This helps clarify the degree to which the norming results can be generalized to the Annual Survey population. In the third section the 1983 data are summarized by presenting normative information related to selected subgroups of the hearing impaired student population.

PATTERNS OF ACHIEVEMENT: 1974 and 1983

Figures 8–3 and 8–4 summarize, for reading comprehension and mathematics computation, the distributions of both hearing and hearing impaired students at three age levels on the sixth and seventh editions of the Stanford Achievement Test, as determined by the relationships among the various normed scales that were developed. In these figures, the seventh edition scaled scores are defined as the interval level standard against which all of the other scales are plotted. Horizontal lines representing the seventh edition scaled scores are drawn in the center of each of these graphs; they range from 400 to 800.

Conversions from the seventh edition scales to all the sixth edition scales appear above this center line; conversions to the other seventh edition scales appear below this line. Estimates of the equivalence between any two sixth edition or seventh edition scales can be made by drawing a vertical line between any two horizontal scale lines that appear on this graph. For example, a student with a 120 scaled score on the sixth edition Reading Comprehension subtest (Figure 8–3), would have roughly the same level of achievement in reading comprehension as a student who scored between 510 and 520 on the seventh edition Reading Comprehension subtest. Or, to take a mathematics example (Figure 8–4), a student scoring 140 in mathematics computation on the sixth edition would have roughly the same level of achievement in mathematics computation as a student scoring between 560 and 570 on the seventh edition test.

The importance of these scaled score conversions can be seen by looking at the norm distributions of both hearing and hearing impaired students on both editions of the test. In general, both hearing and hearing impaired students showed gains between the two normings. Consider the two examples. When the sixth edition was normed with hearing students, a 120 scaled score in reading comprehension represented the median performance of students well into the second grade. When the seventh edition was normed with hearing students, a 515 scaled score (roughly equivalent to the sixth edition score of 120) represented the median performance of students at the end of the first grade. That is, hearing students in the seventh edition standardization sample appear to have acquired reading comprehension skills at a faster pace than did subjects for the sixth edition standardization. A similar shift in the norming distribution occurred with mathematics computation, as indicated in Figure 8–4.

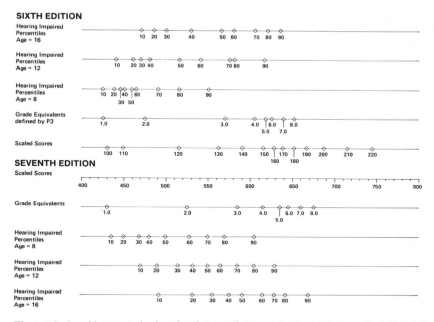

Figure 8–3. Norm equivalencies for reading comprehension measured by the sixth and seventh editions of the Stanford Achievement Test. Seventh edition scaled scores are used as standard equal-intervals.

A study of the percentile ranks for hearing impaired students shows similar shifts. The deciles for 8-, 12-, and 16-year-old hearing impaired students for both the sixth and seventh edition standardizations have been plotted in Figures 8–3 and 8–4. In 1974, when the sixth edition was standardized with hearing impaired students, a 120 scaled score performance in reading comprehension represented approximately the 50th percentile among 12-year-old hearing impaired students (see Fig. 8–3). However, in 1983, when the seventh edition was standardized with hearing impaired students, a 515 scaled score performance, equivalent to the 120 scaled score of the sixth edition, corresponded only to the 30th percentile among 12-year-olds.

In mathematics computation, the results are similar: For example, the 140 scaled score of the sixth edition represented the 80th to 90th percentile among hearing impaired 8-year-olds in 1974. The seventh edition equivalent, 560, represented the 60th to 70th percentile among hearing impaired students of the same age. These shifts in the normed scale values appear all along the reading and mathematics scales for hearing impaired students at all ages. It appears then that the norms have shifted upward for hearing impaired students.

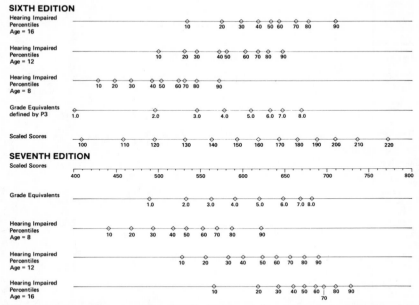

Figure 8–4. Norm equivalencies for mathematics computation measured by the sixth and seventh editions of the Stanford Achievement Test. Seventh edition scaled scores are used as standard equal-intervals.

The fact that both hearing and hearing impaired students showed apparent gains in their achievement, as evidenced by the scale equivalencies and norm conversions depicted in Figures 8–3 and 8–4, has resulted in the following situation: The relationships between percentile ranks for the hearing impaired and grade equivalent scales for the hearing have not changed. Previously published research that used the sixth edition hearing impaired norming data (Trybus and Karchmer, 1977) noted that median reading comprehension performance of hearing impaired students beyond the age of 14 leveled off at about the third- to fourth-grade equivalent. The more current 1983 norming data show the same result. Therefore, while hearing impaired students have gained, they have not gained relative to their hearing cohorts.

GAINS IN ACHIEVEMENT: REAL OR ARTIFICIAL?

The gains shown in Figures 8–1 and 8–2 are dramatic. However, the plotted scaled scores are derived from two different sample populations taking two different tests at two different points in time. Under these circumstances, no comparisons can be made with complete confidence.

Additionally, the lines that represent the 1974 norming in Figures 8-1 and 8-2 rely on the validity of the conversion tables for their interpretation. Caution is needed before any claims can be made about possible gains in the academic achievement of hearing impaired students over the last 10 years.

This section presents the results of three analyses. Each analysis looks at alternative explanations for the gains depicted in Figures 8-1 and 8-2. The first analysis compares the characteristics of the two norming samples and presents the achievement results for students with selected characteristics from both samples. If the two groups differ on characteristics known to affect achievement, then the observed mean differences noted in Figures 8-1 and 8-2 may be artifacts of these sample differences. Included in this analysis is a discussion of how well the 1983 norming sample represented the Annual Survey population from which it was selected.

The second analysis examines differences in the testing situations between the sixth and seventh edition normings. The focus of this analysis is the assignment of students to levels of the full-battery test. For both the 1974 and 1983 normings, screening tests were used to assign students to test battery levels. However, the specific screening procedures changed markedly. Since a student's obtained scaled score is dependent, to some extent, on the test level to which the student is assigned, it is possible that differences in achievement levels may be attributed to differences in the distributions of test level assignments. The third analysis examines more directly the validity of the conversion tables provided by the test publisher when they are applied to the test scores of hearing impaired students.

Analysis #1: Comparisons of the Characteristics Between the Two Norming Samples and the 1983 Target Annual Survey Population

Stratification Variables. When the Stanford Achievement Test was normed in 1974, care was taken to assure that different types of educational programs were adequately represented. Three program types were identified: residential schools, day schools, and local schools (including both self-contained special education classrooms and mainstream classrooms in public and private schools). In 1983 a new stratification variable was added: region of the country. Four regions identified by the U.S. Bureau of the Census definitions were used: Northeast, Midwest, South, and West. A comparison of the distributions of the two norming samples on the two variables used to stratify the population in 1983 reveals that they are similar with respect to their program type but different with respect to their regional distributions.

Table 8-2 shows, for the two norming samples and for the 1983 Annual Survey population, the proportions of students in each of the eight

Table 8–2. Comparisons of 1974 and 1983 Norming Samples on Proportions Contained within Each Stratification Group

Stratification Groups	1974 (%) N = 6,870	1983 (%) N = 7,557	1983 Annual Survey (%) N = 43,830*
Program Type Totals across Regions			
Special schools			
(residential and day)	60.2	61.8	37.5
Local school districts	39.8	38.2	62.5
Northeast			
Special schools			
(residential and day)	13.0	14.1	9.1
Local school districts	3.8	7.5	12.6
Total	16.8	21.6	21.7
Midwest			
Special schools			
(residential and day)	9.2	15.5	6.9
Local school districts	13.2	10.5	16.6
Total	20.4	26.0	23.5
South			
Special schools			
(residential and day)	28.8	22.2	14.7
Local school districts	13.6	12.7	21.6
Total	42.4	34.9	36.3
West			
Special schools			
(residential and day)	9.2	10.0	6.7
Local school districts	9.2	7.6	11.8
Total	18.4	17.6	18.6

*This number represents students in the target Annual Survey population who were between the ages of 7 and 19 years in the spring of 1983 and who were reported to the survey by residential, day, or local district special education programs.

cells formed by crosstabulating the two stratification variables. For simplification, residential and day school students have been combined into one category, called "special schools"; self-contained and mainstream classrooms have been combined into a category called "local school districts." Also, note the defined "target" Annual Survey population of 43,830 hearing impaired students. Students for whom the Stanford Achievement Test is not appropriate were eliminated from the Annual Survey data base before sampling was done. (See Allen, 1986, for a complete description of the sampling procedure.) In the current chapter, descriptions of the Annual Survey data base are limited to this target subgroup. Therefore, proportions reported in various demographic categories may differ slightly from those reported in other chapters in this book that are based on the same reporting year, 1983.

The marginal proportions for program type and region are also shown in Table 8–2. Overall, students attending special schools accounted for 60.2 percent of the sample in 1974 and 61.8 percent in 1983. The two samples are highly similar in this respect. As regards region, considerable variation can be noted. In 1974, 42.4 percent of the sample came from the South. This compares to 34.9 percent in 1983, a figure much closer to the 36.3 percent noted for the Annual Survey population. Similarly, representation from the Northeast and Midwest was less in 1974 than in 1983.

The individual cell proportions show more specifically how the samples differed with respect to the stratification variables. In 1974 southern residential and day school students accounted for 6.6 percent more of the sample (28.8 percent versus 22.2 percent) than they did in 1983. At the same time, residential and day students in the midwestern region accounted for 6.3 percent less of the sample in 1974 than in 1983. Finally, the 1974 sample had 3.7 percent fewer northeastern students attending local schools. All other cell comparisons between 1974 and 1983 show proportional differences less than 3 percent.

A striking difference can be noted between the proportions of students attending different types of educational programs in the two samples versus the proportions of Annual Survey students in those categories. While roughly 60 percent of both norming samples came from special schools, the target Annual Survey population had only 37.5 percent from special schools. This difference resulted from the method used to select the samples. Stratification is a sampling process by which various subgroups are identified. The purpose of stratification is to ensure that statistics computed for each subgroup adequately estimate parameters derived from the subgroup of the population. Stratification does not ensure that the resulting sample will be composed of proportions of subjects in each subgroup equal to those found in the population. The final part of this section discusses the implications of these program differences for the test results. It includes an analysis of the 1983 sample weighted to represent more adequately the Annual Survey population.

The relevant question at this point is whether the differences noted between the two samples with respect to the stratification variables account for the differences in achievement levels between the two years. To answer this question, scaled scores from both normings were combined into one distribution. To remove the effect of age, the scores were then converted to z-scores based on age groupings. The resulting values represent the number of standard deviations above and below the mean of a given age group. For example, if an 11-year-old obtains a converted score of -1.3, the number indicates that that student's score was 1.3 standard deviations below the mean for all 11-year-olds, including those in both the 1974 and the 1983 samples.

Table 8–3 shows, for reading comprehension and mathematics computation, the mean age-adjusted z-scores for each of the stratification groups for the two years. Because all of the scores have been converted

Table 8–3. Comparisons of Reading and Mathematics Performance across Norming Year for Stratification Groups of the Two Hearing Impaired Norming Samples*

	Reading	Math	Northeast Reading	Northeast Math	Midwest Reading	Midwest Math	South Reading	South Math	West Reading	West Math
Overall: Grand Mean	0.00	0.00								
By Norming Year										
1974	− 0.30	− 0.32								
1983	+ 0.20	+ 0.25								
By Region and Norming Year										
1974			− 0.51	− 0.46	− 0.02	− 0.10	− 0.40	− 0.40	− 0.08	− 0.14
1983			+ 0.35	+ 0.36	+ 0.33	+ 0.33	+ 0.20	+ 0.20	+ 0.18	+ 0.25
By Region, School Type, and Norming Year										
Special schools										
1974			− 0.80	− 0.65	− 0.15	− 0.21	− 0.45	− 0.43	− 0.25	− 0.22
1983			+ 0.10	+ 0.22	+ 0.14	+ 0.22	+ 0.12	+ 0.19	− 0.05	− 0.02
Local school districts										
1974			+ 0.36	+ 0.05	+ 0.04	+ 0.04	− 0.35	− 0.41	+ 0.08	+ 0.10
1983			+ 0.76	+ 0.68	+ 0.58	+ 0.49	+ 0.26	+ 0.20	+ 0.45	+ 0.52

*Numbers reported are age-adjusted z-scores.

to z-scores, the overall grand mean is equal to zero. The separate grand means (converted to z-scores) for the 1974 and 1983 samples correspond to the mean differences already noted in Figures 8-1 and 8-2. For both reading comprehension and mathematics computation, the 1983 sample averaged roughly 0.2 standard deviations above their respective age-based means, whereas the 1974 sample averaged about 0.3 standard deviations below their respective age-based means. That is, the advantage shown by the 1983 norming sample, overall, translates to about one half a standard deviation for all age groups combined.

The means for each region for the two norming years are also indicated in Table 8-3. The changes in scaled scores from 1974 to 1983 differ markedly by region. For both reading and mathematics, the difference in the means for the Northeast between normings is greater than 0.8 standard deviations, whereas in the West the difference is only about 0.26 standard deviations for reading comprehension. Thus regional performance did not change at a constant rate across the normings. (This result should not be interpreted too broadly, because region was not a stratification variable in 1974.)

The means for each program type within each region for the two norming years are also given. In this regard, considerable variation can be noted. For example, in the Northeast students attending local public school districts outperformed, by far, students attending special schools. This result occurred for both normings, although the overall level for both program types was higher in 1983. In the South, however, the performance of local public school students and special school students did not differ significantly, a result also consistent across the two normings. These findings suggest that there may be regional differences related to placement in special versus local public school programs. Furthermore, these differences have persisted over the last decade.

Table 8-4 shows the percentage within each region attending the different program types in each norming. For example, of the students selected from the Northeast in 1974, 77 percent attended special schools and 23 percent attended local public schools. In 1983 the percentage of northeastern students attending special schools dropped to 65 percent, with 35 percent attending local schools. These differences do not necessarily reflect differences in enrollment patterns between the two norming years. Rather, they reflect the different methodologies used to stratify the population in the two projects.

The information in Tables 8-3 and 8-4 can be used to explore the possible effects of sample differences on the overall achievement differences discussed above. Three sample differences are of particular interest: (a) the underrepresentation of local public school students in the Northeast in the 1974 norming, (b) the underrepresentation of residential and

Table 8-4. Percentage of Hearing Impaired Students within Region Attending Special and Local Schools for Each Norming Year

	Northeast		Midwest		South		West	
	1974	1983	1974	1983	1974	1983	1974	1983
Special schools	77	65	41	60	68	36	50	57
Local schools	23	35	59	40	32	64	50	43

day school students from the Midwest in the 1974 norming; and (c) the overrepresentation of southern residential and day school students in the 1974 norming.

It is true that in the Northeast the overrepresentation of special school students lowered the mean reading and mathematics scores of the Northeast Region in the 1974 sample; however, if the proportions of students from the Northeast attending special and local schools were .65 and .35, respectively, as they were in 1983, the mean Northeast 1974 performance would still be considerably less than the mean 1983 performance. This conclusion can be derived from the fact that the mean performance for local school district students in 1974 was still between 0.4 and 0.5 standard deviations below the performance shown in 1983 by the same group.

It was noted that special school students were underrepresented in the Midwest in 1974. The percentages indicated in Table 8-4 show that residential and day school students accounted for 41 percent of the midwestern students selected in 1974 and 60 percent of this region's students in 1983. In this situation a weighting of the 1974 midwestern sample to represent a 60/40 split in favor of special school students would actually lower the overall mean for the Midwest Region. This would have the effect of increasing the differences noted in the national means between the two norming projects. However, in 1974 the midwestern means for special and local school district students differed by less than a quarter of a standard deviation. Therefore, weighting the sample would alter the national results by only a small amount.

In the South the overrepresentation of students enrolled in special schools in 1974 should have had very little effect on the regional means. This was true because, as noted earlier, the achievement levels in both reading and mathematics of special school students and local school students did not differ appreciably in the South. The means for special and local school students in the South in 1974 differed by about 0.1 standard deviation.

In sum, the two norming samples differed with respect to the proportions of students in each of the stratification groups. However, a study of the achievement levels of students within each group for the two norming years reveals that a weighting of the 1974 norming sample to approximate the 1983 norming sample with respect to its stratification characteristics would not eliminate the achievement differences. After an examination of the demographic characteristics of the two samples in more detail, the chapter describes a more comprehensive statistical analysis that explores the effect of norming year on achievement with all of the stratification and demographic variables taken into account.

Demographic Variables. Since both the 1974 and 1983 norming projects were linked to the Annual Survey of Hearing Impaired Children and Youth, both samples can be examined to determine if they differed in important demographic and handicapping characteristics. Again, if it can be shown that the samples differed with respect to important characteristics, then it might be concluded that these differences explain why the samples also differed in their achievement.

Table 8–5 presents the demographic profiles of the 1974 and 1983 norming samples along with the profiles of the target 1983 Annual Survey population. The samples have been broken down by age, sex, ethnicity, degree of hearing loss, presence of additional handicaps, age at onset of hearing loss, and cause of deafness. The percentages reported in Table 8–5 add up to 100 percent within each cell. The total on which the percentages are based is given, as well as the proportion of missing data for each variable within each group. Differences between the two samples, as well as differences between the 1983 sample and the 1983 Annual Survey target population, are discussed separately for each variable.

Age. Predictably, the age distributions within the two norming samples differed because of the cohort of students born in 1964 and 1965, when an epidemic of rubella among pregnant mothers caused a dramatic increase in the incidence of deafness. The 20.3 percent bulge in the 9-year-old category in 1974 is directly related to the higher percentages (12.2 and 16.9) of 17- and 18-year-olds in 1983. In the other age groups the percentages are comparable. In comparison to the target Annual Survey population, the 1983 sample represents fairly well the age groups from 8 to 18 years and underrepresents the 7- and 19-year-old students. This can be explained by the fact that when testing materials were sent to the programs who participated in the norming, instructions to the test administrators required the administration of the test to students between the ages of 8 and 18 years. Administration to other age groups was declared optional; norms were not computed for these age groups. In this chapter, the 7- and 19-year-olds have been included in the demographic comparison groups; the achievement results for these groups are not discussed.

Sex. The distributions of males and females in the two norming samples and in the target Annual Survey population are virtually identical.

Ethnicity. The proportional breakdowns for whites, blacks, Hispanics, and other (or multiethnic) students are quite similar for the two norming samples and for the target Annual Survey population. The two norming groups show virtually identical proportions of white and Hispanic stu-

Table 8–5.   Demographic Profiles of 1974 and 1983 Hearing Impaired Norming Samples, Compared to 1983 Annual Survey Sample*

Demographic Profile	1974 (%)	1983 (%)	1983 Annual Survey (%)
Age (years of age)			
7	1.6	2.3	5.5
8	7.7	4.7	6.2
9	20.3	5.3	6.4
10	7.6	7.8	6.3
11	6.3	7.7	7.3
12	7.0	7.8	7.5
13	7.3	8.2	7.8
14	8.4	8.8	7.8
15	11.7	8.3	7.5
16	7.2	8.7	7.5
17	5.7	12.2	11.1
18	4.6	16.9	14.2
19	4.5	3.4	5.0
	N = 6,870 (0% missing)	N = 7,624 (1.7% missing)	N = 43,830 (0% missing)
Sex			
Male	53.3	53.3	53.7
Female	46.7	46.7	46.1
	N = 6,852 (0.3% missing)	N = 7,730 (0.3% missing)	N = 43,830 (0% missing)
Ethnic Background			
White	65.0	65.9	67.7
Black	16.7	18.3	18.5
Hispanic	12.1	12.2	10.0
Other, or multiethnic	6.1	3.6	3.7
	N = 6,870 (0% missing)	N = 7,740 (0.2% missing)	N = 42,558 (2.9% missing)
Hearing Loss			
Less-than-severe	20.3	17.6	34.3
Severe	27.6	25.3	21.3
Profound	52.1	57.1	44.4
	N = 6,646 (3.3% missing)	N = 7,662 (1.2% missing)	N = 43,047 (1.8% missing)
Additional Handicaps			
None	72.4	73.8	68.8
Physical only	10.0	9.9	8.8
Cognitive-Behavioral (with and without physical)	17.6	16.3	22.4
	N = 6,035 (12.2% missing)	N = 7,523 (1.7% missing)	N = 42,099 (3.9% missing)

(continued on next page)

Table 8–5 (*continued*).

Age at onset of hearing loss			
Prelingual (0–2 years)	93.9	94.8	92.8
Postlingual (3 years or older)	6.1	5.2	7.2
	N = 5,917 (13.9% missing)	N = 6,915 (10.9% missing)	N = 35,787 (18.4% missing)
Cause of Deafness			
Maternal rubella	36.1	35.6	30.0
Meningitis	11.3	12.1	10.9
Heredity	16.3	19.2	18.3
Otitis media	1.9	2.3	4.6
Other, at birth	19.4	12.4	14.5
Other, after birth	9.2	9.4	10.6
Other, not listed	5.8	9.0	11.1
	N = 3,208 (46.7% missing)	N = 5,080 (34.5% missing)	N = 36,868 (38.7% missing)

*See note for Table 8–2.

dents. The 1983 sample shows a 1.6 percent higher proportion of blacks; the 1974 sample shows a 2.5 percent higher proportion of students reported as other or multiethnic. The target Annual Survey population differs only slightly in its ethnic makeup from the 1983 norming sample. The proportion of blacks and students classified as other or multiethnic is the same. There is a slightly higher percentage of Hispanic students in the 1983 sample (12.2 percent versus 10.0 percent in the Annual Survey) and a slightly lower percentage of whites (65.9 percent versus 67.7 percent in the Annual Survey).

Degree of Hearing Loss. The distributions of students within each hearing loss group for the two samples and for the target Annual Survey population were different. The 1983 norming sample had 5.0 percent more students with profound hearing loss than the 1974 sample (57.1 percent versus 52.1 percent), and 2.7 percent fewer students with a less-than-severe hearing loss (17.6 percent versus 20.3 percent). Also, the 1983 norming sample showed 12.7 percent more students with profound hearing loss (57.1 percent versus 44.4 percent) than did the target Annual Survey population and 16.7 percent fewer students with less-than-severe loss (17.6 percent versus 34.3 percent). This finding is related to the fact, discussed previously, that students from local schools, who would be expected to have mild degrees of hearing loss, were underrepresented in the norming sample. It is also related to the fact that students with mild degrees of loss are not typically selected for testing with a measure designed for use with special populations. The implications of this difference between the

1983 norming sample and the Annual Survey population are discussed in a later section.

Additional Handicap Status. The two norming samples do not differ by more than 1.5 percent in any of the three additional handicap categories (none, additional physical handicaps only, additional cognitive or behavioral handicaps). However, the 1983 sample differs somewhat from the target Annual Survey population, with 5.0 percent more students reporting no additional handicaps (73.8 percent versus 68.8 percent). Also, the sample contained 6.1 percent fewer students with cognitive-behavioral handicaps (16.3 percent versus 22.4 percent). A segment of the target Annual Survey population was perhaps considered too cognitively handicapped by their teachers to be administered the Stanford Achievement Test. This resulted in a sample that was, overall, less handicapped than the Annual Survey population.

Age at Onset of Hearing Loss. The distributions of prelingually and postlingually deaf students in the two norming samples and in the target Annual Survey population are very similar. The overwhelming majority of these students became hearing impaired before the acquisition of language.

Cause of Deafness. In discussing the reported causes of deafness for the two samples, it is important, first of all, to take note of the large percentages of missing data. The implications of this missing data for generalizing to the population at large are discussed elsewhere in this book in Chapter 2. Here, it should be pointed out that the proportion of missing data was drastically reduced from 1974 to 1983 (from 46.7 percent to 34.5 percent). With these high proportions of missing data it is difficult to make judgments related to the comparability of the samples. However, if it is assumed that the actual distribution of causes among the missing cases is the same for all groups, then it is possible to compare the resulting adjusted values as they are entered in Table 8–3. Such a comparison shows that the four specific causes studied—maternal rubella, meningitis, heredity, and otitis media—are very similarly distributed in the two norming samples.

As for the Annual Survey comparisons, there is a slight increase in the 1983 sample in the proportion of students for whom maternal rubella was listed as the cause of deafness (35.6 percent versus 30.0 percent). This resulted possibly from the fact that persons with rubella-caused deafness tend to have accompanying additional handicaps in greater numbers than persons with other listed causes of deafness. Therefore, they are perhaps more likely to be enrolled in special schools; as noted previously, special schools are overrepresented in the 1983 norming sample. On the other hand, the 1983 norming sample had a smaller proportion of students with additional handicaps. The differences are really not explainable. It is questionable how important these differences are to the achievement levels of students in the samples.

Summary. In only two instances did the proportions of students in the two samples differ on any characteristic by more that 2 percentage points. This was true within the age categories because of the presence of the rubella cohort, and within the hearing loss categories, in which it was noted that the 1983 sample had 5 percent more students with profound hearing losses. These findings do not appear to explain the achievement differences noted between the two samples. If anything, the greater proportion of students with profound hearing losses in 1983 would suggest there might be lower achievement in the more recent norming. However, the opposite was true, lending support to the hypothesis that hearing impaired students have shown gains in their reading and mathematics achievement levels over the last 10 years.

Statistical Analysis. To this point, the chapter has examined the characteristics of the two norming samples in search of possible explanations for the gains in scaled score performance described at the beginning, and there has been no compelling reason to argue against the gain hypothesis. This section looks at the statistical effect of norming year on achievement levels in a regression analysis that controls for differences in the samples of all of the variables described so far. This analysis makes it possible to assess the strength of the relationship between norming year and achievement level and sets the stage for the final section of this chapter, which studies the achievement patterns of different subgroups of the hearing impaired student population.

Tables 8–6 and 8–7 present the results of the regression analyses performed on the reading comprehension and mathematics computation scores. In these tables the age-adjusted z-scores are the dependent measures, and the categorical independent measures are converted to dichotomized dummy variables for the purpose of this analysis. Descriptions of the dichotomies that were defined also appear in Tables 8–6 and 8–7 for the variables that were significant predictors of achievement. Only those variables that attained a level of significance at the .001 level are included. This conservative level of significance was adopted as the inclusion criteria because the sample size was very large, allowing factors with very small beta weights to obtain significance at the .05 or .01 levels.

. To test for the effect of norming year on achievement, two regression analyses were run for each subject area. In the first analysis, norming year was not included as an independent variable. In the second analysis it was. The increase in multiple R-square between the two analyses is equal to the proportion of variance accounted for by norming year. As indi-

Table 8–6.   Significant Effects in Regression Analysis for Reading Comprehension

Description of Dichotomous Variables	Beta Weight	Significance
1. Attending a local school district (versus attending a special school)	.14	< .001
2. Living in the South (versus living in other regions of the country)	− .08	< .001
3. Being female (versus being male)	.11	< .001
4. Being member of minority ethnic group (versus being white)	− .23	< .001
5. Having profound hearing loss: > 90 dB average threshold in the better ear (versus having a less than profound loss)	− .07	< .001
6. Becoming hearing impaired before the age of 3 years (versus becoming impaired at *or* after the age of 3)	− .07	< .001
7. Having one or more additional physical handicaps (versus having no additional handicaps *or* having additional cognitive handicaps)	− .10	< .001
8. Having one or more additional cognitive handicaps, with or without additional physical handicaps (versus having no additional handicaps *or* having additional physical handicaps only)	− .25	< .001
9. Being tested in 1983 (versus being tested in 1974)	.25	< .001
Multiple R-square for model that *does not* include norming year as an independent measure	.18	
Multiple R-square for model that *does* include norming year as an independent measure	.25	
Proportion of variance attributable to norming year, independent of all other effects	.07	

cated in Tables 8–6 and 8–7, norming year independently accounted for 7 percent of the variance in reading comprehension scores and 8 percent of the variance in mathematics computation scores. These figures indicate a strong association between norming year and achievement levels in reading and mathematics.

The beta weights for the other variables show the degree to which they account for the achievement levels of hearing impaired students. It is helpful to divide the variables into three categories: weak predictors (i.e., those with beta weights less than .10), moderate predictors (i.e., those with beta weights between .10 and .19), and strong predictors (i.e., those with beta weights of .20 or higher). It should be kept in mind that all reported weights were significant at the .001 level. The following summarizes the results for reading comprehension and mathematics computation. The sign represents the direction of the relationship, that is, (+) indicates a positive correlation with achievement and (−) represents a negative correlation with achievement.

Table 8–7. Significant Effects in Regression Analysis for Mathematics Computation

Description of Dichotomous Variables	Beta Weight	Significance
1. Attending a local school district (versus attending a special school)	.11	<.001
2. Living in the South (versus living in other regions of the country)	−.09	<.001
3. Being member of minority ethnic group (versus being white)	−.17	<.001
4. Having one or more additional *physical* handicaps (versus having no additional handicaps *or* having additional cognitive handicaps)	−.11	<.001
5. Having one or more additional cognitive handicaps, with or without additional physical handicaps (versus having no additional handicaps *or* having additional physical handicaps only)	−.30	<.001
6. Being tested in 1983 (versus being tested in 1974)	.27	<.001
Multiple R-square for model that *does not* include norming year as an independent measure	.15	
Multiple R-square for model that *does* include norming year as an independent measure	.23	
Variation attributable to norming year, independent of all other effects	.08	

Reading Comprehension
    Weak Predictors
        Living in the South (−)
        Having profound hearing loss (−)
        Having a prelingual age at onset of deafness (−)
    Moderate Predictors
        Attending local school (+)
        Being female (+)
        Having an additional physical handicap (−)
    Strong Predictors
        Being a member of a minority ethnic group (−)
        Having an additional cognitive-behavioral handicap (−)
        Being tested in 1983 (versus 1974) (+)
Mathematics Computation
    Weak Predictors
        Living in the South (−)
    Moderate Predictors
        Attending a local school (+)
        Being a member of a minority ethnic group (−)
        Having an additional physical handicap (−)
    Strong Predictors
        Having an additional cognitive-behavioral handicap (−)
        Being tested in 1983 (+)

Ethnic status and additional handicap status exerted strong influences on reading comprehension achievement in both 1974 and 1983. Sex and program type were somewhat less important: Females outscored males, and local school students outscored students enrolled in special schools. Finally, hearing loss, age at onset of hearing loss, and region had weaker, but statistically significant, effects.

For mathematics computation the set of significant predictors was different. Sex, hearing loss, and age at onset of hearing loss were not statistically significant. Also, ethnic status showed somewhat less of an effect. Otherwise, additional handicap status continued to exert a strong influence on achievement, program type exerted a moderate influence, and region exerted a weak influence. A more in-depth discussion of the achievement patterns of students with these characteristics appears in the final section of this chapter.

Sample Representativeness. In the discussion of the sample characteristics, three differences between the 1983 norming sample and the target Annual Survey population were noted that may hinder the ability to generalize the results of the 1983 norming project: (a) the Annual Survey population had a greater proportion of students who attended local schools than did the 1983 norming group, (b) the Annual Survey population had a greater proportion of students with less-than-severe hearing loss, and (c) the Annual Survey population had a greater proportion of students with cognitive-behavioral additional handicaps. Possible reasons for these differences have already been noted. That is, students with low levels of impairment were systematically excluded from the norming because they are not normally administered tests designed for special populations, and students with compounding cognitive-behavioral additional handicaps also are not selected for testing with standardized tests because of their inability to handle these tests.

To examine these biasing factors, the 1983 norming sample was weighted to more accurately reflect the Annual Survey population on the three variables of concern: program type, additional handicap status, and level of hearing loss. Each student in the sample was classified according to the three weighting variables and then assigned a weighting factor that was the ratio of proportion of students in the Annual Survey population to the proportion of students in the sample who possessed the same set of characteristics vis-a-vis the three variables.

Table 8–8 summarizes the results of the weighted sample analysis. It shows, for 8-, 12-, and 16-year-olds, the scaled scores associated with the 20th, 50th, and 80th percentiles in reading comprehension and mathematics computation. Separate entries are included for both the weighted and unweighted samples. The table shows clearly that weighting the sample had little effect on the scaled score distributions. The weighted percentiles never deviate from the unweighted percentiles by more

Table 8–8. Reading Comprehension and Mathematics Computation Scaled Scores Associated with 20th, 50th, and 80th Percentiles for 8-, 12-, and 16-year olds: Comparisons of Weighted and Unweighted Samples

	Age 8		Age 12		Age 16	
Percentile	Unweighted Sample	Weighted Sample	Unweighted Sample	Weighted Sample	Unweighted Sample	Weighted Sample
Reading Comprehension						
80th	552	553	606	613	641	646
50th	490	499	549	562	594	596
20th	447	452	489	495	531	531
Math Computation						
80th	567	570	673	672	710	709
50th	533	537	623	623	673	671
20th	467	473	556	559	618	613

than 13 scaled score points (549 versus 562 for the 50th percentile in reading comprehension for 12-year-olds represents the largest deviation). Most comparisons show differences of less than 4 points.

These findings suggest that the score distributions from unweighted samples are adequate estimates of the population distributions. However, the weighting technique assumes that the students in the sample with additional handicaps are representative of those outside the sample with additional handicaps. This assumption also holds for the program type and hearing loss variables. These assumptions may not be true. As pointed out before, teachers exercised some judgment in selecting students for testing. Thus weighting the sample would not allow an accurate estimation of the performance of the students who were not sampled, even if subgroups of the norming sample who share handicapping, audiological, and program characteristics could be identified. The factor of teacher selection is unaccounted for. Because the weighting cannot completely remove the effects of possible sample bias, another descriptor must be added to the definition of the target population (i.e., students selected for achievement testing with a test designed for special use). The 1983 norming project can be seen as one in which the broad middle range of hearing impaired students who receive special education was sampled. Students at both extremes, that is, students with severe cognitive-behavioral handicaps and students with low levels of loss, have been systematically excluded.

Analysis #2: Comparisons of the Screening Results Between the Two Normings

Both the 1974 and 1983 normings of the Stanford Achievement Test involved adapting procedures for administering the test so that the results would more fairly assess the achievement levels of hearing impaired students. Central to the problem of ensuring fairness is the issue of test level assignment. When hearing students take the Stanford test, they are assigned a test level on the basis of their age or grade in school. Such a procedure is not advisable for hearing impaired students for two reasons. First, their achievement levels lag behind their hearing counterparts, and, second, their growth in different subject areas is often uneven. (Figures 8–1 and 8–2 demonstrate these facts clearly.) Assigning a student a test booklet containing a battery of tests designed for a single grade in school will not fairly assess the student's achievement in all areas if the student shows an uneven growth pattern across achievement areas.

The two norming projects chose different solutions to the problem of test level assignment. In 1974 two Reading Comprehension subtests from the Form B Stanford Achievement Test (sixth edition) battery were used as screening tests. Additionally, subtests from different levels of the battery were recombined into the different full-battery test booklets to more adequately reflect the growth patterns of hearing impaired students in the different subject areas. Six levels of an adapted test battery were created. These levels were parallel to the six levels of the regular Stanford (Form A) with respect to Reading Comprehension but were different with respect to Mathematics Computation. More specifically, levels 1 through 4 of the adapted test contained the Primary 1, Primary 3, Intermediate 1, and Intermediate 2 levels of Mathematics Computation subtests. Both levels 5 and 6 of the adapted test contained the Advanced level Mathematics Computation subtest. The regular Primary 2 level Mathematics Computation subtest was omitted.

For the 1983 norming, test booklets were not reconstructed and subtests were not rearranged. Instead, separate short screening tests in both reading and mathematics were developed for screening students into regular seventh edition full-battery levels. The items for these screening tests were taken from the bank of items that had been piloted by The Psychological Corporation during the item tryout associated with the development of the seventh edition of the Stanford Achievement Test.

The difference in these two procedures is illustrated by the following example. A student in 1974 takes the 1974 screening test. The student screens into Level 2. Because of the reconstruction of the battery, the student takes the Primary 2 Reading Comprehension subtest and the Primary 3 Mathematics Computation subtest. In 1983 the student would have taken two screening tests. It is therefore possible for this student to screen into the Primary 2 Reading Comprehension subtest and the Advanced Mathematics Computation subtest. The student would then take the relevant subtests from the regular Stanford Achievement Test materials.

The question being considered in the current discussion is whether these two different screening procedures have resulted in spurious scaled score distributions. Scaled scores are, to some extent, dependent on level assignment. If a student scores at chance on a test level that is too difficult, the scaled score assigned to that student will overestimate the student's true ability level. Therefore, it is possible that the 1983 screening procedures systematically placed students in levels of the test that were too difficult, resulting in spuriously high mean scores.

To study this potentially biasing problem, two analyses are presented. The first is a study of the distributions of test level assignment in reading and mathematics for the two norming projects. This analysis determines if, in fact, students tended to be assigned to higher levels of the battery in 1983. The second analysis considers the accuracy of test level assignment of both norming projects. It defines acceptable raw score ranges for each of the subtests at each of the levels and is used to study the proportions of each sample scoring in acceptable and unacceptable ranges.

Tables 8–9 and 8–10 present the Reading Comprehension and Mathematics Computation test level assignments for students in each age group within each norming sample. The tables clearly demonstrate that students in the 1983 sample were assigned to higher test levels than they were in 1974. For example, 98.7 percent of the 8-year-olds in the 1974 sample were assigned either to Primary 1 or Primary 2 levels for Reading Comprehension. In 1983 the percentage of 8-year-olds taking the lower two levels of the test was 83.1. The 1983 sample therefore contained 15.6 percent more 8-year-old students taking levels of the Stanford Reading Comprehension subtest higher than Primary 2.

In Mathematics Computation (Table 8–10), there are no entries for Primary 2 for the 1974 sample; this is because the Primary 2 Mathematics Computation subtest was not included in the restructuring of the sixth edition of the Stanford Achievement Test. Combining the lower three levels of the test, it can be seen that 98.7 percent of the 8-year-olds were assigned to these levels in 1974. In 1983, 91.8 percent of the 8-year-olds were assigned to the lower three levels, 6.9 percent fewer 8-year-olds than were assigned to these levels in 1974.

The differences in the distributions of test level assignments between 1974 and 1983 are significant enough to explain the differences in means described at the beginning of the chapter. Table 8–11 presents data relevant to the question of whether the differences in test level assignments reflect true differences in the abilities of the students or whether the differences arise out of errors in test level assignment in either of the two years. For reading and mathematics separately, students were divided into three categories, depending on the raw scores they obtained. If they scored 25 percent or fewer of the items correct, they were classified as being in the chance level. If they scored more than 90 percent of the items correct, they were classified as scoring in the top-out category. All other students were classified as being in the acceptable range.

Table 8–11 presents, for reading and mathematics separately, the proportions of students in each category for each test level for the two

Table 8–9. Reading Test Level Assignment for Hearing Impaired Students in the 1974 and 1983 Normings of the Stanford Achievement Test (Sixth and Seventh Editions)

Age (year)	Total (N) 1974	1983	Primary 1 (%) 1974	1983	Primary 2 (%) 1974	1983	Primary 3 (%) 1974	1983	Intermediate 1 (%) 1974	1983	Intermediate 2 (%) 1974	1983	Advanced (%) 1974	1983
8	530	354	75.5	56.5	23.2	26.6	0.9	10.5	0.2	5.4	0.0	0.0	0.2	1.1
9	1395	400	67.0	44.8	29.7	27.3	2.6	14.3	0.7	11.3	0.0	0.5	0.0	2.0
10	520	436	50.2	37.4	38.7	28.2	7.7	16.1	2.5	13.3	0.6	1.6	0.4	3.4
11	436	578	38.3	32.5	46.6	27.3	8.7	21.3	3.2	13.8	1.6	1.7	1.6	3.3
12	484	584	26.9	23.5	50.0	26.0	10.7	30.0	7.2	12.3	2.5	2.4	2.7	5.8
13	499	622	22.8	19.5	50.3	25.4	13.8	26.2	6.6	15.0	2.0	2.4	4.4	11.6
14	580	661	17.8	15.1	49.5	22.7	13.8	25.6	7.4	15.4	5.0	5.0	6.6	16.2
15	801	628	14.9	12.1	47.1	18.4	12.7	28.0	8.4	17.3	9.9	4.0	7.1	20.3
16	494	655	11.3	14.4	42.3	17.3	12.6	25.7	9.5	15.9	12.8	5.6	11.5	21.2
17	394	915	10.7	13.9	33.8	16.9	16.2	25.7	10.4	18.9	13.2	4.9	15.7	19.7
18	319	1277	8.8	13.3	32.6	18.2	12.2	28.5	13.2	17.9	14.7	5.5	18.5	16.6

Table 8–10.   Mathematics Test Level Assignment for Hearing Impaired Students in the 1974 and 1983 Normings of the Stanford Achievement Test (Sixth and Seventh Editions)

| | Total | | Primary 1 | | Primary 2* | Primary 3 | | Intermediate 1 | | Intermediate 2 | | Advanced | |
| | | | (%) | | (%) | (%) | | (%) | | (%) | | (%) | |
Age (year)	1974 (N)	1983	1974	1983	1983	1974	1983	1974	1983	1974	1983	1974	1983
8	530	357	75.5	68.3	15.1	23.2	8.4	0.9	7.6	0.2	0.6	0.2	0.0
9	1395	399	67.0	48.6	17.5	29.7	20.1	2.6	12.0	0.7	1.3	0.0	0.5
10	520	425	50.2	37.2	13.2	38.7	28.2	7.7	16.2	2.5	3.8	1.0	1.4
11	436	574	38.3	22.3	15.7	46.6	24.7	8.7	27.5	3.2	7.8	3.2	1.9
12	484	579	26.9	18.0	10.0	50.0	24.7	10.7	30.1	7.2	12.6	5.2	4.7
13	499	619	22.8	10.8	10.0	50.3	23.4	13.8	28.6	6.6	16.5	6.4	10.7
14	580	654	17.8	6.9	6.9	49.5	21.7	13.8	28.7	7.4	17.7	11.6	18.0
15	801	623	14.9	7.1	5.3	47.1	16.1	12.7	28.7	8.4	20.9	17.0	22.0
16	494	644	11.3	7.1	5.4	42.3	14.6	12.6	25.3	9.5	20.8	24.3	26.7
17	394	903	10.7	6.0	4.8	33.8	13.2	16.2	29.3	10.4	19.4	28.9	27.4
18	319	272	8.8	6.7	5.9	32.6	14.2	12.2	29.7	13.2	19.5	33.2	24.0

*In the sixth edition of the test, as adapted for hearing impaired students, the Primary 2 Mathematics Computation subtest was not included in the battery because of the restructuring of the subtests.

Table 8–11. Percent Scoring in Each of Three Performance Categories for Reading Comprehension and Mathematics Computation at Each of the Six Stanford Achievement Test Battery Levels for the 1974 and 1983 Norming Samples

	N		Chance* (%)		Acceptable* (%)		Top-out* (%)	
	1974	1983	1974	1983	1974	1983	1974	1983
Reading Comprehension								
Primary 1	2372	1335	4.8	0.9	94.9	96.0	0.9	3.1
Primary 2	2641	1694	8.0	2.3	91.5	97.6	0.5	0.1
Primary 3	624	1788	0.0	1.3	99.2	98.6	0.8	0.1
Intermediate 1	404	455	4.2	1.3	95.8	98.5	0.0	0.1
Intermediate 2	370	268	2.2	4.5	97.3	95.1	0.5	0.4
Advanced	355	959	1.4	5.0	94.4	93.7	4.2	1.3
Overall	6766	6499	5.2	2.1	94.0	96.9	0.8	1.0
Mathematics Computation								
Primary 1	2201	958	19.1	1.6	64.8	76.1	16.0	22.3
Primary 2	—†	516	—†	0.0	—†	88.0	—†	12.0
Primary 3	2601	1399	5.1	1.1	75.2	77.3	19.7	21.6
Intermediate 1	625	1648	5.0	1.1	73.1	85.9	21.9	13.0
Intermediate 2	402	1094	4.2	0.5	83.1	83.9	12.7	15.6
Advanced	721	1178	3.1	0.9	90.0	91.7	6.9	7.4
Overall	6550	6793	9.5	1.0	73.5	83.6	16.8	15.4

*Chance = <26% items correct; Acceptable = 26%–90% items correct; Top-out = >90% items correct.
†See note for Table 8–10.

norming samples. In reading, both screening procedures resulted in high proportions of students being acceptably screened (94.0 percent in 1974 and 96.9 percent in 1983). In mathematics computation the results are not as good. Whereas 83.6 percent of the 1983 sample scored in acceptable ranges on their mathematics computation subtests, only 73.5 percent of the 1974 sample did so. This result is not surprising because the screening procedures in 1974 involved the administration of a reading test only. What is surprising is the larger number of students in 1974 who scored at chance level on the mathematics computation tests. As described earlier, chance level performance yields scaled scores that tend to overestimate rather than underestimate performance. Thus, if these students had been more appropriately placed, their 1974 scores in mathematics computation would actually have been lower. This analysis therefore provides support for the gain hypothesis: Students were assigned to higher levels of the test in 1983, and these higher test level assignments seem to be rooted in higher actual ability.

Analysis #3: An Assessment of the Validity of the Conversion Tables When Applied to Hearing Impaired Students

Throughout this chapter, a great deal of faith has been placed in the test publisher's tables that convert the sixth edition scales to the seventh edition scales. These tables were developed by using sophisticated item response theory analyses in which large national samples of hearing students were administered tests containing items from both the sixth and seventh editions of the tests. The items were statistically linked, and the resulting conversion tables reflect the relationship between the two scales when applied to hearing students.

The data from the two norming samples of hearing impaired students cannot be employed adequately to study the appropriateness of the conversion tables when applied to hearing impaired students. These data come from two different samples, and the 9-year lapse between the two administrations makes a study of the validity of the conversions impossible. There exists, however, a small data set of 512 students within the 1983 norming sample for whom data on both the sixth and seventh editions are available. A study of these students' performance on both tests helps in understanding the relationship between the two scales. The students in this subgroup attended programs participating in the pilot testing of the screening tests that have become part of the procedures for administering the Stanford Achievement Test to hearing impaired students. As part of that pilot project these students had been administered the sixth edition of the adapted Stanford Achievement Test in the spring of 1982. In the following spring, they were administered the seventh edition of the test as part of the norming project.

Students who have taken both the sixth and seventh editions of the Stanford Achievement Test at about the same time should show converted sixth edition scaled scores that are roughly equivalent to the scaled scores they obtain on the seventh edition. For the pilot sample students it is not reasonable to assume that their sixth and seventh edition performances would be equivalent, as an entire year elapsed between their two test administrations. It is possible, however, to estimate the amount of longitudinal change that would be expected after a year's interval by examining the cross-sectional differences shown by students in adjacent age categories from the norming sample itself. It is possible to see the degree to which the pilot sample's gain from 1982 to 1983 matched the expected cross-sectional gain. If the means of the longitudinal differences are greater than the differences between the means of the adjacent age categories, it can be concluded that the converted scores from the sixth edition are not as accurate as investigators would like them to be and that the scores have underestimated the performance of students taking the sixth edition.

Table 8–12 shows the results of these comparisons. For almost all age groups for both reading comprehension and mathematics computation, the longitudinal differences between the pilot subjects' converted sixth and seventh edition scores are greater than the differences determined by cross-sectional analysis. For reading comprehension, the average difference between the longitudinal and cross-sectional columns of Table 8–12 is 24.6 points. For mathematics computation, the average difference between the two columns is 12.3 points.

If it is believed that students should gain, from year to year, an amount equal to the cross-sectional differences shown by the norming sample, then it is possible that the conversion tables may, on average, be underestimating sixth edition reading comprehension performance by approximately 25 points and mathematics computation performance by about 12 points. As noted previously, the apparent advantage shown by 1983 norming sample students was about one half a standard deviation within each age group, which translates to about 30 to 40 points. (The overall standard deviations for the norming sample are 67.9 scaled score points for reading comprehension and 74.6 for mathematics computation.) Thus, much of the gain between 1974 and 1983 may, in fact, be attributable to questionable score conversions. This conclusion is not as strong for mathematics computation, in which the average 12-point discrepancy between the cross-sectional and longitudinal columns in Table 8–12 represents only about a third of the difference in performance levels noted in "Analysis 1" earlier in the chapter.

This study of the pilot sample is not conclusive. There are several limitations to the analysis just described. First, it is not clear that the pilot sample adequately represented the 1983 norming sample and, by implication, the target Annual Survey population itself. The pilot screening test project involved administering the sixth edition to nearly 1300 students.

Table 8–12.   Comparison of the Mean Differences between the Sixth and Seventh Edition Scaled Scores after a 1-Year Interval with Cross-sectional Differences of Adjacent 1983 Norming Age Categories

Age (years)	Reading Comprehension		Math Computation	
	*Longitudinal**	*Cross-sectional†*	*Longitudinal*	*Cross-sectional*
8 to 9	22.6 ($N=17$)	15.4	25.5 ($N=16$)	10.6
9 to 10	37.4 ($N=19$)	16.4	3.6 ($N=19$)	30.0
10 to 11	34.1 ($N=45$)	5.3	21.8 ($N=45$)	17.5
11 to 12	45.3 ($N=54$)	14.1	26.5 ($N=53$)	21.3
12 to 13	39.7 ($N=59$)	11.7	37.9 ($N=58$)	13.5
13 to 14	41.8 ($N=61$)	11.0	31.8 ($N=58$)	11.1
14 to 15	34.9 ($N=55$)	9.0	29.5 ($N=49$)	7.0
15 to 16	16.4 ($N=43$)	0.0	32.5 ($N=43$)	13.0
16 to 17	30.7 ($N=54$)	−1.3	33.7 ($N=53$)	14.0
17 to 18	18.8 ($N=71$)	−6.0	20.3 ($N=70$)	1.7

*Longitudinal differences represent the mean scaled score "gain" in pilot sample students from converted sixth edition scaled scores in 1982 to seventh edition scaled scores in 1983.

†Cross-sectional differences are computed from the 1983 norming sample data by subtracting the mean scaled scores of each age cohort by the mean scaled score of the next higher age group.

All of the programs that served these students were invited to participate in the norming during the following year. It could be argued that programs that agreed to participate in the norming project were those that had had good experiences with the pilot project the year before. This may have biased the sample in favor of higher achieving students who could be expected to gain more than the amount suggested by the cross-sectional differences.

Another concern is the assumption that the cross-sectional differences from year to year are good estimates of longitudinal growth. There is evidence that the special education population is not stable, that is, the group of students that enter the Annual Survey data base at the age of 8 years are not the same students in the data base 10 years later. Students who prove themselves capable of regular classroom work are transferred into the mainstream; students who have begun in the mainstream but have been unable to keep up with hearing peers are transferred into special education. At the beginning of the chapter, one of the conclusions after examining Figures 8–1 and 8–2 was the possibility that the academic achievement of hearing impaired students levels off. It is possible that movement in and out of special education results in a more handicapped, and therefore lower achieving, population among the older age groups. (This topic is discussed more fully in Chapter 3.) If so, then the leveling off is artificial, and the cross-sectional means are not good representations of longitudinal growth.

These two concerns, the representativeness of the pilot sample used in this analysis and the use of the cross-sectional differences to estimate expected longitudinal growth, shed doubt on the conclusion that the conversion tables are inappropriate. Nonetheless, all of the arguments in favor of a gain hypothesis have relied on the validity of the conversion tables. If the analysis presented here has not proved the invalidity of these tables, these results should prompt caution about the strength of the conclusions. The sixth and seventh editions of the Stanford Achievement Test are not the same test, and the two samples, despite their similarities, were different groups of students. Thus, the evidence presented in favor of the gain hypothesis can never be completely convincing.

A review of the evidence shows that the two samples used to norm the sixth and seventh editions of the Stanford Achievement Test were very similar with respect to the distributions of students attending different types of educational programs. Also, although the samples differed with respect to their regional breakdown, achievement differences between the stratification cells that make up the two samples were not great enough to discount the gain hypothesis. In regard to the demographic and handicapping characteristics, the two norming samples were extremely similar. There was, however, a higher proportion of students with profound hearing loss in the 1983 sample. This finding argued in favor of a gain hypothesis because the achievement differences were noted despite a more severely handicapped sample. A statistical analysis that included both the demographic and stratification variables revealed that norming year accounted for a significant proportion of achievement variation in reading comprehension and mathematics computation.

The screening procedures used to assign students to test level changed markedly between the two normings. Nonetheless, both screening procedures resulted in a very high proportion of students scoring in acceptable ranges of the reading comprehension subtests. In mathematics, the results were not so encouraging, especially for the 1974 sample, in which only 74 percent scored in an acceptable range. For this test a higher proportion of students in the 1974 sample scored in the chance range. Typically, chance level performance overestimates the actual abilities of a given student. Thus, there is further support for the gain hypothesis, as the mean scaled scores for mathematics computation reported for the 1974 group may be inflated.

Finally, there are questions left unanswered about the validity of the conversion tables used to link the sixth and seventh editions of the test. It is possible that use of the conversion tables underestimates the achievement level of the 1974 scores.

In summary, there is good reason to believe that hearing impaired students' achievement levels were higher in 1983 than they were in 1974 when the sixth edition of the Stanford Achievement Test was normed. Unfortunately, the degree of uncertainty introduced by the conversion tables does not permit direct assessment of the amount of achievement gain that has taken place.

ACHIEVEMENT PATTERNS OF VARIOUS SUBGROUPS OF THE 1983 NORMING SAMPLE

The purpose of this section is to provide some summary normative data for various subgroups of the hearing impaired student population based on the 1983 norming. The previous section took note of some factors that significantly affected achievement for the combined 1974 and 1983 samples in a regression analysis that controlled statistically for other important demographic variables. The fact that so many of the variables had significant effects on the reading and mathematics achievement levels of hearing impaired students indicated clearly that this population of students is heterogeneous with respect to variables that influence achievement.

Questions are often asked about the published hearing impaired percentile ranks related to the definitions of the target norming population. Answers to these questions help educators decide on the usefulness of the percentile rank in various test reporting contexts (e.g., individualized education plans, parent conferences, district or statewide reports). Behind these questions lie concerns over whether individual students or groups of students fit the target group to such an extent that the percentile ranks have meaning. In many cases it is difficult to ascribe meaning to the percentile rank because students are individuals with unique characteristics, and the norming sample was composed, as noted, of students with widely differing characteristics.

Clearly, the usefulness of normative data is enhanced if subgroups upon which normative comparisons are made can be defined more specifically. The purpose of this section, therefore, is to summarize the percentile distributions of the various subgroups discussed previously. These summaries focus on the scaled scores of 8-, 12-, and 16-year-olds and report the 20th, 50th, and 80th percentiles of the various groups under analysis. (See Allen, 1986, for complete decile tables for all ages of the different population subgroups.)

The tables and figures summarize the percentile distributions for the following subgroups:

Region of the U. S. (Table 8–13 and Fig. 8–5), including Northeast, Midwest, South, and West

Program type (Table 8–14 and Fig. 8–6), including special schools (residential and day) and local school districts

Ethnic group (Table 8–15 and Fig. 8–7), including whites, blacks, and Hispanics

Degree of hearing loss (Table 8–16 and Fig. 8–8), including less-than-severe and severe and profound (combined)

Additional handicap (Table 8–17 and Fig. 8–9), including no additional handicaps and additional handicaps (physical or cognitive-behavioral).

Because the specific percentiles require dividing the population by two variables (age plus the variable of interest), it was sometimes necessary to combine categories to ensure that the total sample size upon which the norms were based was of adequate size. For example, note that severely and profoundly deaf students are combined, as are the physical and cognitive-behavioral categories for additional handicap. The variable of age at onset could not be included because the overwhelming majority of students in the sample (94.8 percent) were prelingually deaf.

Region

No consistent pattern can be determined from Table 8–13 and Figure 8–5; that is, in no region was the distribution of scores lower or higher in reading and mathematics across all age groups. It is interesting to note that among 8-year-olds the northeastern students showed considerably more variation in both reading and mathematics, indicating a more heterogeneous population of students enrolled in special education at this age. Interestingly, the 16-year-old northeastern subgroup shows the least amount of variation in test scores, especially in reading comprehension. Perhaps, as students get older, there is more migration out of special education in the Northeast such that the older students are more homogeneous. Regional differences in the migration of students in and out of special education is a fruitful topic for future research.

What is true for the medians in these plots is not necessarily true for the other percentile ranks. For example, the 50th percentile mathematics computation score for 8-year-olds in the Midwest is 37 points above the 50th percentile score for 8-year-old students in the Northeast. Yet the 80th percentile score is identical for both groups. The higher achieving students in both regions scored about the same on the test, whereas the lower achievers scored much higher in the Midwest, resulting in a sizeable difference in the reported medians. This example shows that the median alone

Table 8–13. 20th, 50th, and 80th Percentiles in Reading Comprehension and Mathematics Computation for Hearing Impaired Students in Different Regions of the U.S., Stanford Norming Project, Spring 1983

Percentile	Age 8				Age 12				Age 16			
	NE	MW	S	W	NE	MW	S	W	NE	MW	S	W
Reading Comprehension Scaled Scores												
80th	566	549	543	548	614	608	597	599	646	646	635	638
50th	500	499	493	475	555	555	543	544	618	591	590	585
20th	442	454	454	449	494	510	478	483	557	545	530	513
Mathematics Computation Scaled Scores												
80th	590	590	585	582	683	678	654	664	721	713	698	710
50th	514	551	527	527	635	639	602	632	686	672	670	671
20th	446	497	475	464	580	555	550	567	636	617	620	610

Note: NE = Northeast, MW = Midwest, S = South, and W = West.

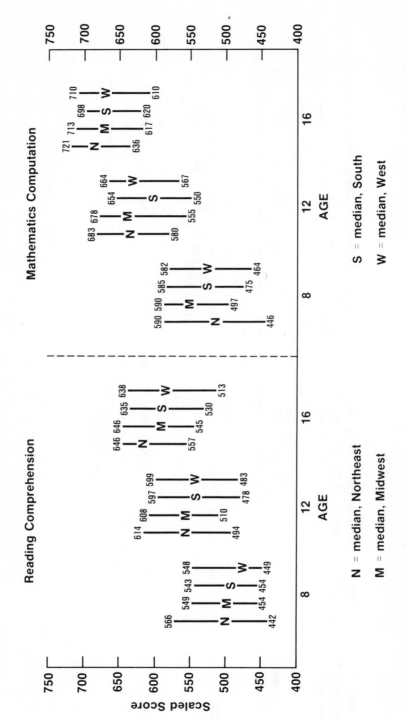

Figure 8–5. 20th to 80th percentile ranges for hearing impaired 8-, 12-, and 16-year-olds in different regions of the United States, Stanford Norming Project, Spring 1983.

Table 8-14.   20th, 50th, and 80th Percentiles in Reading Comprehension and Mathematics Computation for Hearing Impaired Students in Different Types of Special Education Programs, Stanford Norming Project, Spring 1983

Percentile	Age 8		Age 12		Age 16	
	Special Schools	Local Districts	Special Schools	Local Districts	Special Schools	Local Districts
	Reading Comprehension Scaled Scores					
80th	533	563	589	618	635	656
50th	485	510	536	572	589	604
20th	447	456	480	503	526	545
	Mathematics Computation Scaled Scores					
80th	567	603	667	679	707	717
50th	517	550	613	635	669	681
20th	455	491	551	568	611	634

is insufficient to characterize the achievement levels of students in a given group.

Program Type

As indicated in Table 8-14 and Figure 8-6, the distributional differences between special school and local school students are consistent and fairly straightforward. Local school students show advantages in both reading and mathematics for all age groups. This finding in no way implies a causal relationship between program type and academic achievement. It simply describes a fact: At the current time the population of students receiving special educational services within the local schools achieve at higher levels, on average, than do students attending special schools. Many factors affect achievement, as it is hoped this chapter has made clear. Figure 8-6 should not, therefore, be interpreted as an endorsement for local school over residential or day school placement.

Ethnicity

Table 8-15 and Figure 8-7 present the results for the different ethnic groups within the broader population. The previous regression analysis indicated that ethnic status was one of the strongest predictors of achievement. This fact is dramatically illustrated by these percentile distributions. For exam-ple, the 50th percentile reading comprehension scores for Hispanic 12-year-olds is 11 scaled score points less than the 50th percentile for white 8-year-olds. Hispanics perform more poorly than do blacks in reading compre-hension, but their performance is similar to black students' performance in mathematics computation. Finally, the distributions are far less varied for mathematics computation. This is consistent with the regression

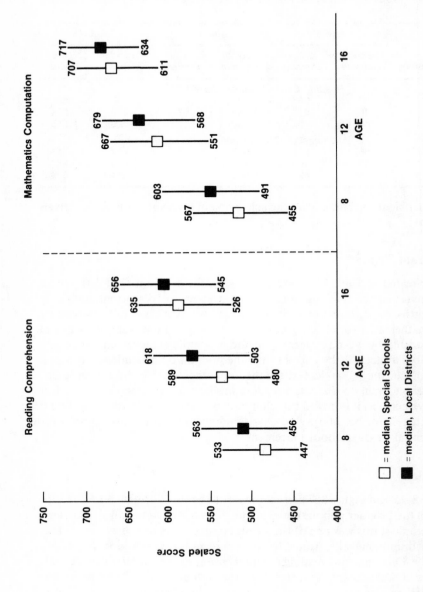

Figure 8–6. 20th to 80th percentile ranges for hearing impaired 8-, 12-, and 16-year-olds in different types of special education programs, Stanford Norming Project, Spring 1983.

Table 8–15. 20th, 50th, and 80th Percentiles in Reading Comprehension and Mathematics Computation for Hearing Impaired Students in Different Ethnic Groups, Stanford Norming Project, 1983

Percentile	Age 8			Age 12			Age 16		
	White	Black	Hispanic	White	Black	Hispanic	White	Black	Hispanic
Reading Comprehension Scaled Scores									
80th	564	511*	482*	615	570	570	646	608	595
50th	510	468*	450*	569	525	499	608	566	531
20th	462	442*	430*	512	470	471	556	491	476
Mathematics Computation Scaled Scores									
80th	599	544*	553*	683	631	640	715	688	693
50th	550	501*	490*	642	588	596	680	646	657
20th	493	456*	453*	571	529	553	631	577	614

* N is <50.

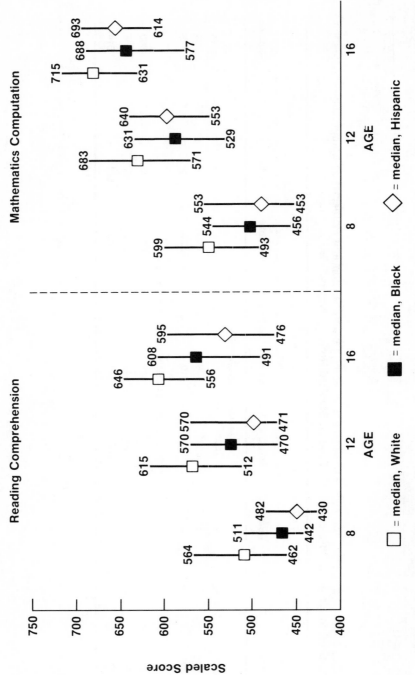

Figure 8–7. 20th to 80th percentile ranges for hearing impaired 8-, 12-, and 16-year-olds in different ethnic groups, Stanford Norming Project, Spring 1983.

Table 8–16.   20th, 50th, and 80th Percentiles in Reading Comprehension and Mathematics Computation for Hearing Impaired Students with Different Degrees of Hearing Loss, Stanford Norming Project, 1983

Percentile	Age 8		Age 12		Age 16	
	Less-Than-Severe	Profound	Less-Than-Severe	Profound	Less-Than-Severe	Profound
Reading Comprehension Scaled Scores						
80th	572	540	626	602	647	639
50th	518	488	583	544	606	590
20th	458	449	527	486	552	528
Mathematics Computation Scaled Scores						
80th	595	585	666	673	700	709
50th	540	528	619	625	659	673
20th	496	465	567	557	594	622

analyses, in which the beta weights reported for minority status were less significant for mathematics computation.

Again, it should be stressed that these analyses do not imply cause. Ethnicity is a surrogate variable for other characteristics, most notably socioeconomic status. Also, it is known that black hearing impaired students have higher proportions of additional handicaps. (See Chapter 3.) Thus, it should not be concluded that racial background and achievement are causally related.

Hearing Loss

Students with severe and profound hearing loss performed more poorly in reading comprehension than did students with less-than-severe loss, as indicated in Table 8–16 and Figure 8-8. In mathematics the differences were not as great. In fact, the severe and profound 16-year-olds scored higher than their age cohorts with less-than-severe hearing loss. It is known that, among students receiving special education, those with less-than-severe hearing losses have a higher likelihood of having additional handicaps. This may explain why among older students in the norming sample those with less-than-severe losses perform more poorly on achievement tests than those with profound losses. The fact that this finding is observed only among 16-year-olds suggests that hearing impaired students with less-than-severe losses and no additional handicaps (and therefore higher expected achievement scores) are most likely to leave special education in their high school years.

Additional Handicap Status

Table 8–17 and Figure 8-9 show the results for students with and without additional handicaps. Quite clearly students with additional handicaps

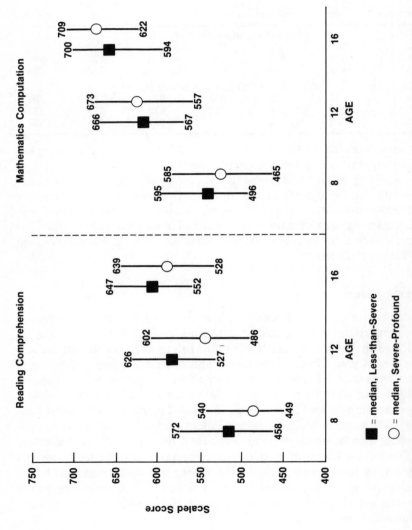

Figure 8–8. 20th to 80th percentile ranges for hearing impaired 8-, 12-, and 16-year-olds with different degrees of hearing loss, Stanford Norming Project, Spring 1983.

Table 8–17.   20th, 50th, and 80th Percentiles in Reading Comprehension and Mathematics Computation for Hearing Impaired Students with and without Additional Handicaps

Percentile	Age 8		Age 12		Age 16	
	No AHC	*AHC**	*No AHC*	*AHC**	*No AHC*	*AHC**
	Reading Comprehension					
80th	553	517†	612	573	644	612
50th	498	466†	565	519	601	545
20th	453	438†	503	470	548	472
	Mathematics Computation					
80th	594	563†	679	638	714	683
50th	539	485†	636	569	680	630
20th	489	429†	583	526	640	546

*AHC = additional handicapping condition. This group includes students with physical handicaps and students with cognitive handicaps.

†N is <50.

achieve at lower levels than do students with no additional handicaps. Also, the differences between the two groups seem to widen as the students become older. For example, the median reading comprehension performance of 16-year-olds with additional handicaps is 56 points below the median performance of 16-year-olds with no additional handicaps. For 8-year-olds the same comparison shows a difference of only 32 points. Thus, it appears that hearing impaired students in special education who have compounding additional handicaps fall farther and farther behind as they move through school.

CONCLUSION

The beginning of this chapter drew some tentative conclusions based on the study of Figures 8–1 and 8–2. Those conclusions are now reconsidered based on the inquiries into the norming samples of 1974 and 1983.

The first conclusion was that hearing impaired students lag behind their hearing counterparts in reading and mathematics. This is undoubtedly a fair statement to make; however, as noted, it is inappropriate to draw conclusions based on the study of measures of central tendency alone. In situations in which there are far greater proportions in the lower deciles in one group, the median for that group will be lowered. It may be that students in the upper deciles perform comparably to their hearing counterparts. Also, accurate definitions of the term hearing impaired students are difficult to come by. Careful descriptions of subgroups of the population allow for more meaningful discussions of student performance.

The second conclusion was that the deficit between hearing and hearing impaired performance is more profound in reading than in mathe-

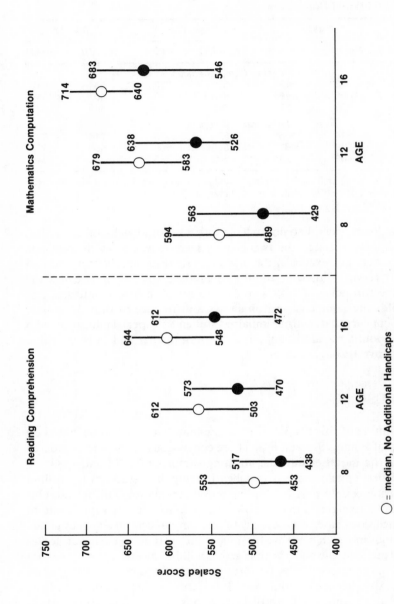

Figure 8–9. 20th to 80th percentile ranges for hearing impaired 8-, 12-, and 16-year-olds with and without additional handicapping conditions, Stanford Norming Project, Spring 1983.

matics. This is clearly true. Throughout the entire chapter, mathematics computation achievement level was higher than reading comprehension level, no matter what subgroup was being discussed.

The third and fourth conclusions noted a leveling off in the achievement capabilities of hearing impaired students in reading comprehension and mathematics computation. This conclusion is questionable. There is reason to believe that the cross-sectional mean performance of each age group, represented by the mathematics and reading curves drawn in Figures 8–1 and 8–2, are not adequate representations of longitudinal growth. This entire book grapples with the task of describing an unstable heterogeneous population. The leveling off seen in Figures 8–1 and 8–2 representing the performance of older hearing impaired students may result from the increasing proportions of students with additional and more severely handicapping characteristics. A more radical interpretation is that students who cannot achieve beyond a third- or fourth-grade reading level are the very students who stay in special education. Thus the results of the Stanford norming project may simply validate this selection process. In any case, it should not be concluded of any young hearing impaired student that he or she will never achieve beyond a certain level.

The final conclusion was that hearing impaired students have shown gain in their reading and mathematics achievement over the last 10 years. Happily, much of the evidence explored pointed to the truth of this statement. It is true that some ambiguity exists related to the validity of the conversion tables. Nonetheless, it appears reasonable from the evidence presented that students demonstrated higher achievement levels on the seventh edition of the Stanford Achievement Test than on the sixth edition.

REFERENCES

Allen, T. (1986). *Understanding the scores: Hearing-impaired students and the Stanford Achievement Test (7th Edition).* Washington, DC: Gallaudet College Press.

Allen, T., and Karchmer, M. (1981). Influences on academic achievement of hearing-impaired students born during the 1963–65 rubella epidemic. *Directions, 2,* 40–54.

Allen, T., and Osborn, T. (1984). Academic integration of hearing impaired students: Demographic, handicapping, and achievement factors. *American Annals of the Deaf, 129,* 100–113.

Gardner, E.F., Rudman, H.C., Karlsen, B., and Merwin, J.C. (1982). *Stanford Achievement Test* (7th ed.). New York: Harcourt Brace Jovanovich.

Karchmer, M., Milone, M., and Wolk, S. (1979). Educational significance of hearing loss at three levels of severity. *American Annals of the Deaf Directory of Programs and Services, 124,* 97–109.

Madden, R., Gardner, E., Rudman, H., Karlsen, B., and Merwin, J. (1972). *Stanford Achievement Test for Hearing Impaired Students.* New York: Harcourt Brace Jovanovich.

Trybus, R., and Karchmer, M. (1977). School achievement scores of hearing impaired children: National data on achievement status and growth patterns. *American Annals of the Deaf Directory of Programs and Services, 122,* 62–69.

Chapter 9

Minimum Competency Testing Programs and Hearing Impaired Students

Carol A. Bloomquist

By late 1985 as many as 40 states in the United States had established minimum competency testing (MCT) programs in response to widespread public dissatisfaction with the quality of American education. Nurtured by the demand for educational accountability, these MCT programs are structured according to state and local mandates. Although the programs vary considerably, most MCT programs include common elements: (a) identification of a set of skills that students should master by a particular time in their school career, (b) development or adoption of tests to measure student mastery of those skills, (c) creation of standards for acceptable test performance that represent student achievement of the set of skills, and (d) construction of a link between mastery of the specified skills and remedial instruction, grade promotion, or high school graduation.

While states were legislating MCT programs, the courts were strengthening the constitutional and statutory rights of handicapped students in the public schools. For example, the Education for All Handicapped Children Act of 1975 (U.S. Public Law 94-142) legislated that all states comply with new requirements to ensure that a free, appropriate public education is available for all handicapped students in the least restrictive environment. In addition, Section 504 of the 1973 Rehabilitation Act (U.S. Public Law 93-112) prohibited discrimination on the basis of a disability in any program receiving federal assistance. In general, these mandates were created to ensure appropriate educational programming for students

The author gratefully acknowledges Corinne S. White for making available a collection of background literature and notes that formed the foundation for this chapter.

with special needs. As a consequence, each student's needs receive separate evaluation, and individualized educational goals are defined in terms of an individualized educational plan (IEP).

In sharp contrast to the IEPs for handicapped students are MCT programs that suggest that all students should meet a uniform set of minimum standards and be evaluated by means of a uniform assessment instrument. The purpose of this chapter is to describe ways in which MCT programs and laws protecting handicapped students have converged to affect hearing impaired students.

The chapter is divided into three sections. First, an overview of statewide minimum competency testing programs is presented. Second, legal issues and recent court decisions associated with hearing impaired students and MCT programs are described. Third, several different practices that have been used in states implementing MCT programs with hearing impaired students are summarized. The aim is to present information that may be useful to educators of deaf students rather than to debate various issues associated with the testing of hearing impaired students in MCT programs. The fact is that important decisions are made about hearing impaired students in those states mandating MCT programs. The question is, How can it be assured that these decisions are based on accurate and sufficient information?

OVERVIEW OF STATE MINIMUM COMPETENCY TESTING PROGRAMS

As of November 1985, 40 states had required students to be tested in such basic skills as reading, writing, and mathematics or in such "life skills" as writing a check, reading a road map, and computing a retail sales tax, or in both (Pipho, 1985). Results of these tests are then typically used to determine student eligibility for remedial instruction. Although the tests have various names, for the purpose of the discussion in this chapter testing programs included under the rubric of MCT conform to the characteristics delineated in the National Institute of Education Issues Clarification Hearing on Minimum Competency Testing (1981) and refer to those testing programs mandated by a state in which

1. all or almost all students at designated grades are required to take paper and pencil tests designed to measure basic academic skills, life or survival skills, or functional literacy;
2. a passing score or standard for acceptable levels of student performance has been established;

3. test results may be used to certify students for grade promotion, graduation, or diploma award; to classify students for or place students in remedial or other special services; to allocate compensatory funds to districts; to evaluate or certify schools or school districts; or to evaluate teachers.

During the past decade states have moved from legislating MCT programs that link skills with high school diplomas to implementing programs that detect inadequate achievement throughout the school career. More specifically, the focus of MCT programs shifted, according to Pipho in 1978 and 1983, in the following manner:

1. From 1975 through 1977, the emphasis was on testing students to determine whether they would receive high school diplomas.
2. The peak years for legislative and state board of education mandates were 1977 and 1978, when 25 states adopted the testing.
3. Only two states have moved to require minimum competency testing since 1978.
4. In 1978 and 1979, only two states moved to tie high school graduation to passage of minimum competency tests.
5. In the early eighties, states have emphasized creating an early warning testing program that would report on students' progress at the elementary, junior, and senior high school levels, for the purpose of making better decisions for improving the instructional program and providing remediation.

In 1985 Pipho reported that the shift in focus of MCT programs was continuing. He found more concern "with higher-order thinking skills, with gifted and talented programs, with more graduation requirements. . . . The emphasis seems to be away from minimum competency" (cited in Olson, 1985, p. 9).

This shift in focus does not mean that few states use the tests to certify students for high school diplomas. As many as 16 states have had exit tests, and 7 others have approved them as a local option. Another 2 states require passing the tests for a gold seal, or proficiency endorsement, on diplomas (Pipho, 1985). In general, noted Pipho (1978), the states "tended to pass legislation or state board rulings that are consistent with their own governance structures. For the most part, the states up and down the Midwest with the largest number of school districts have tended not to pass statewide mandates unless these mandates lean heavily toward local control" (p. 587).

The process of developing and implementing competency programs has required several years of state-sponsored activities. For example, creating test item specifications for a minimum competency test typically has involved not only a statewide committee of educators and interested lay citizens but also a strenuous debate over which basic skills should be taught at what grade levels and what skill levels should be considered minimum. Although most states have decided to test reading, writing, and mathematics skills, some state mandates also require minimum competency testing in such subjects as spelling, government, citizenship, career training, life or survival skills, and consumer economics.

Throughout each step in the development and implementation of MCT programs, the major focus has been on the students in "regular education." As late as 1979 little attention had been paid to the concept of minimum competencies for special education students in general, and hearing impaired students in particular (National Association of State Directors of Special Education, 1979; Olsen, 1980). Only one state—Florida—has developed and validated a separate test for its hearing impaired students (Watson, 1979). Although it cannot be assumed that MCT programs designed for and validated with nonhandicapped students are appropriate for students with disabilities, the consideration of special students has been relatively recent. In contrast with the previous decade, during the 1980s most of the states with MCT programs have established policies for the testing of handicapped students, many of them requiring IEP committees to decide the appropriateness of the test on a case-by-case basis.

Table 9–1 highlights selected MCT activities by state for the 40 states requiring such tests. It should be noted that many of the states listed do not label their programs as MCT programs; but because their programs fall under the general definition used in this chapter, they have been included in Table 9–1.

To suggest the magnitude of the potential impact that each state's MCT program might have on hearing impaired children, the numbers of such children ages 3 through 21 years served under U.S. Public Law 89-313 and U.S. Public Law 94-142 (known as the official "child counts") for the school year 1983–1984 are provided in the first column. Of the 72,082 hearing impaired children reported in the United States, 65, 924 (91 percent) attended schools in the 40 states having MCT. The vast majority of hearing impaired students in the United States are touched by MCT programs.

The next seven columns in Table 9–1 present information regarding the government level that sets the standards and the grade levels and skill areas tested for each state having MCT. While 25 of the states listed have adopted only statewide MCT standards, 14 empower local school districts to set district standards. Essentially all of the states administer their tests several times, most beginning at the elementary level and continuing into the secondary level. In most cases students are singled out at each level

Table 9-1. State Activity in Minimum Competency Testing[1]

Hearing Impaired Students[2]	States Using Minimum Competency Testing	Government Level Setting Standards	Levels Assessed	Subject Areas Assessed				Expected Uses				First Graduating Class Assessed[5]
				Reading	Math	Writing[3]	Other	High School Graduation	Regular Diploma Requirement for Hearing Impaired	Remediation	Other[4]	
1,115	Alabama	State	3,6,9,11	x	x	x		x	x	x	x	1985
1,060	Arizona	State/local	8,12	x	x	x		x	LO[6]			1976
655	Arkansas	State	3,4,6,8	x	x	x	x			x	x	
7,178	California	State/local	4–11	x	x	x		x	LO	x	x	1979
993	Colorado	Local	9,12	LO	LO	LO	LO	LO	LO			
971	Connecticut	State	4,6,8	x	x	x				x	x	1981
319	Delaware	State	8,11	x	x	x		[7]	[7]		x	1983
2,003	Florida	State/local	3,5,8,10	x	x			x	x		x	1983
1,678	Georgia	State	1,3,6,8,10	x	x			x	x	x	x	1985
300	Hawaii[8]	State	3,9–12	x	x	x	x	x	x	x	x	1983
441	Idaho	State	8–12	x	x	x	x	[9]	[10]	x	x	1982
4,163	Illinois	Local	LO	x	x	LO	LO				LO	
1,336	Indiana	Local	3,6,8,10	x	x	x	x			x	x	
717	Kansas[11]	State	2,4,6,8,10	x	x						LO	
1,297	Kentucky[12]	State	K–12	x	x	x	x			x		
1,569	Louisiana	State	2–5,8	x	x	x				x	x	
1,487	Maryland	State	7,9	x	x	x	x	x	x	x	x	1982
1,909	Massachusetts	Local	LO	x	x					x		
3,216	Michigan	State	4,7,10	x	x		x			x	x	
575	Mississippi	State	3,5,8,11	x	x	x	x	x	x		x	1987[13]
1,000	Missouri	State	9+	x	x		x				x	

(continued on next page)

Table 9–1. (continued)

Hearing Impaired Students[2]	States Using Minimum Competency Testing	Government Level Setting Standards	Levels Assessed	Subject Areas Assessed				Expected Uses				First Graduating Class Assessed[5]
				Reading	Math	Writing[3]	Other	High School Graduation	Regular Diploma Requirement for Hearing Impaired	Remediation	Other[4]	
577	Nebraska	Local	5+	x	x	x	x				x	
229	Nevada	State	3,6,9,11	x	x	x		x	x	x		1982
358	New Hampshire[14]	State	4,8,10	x	x		x	LO	LO	LO	LO	1985
1,814	New Jersey	State	9–12	x	x	x		x	x	x	x	1981
458	New Mexico	State	LO,10–12	x	x	LO	x	9	9		x	1979
5,211	New York	State	3,5,6,8–12	x	x	x		x	x	x		1980
2,201	North Carolina	State	1–3,6,8–10	x	x	x		x	x	x		1990
2,644	Ohio	Local	LO,1–11	x	x	x				LO	LO	
834	Oklahoma[16]	None	3,6,9	x	x	x	x			x	x	1978
1,355	Oregon	Local	LO	x	x	x	x	17	17			
3,955	Pennsylvania	State	3,5,8	x	x					x		1990
1,199	South Carolina	State	1,2,3,6,8,10	x	x	x		x	x	x	x	1982
2,035	Tennessee	State	2–8,9+	x	x		x	x	x	x	x	1987
5,213	Texas	State	1,3,5,7,9,11+	x	x	x		x	18	x		1980
849	Utah[19]	Local	LO	x	x	x	x	LO	LO	x		1981
259	Vermont	State	1–12	x	x	x	x	20	20		x	1981
1,476	Virginia	State/local	K–6,10–12	x	x		x	x	x		x	
1,134	Wisconsin	Local	1–4,5–8,9–10	x	x	x		LO	LO	x	LO	
141	Wyoming	Local	LO	x	x	x	x	LO	LO	x		

Source: The data in Column 1 are from the *Seventh Annual Report to Congress on the Implementation of the Education of the Handicapped Act* (p. 199) by the Division of Educational Services, Special Education Programs, 1985, Washington, DC: U.S. Department of Education. The remaining data are from *State Activity: Minimum Competency Testing* (Clearinghouse Notes) by C. Pipho, November 1985, Denver, CO: Education Commission of the States. Adapted by permission.

1. Activity is reported as of November 1985. Many of the states listed do not consider their testing programs to be MCT. These testing programs do, however, fall under the definition of MCT used in this chapter.

2. Number of children ages 3–21 years served under U.S. Public Laws 89-313 and 94-142 designated hard of hearing or deaf, school year 1983–1984.

3. Writing is tested in some states by direct assessment methods.

4. Other uses may include curricular or instructional improvement or grade promotion.

5. Some states have dates for the first high school graduating class to be assessed even though the test is not a graduation requirement.

6. LO indicates local option.

7. In Delaware each LEA administers its own test or assessment instrument to certify competencies. Handicapped students are required to master the competencies to receive a diploma. Mastery is determined through testing or other means based on the IEP.

8. In Hawaii, students have three options: paper and pencil test, performance test, or course. First time taken (grade 9) must be paper and pencil test.

9. Required for proficiency endorsement (gold seal) on diploma.

10. If the Idaho state waiver for a handicapped student is granted, the state proficiency endorsement (gold seal) may be placed on the diploma, but the test waiver has to be recorded on student's transcript.

11. The Kansas Minimum Competency Assessment will be in effect through 1988–1989.

12. Kentucky 1984 legislation requires State Superintendent to recommend process of using test results for promotion and graduation to the 1986 legislature.

13. The first class required to pass for graduation in Mississippi will be the class of 1989.

14. New Hampshire 1985 legislation requires testing in 1985–1986 and 1986–1987.

15. Required unless specifically excluded by IEP.

16. The Oklahoma Schools Testing Program includes students with an IEP only if parental permission is given.

17. Oregon requires districts to certify a student as being competent in specified areas prior to graduation. Some districts use a test to certify competence; others use other means.

18. Not decided as of January 1986.

19. The class of 1988 is the last class under the current testing program in Utah; a new testing program will be in effect beginning with the class of 1989.

20. Beginning in 1989 Vermont students must master the basic competencies to enter high school. Handicapped students are exempt from portions of the test they cannot attempt; other portions must be mastered.

for remediation. For example, South Carolina's Basic Skills Assessment Program is used to identify students for remediation at grades 1, 2, 3, 6, 8, and 10.

An examination of the information provided for the skill areas that were assessed shows that nearly all of the programs test reading, mathematics, and writing skills; about half of the programs test other skill areas as well. Maryland, for example, tests reading, mathematics, writing, and citizenship skills. The specific skills selected for testing often hold special importance for hearing impaired students. Notably, the selection of reading and writing for testing is associated with particular problems for hearing impaired students, because their achievement in these two areas typically lags substantially behind that of hearing students.

The last five columns to the right in Table 9–1 provide information on the uses expected to be made of the test results and the date indicating the first graduating class to be assessed in the MCT program. The states that include passing the MCT as a graduation requirement are using these tests with classes that will graduate in the 1980s. Intended uses of MCT results vary by state. Test results may satisfy a student's high school graduation requirement or identify students for remediation. The MCT results may have other uses such as to qualify students for grade promotion (as occurs in Florida, Georgia, and Louisiana and is a local option in Arkansas and California) or to improve school curriculum and instruction (as specified for Connecticut, Indiana, Michigan, Mississippi, and South Carolina).

Of the 19 states in which a regular high school diploma (or one with a proficiency endorsement) is contingent on passing the MCT, 14 maintain the same MCT requirement for their hearing impaired students. Several states designate the diploma requirement a local option; some associate receiving a regular diploma with the individual student's fulfillment of IEP requirements (which may not include the MCT). In Ohio, for example, local districts have to establish guidelines for test use and a policy regarding handicapped students' participation in testing programs. Many states and local school districts leave the decision as to whether the hearing impaired student may or must take the MCT to those responsible for the student's IEP. As is addressed in the following section, no matter what uses are intended for the test scores, requiring hearing impaired students to take the test or barring them from it may have legal implications.

LEGAL ISSUES ASSOCIATED WITH MCT PROGRAMS

Legal provisions and theories that may be associated with hearing impaired students in MCT programs are treated in this section. To clarify the current legal position of hearing impaired students with regard to their treatment within such programs, recent judicial decisions related to MCT are summarized.

According to Tractenberg (1980), the legal provisions that may prove relevant to MCT programs fall into six categories:

1. Federal and state constitutional due process clauses
2. Federal and state constitutional equal protection clauses
3. State constitutional education clauses
4. State education statutes
5. State education regulations
6. Common law

Each of these sources of law is treated briefly with regard to the application of MCT programs, or specific elements of those programs, to hearing impaired students.

Due Process

A due process clause is contained in the Fourteenth Amendment to the U.S. Constitution and most state constitutions. According to the Fourteenth Amendment, no state shall "deprive any person of life, liberty, or property, without due process of law." Due process has been construed by the judiciary to have substantive and procedural aspects. For substantive due process to be satisfied, the action of the state must be rational and reasonably related to a legitimate state objective. If a state's MCT program tests students on material not taught in the schools, students who fail to demonstrate their competency on that test might charge that their right to substantive due process was violated (Beckham, 1980; Citron, 1983, p. 3; Fenton, 1980, p. 187; McClung, 1978, p. 399; Tractenberg, 1980). Such might be the case for a hearing impaired student whose IEP did not contain the objectives measured by the MCT.

A state is required by procedural due process to act in a fair manner when it deprives a citizen of liberty or property. Procedural due process might demand adequate notice of the MCT requirements in effect (Beckham, 1980, pp. 25–26; Citron, 1983, p. 2; Fenton, 1980, p. 186; McCarthy, 1983, p. 156; McClung, 1978, p. 399; Popham and Lindheim, 1981) or a procedure by which students failing an MCT can challenge the test's scoring or validity.

For due process to be invoked, it must be shown that a person has been deprived of liberty or property by a state action. Denial of a regular diploma, of promotion, or of graduation under an MCT program could constitute a deprivation of property. The U.S. Supreme Court found (*Goss v. Lopez*, 1975) that students have a property interest in their education such that physical exclusion from school can involve due process procedures. However, retention in grade or failure to graduate would less clearly constitute a deprivation of a property interest (McCarthy, 1983).

Deprivation of liberty might be argued based upon the stigmatization allegedly occurring as a consequence of a student's classification as below minimum competency or as ineligible for promotion, graduation, or a regular diploma.

If proof of deprivation of liberty or property is shown, the state's action is not necessarily condemned. Rather, the state is obligated to act fairly and rationally. Deprivations of liberty or property that are rationally related to a legitimate governmental purpose and that afford the affected citizen adequate procedural protections are unlikely to be judged to be in violation of a state or federal due process clause. According to McCarthy (1983), "handicapped students can be required to satisfy academic standards, including passage of an examination to receive a high school diploma. Such children have a federally protected right to individualized *instruction*, designed to address their unique needs, but they are not entitled to individualized *diploma standards*" (p. 146).

Equal Protection

The equal protection clauses of the U.S. Constitution and of several state constitutions require rationality and fairness in the government's treatment of groups or classes of citizens unless there is adequate justification for differential treatment. To challenge a state action under equal protection, one must show that the action classifies persons and treats them differently. The burden of justification for differential treatment rests with the state and increases with the importance of the interest that is subjected to differential treatment. Fundamental interests and suspect classifications, such as those based upon race, require strict scrutiny, the highest order of justification by the state. Under strict scrutiny the state must show a compelling reason for, and no available alternative to, the differential treatment. When interests of lesser importance or classifications not based upon a suspect characteristic are involved, the state faces a lesser burden of justification, perhaps needing only to prove that the classification is rational, even if it is not the best means to achieve the state's objective. The argument for applying strict scrutiny because of the fundamental nature of education is unlikely to succeed in the federal courts (McCarthy, 1983, p. 149; Tractenberg, 1980, pp. 87–88). Although several state courts (e.g., California, 1977; Connecticut, 1977) have considered education to be a fundamental interest, the U.S. Supreme Court ruled in 1973 (*San Antonio Independent School District v. Rodriguez*) that education is not a fundamental right under the constitution, with the result that strict scrutiny would not be applied with regard to an educational interest.

Handicapped students can raise equal protection challenges to MCT programs if they are all excluded entirely from the program (McCarthy, 1983, p. 150; Riegel and Lovell, 1980, p. 21; Tractenberg, 1979, p. 6). They may assert that their exclusion violates equal protection in that the remedial help associated with the MCT program would be unavailable to them. If some classes of handicapped students are included and others excluded with respect to a state's MCT program, then the rationality of the distinction made could be disputed. Tractenberg (1979, p. 7) argued that equal protection issues would be minimized if the state left the applicability of MCT requirements to the IEP process, a practice recommended by other writers as well (Beckham, 1980, p. 22; Olsen, 1980). At the least, challenges would likely proceed through the administrative hearing procedure associated with the IEP and designed to resolve disputes about its appropriateness. In addition to students' inclusion in or exclusion from MCT programs, the type of diploma or certificate awarded hearing impaired students is relevant to equal protection challenges.

State Education Clauses

Frequently the quality or extent of the education required of a state is defined in the state constitution. For example, New Jersey, Ohio, Pennsylvania, and Virginia include "thorough and efficient" in their state constitutions' education clauses; Illinois, Montana, and Virginia include "high quality"; California, Idaho, and Wyoming include "uniform" in theirs. Some state courts have ruled that these clauses defining the required education give students a legally enforceable right to that quality or extent of education.

Among the MCT-related challenges that might be based on state education clauses are several suggested by Tractenberg (1979, 1980). The absence of an MCT program might provoke a challenge in a state with a thorough and efficient clause, following an argument that includes basic skills proficiency as a necessary educational component. The level at which competency standards are set could be challenged as not consistent with a high quality or thorough and efficient education. Local standards could be challenged as violating a uniform educational system mandated for a state. An inadequate remedial program for students who fail the MCT could be challenged in a state that includes basic skills competency in its educational mission. For example, hearing impaired students might be poorly served by a particular remedial program.

State Education Statutes

State education statutes dealing with general educational provisions or with a specific provision other than MCT may establish legal requirements that are applicable to MCT. In addition to these statutes, many states have provisions establishing an MCT program and containing requirements for its implementation. Both of these types of statutes may form the basis for legal challenges to MCT programs.

Some general educational statutes, while not explicitly establishing an MCT program, nevertheless provide a basis for establishing MCT to meet the state's educational obligations as laid out in the statutes. Statutes related to hearing impaired students or other special populations may apply to the participation of such students in an MCT program. For example, it may be stipulated that certain classes of students should be excluded from the MCT program altogether. Other statutes establishing or otherwise directly related to the state's MCT program may be used in an effort to show noncompliance with statutory requirements. It may be argued that an MCT program, as implemented, does not agree with specific requirements or is qualitatively inadequate. For example, a statute may stipulate that a specific minimum number of testing opportunities be available to students or that students be given sufficient prior notice of an MCT requirement.

A mandamus action, the vehicle by which legal challenges based on state education statutes could be brought, requests the court to order public officials to carry out their legal responsibilities (Tractenberg, 1980). Because in some states mandamus is available only to require public officials to perform ministerial, but not discretionary, functions, mandamus actions in those states may be more readily applicable to failures to implement MCT programs or specific MCT requirements than to qualitative inadequacies in those programs.

State Education Regulations

Education regulations sponsored by state education authorities have the force of law in some states and, like statutes, can form a basis for legal challenges related to MCT programs. In fact, they may provide a stronger basis for legal action because regulations tend to deal with educational programs in greater detail than do statutes. Even in states in which education regulations do not have the force of law, they nevertheless may be accorded substantial legal importance in court:

> In states where administrative regulations are not given the force of

law, or in cases of administrative actions (such as guidelines or policy statements) not having the status of formal regulations, the substance of the
administrative judgment should still have weight in a legal proceeding. The
administrative position represents the expert view of the state's educational
authorities. As such, a court would likely find it highly relevant to an interpretation of broad constitutional or statutory provisions.

(Tractenberg, 1980, p. 90)

State education regulations in some states refer in particular to hearing impaired students and specify how the MCT program must be modified to accommodate them.

Common Law

The common law, or judge-made law, is the final source of law discussed
here that may influence judicial responses to an MCT challenge. Because
courts tend to follow prior judicial decisions in similar cases, in facing
a new case a court will consider the judicial precedent, especially cases
decided in the same jurisdiction, along with relevant constitutional, statutory, and regulatory provisions.

Educational malpractice litigation may well be the most likely con-
duit for common law developments. A type of malpractice case relevant
to the hearing impaired student closely parallels professional malpractice
litigation (Beckham, 1980; Tractenberg, 1979). It typically involves a handicapped student whose special needs have not been properly diagnosed
or treated by school or school-related professionals. These cases (e.g., *Hoffman v. Board of Education*, 1978) have been more successful than the malpractice suits with "normal" children (e.g., *Donohue v. Copiague School
District*, 1979; *Peter W. v. San Francisco Unified School District*, 1976).

The difficulties in proving the presence of traditional malpractice elements, joined with the strongly felt public policy concerns of the courts,
have left the courts reluctant to impose liability on school systems for their
students' learning failures. The establishment of an MCT program can
increase the likelihood of a successful malpractice case both by facilitat-
ing proof of the necessary malpractice elements and by allaying some of
the courts' policy concerns. An educational malpractice suit directed at
court-ordered improvements in the educational program would raise fewer
policy concerns than one seeking money damages. Still, the court would
be forced to consider the appropriateness of its intervention in educational
program details and its capacity to so intervene. All in all, the establishment of an MCT program should strengthen the basis for a common law
challenge to inadequate educational programs (Tractenberg, 1979).

IMPLEMENTATION OF STATE MCT PROGRAMS WITH HEARING IMPAIRED STUDENTS

States have implemented the several aspects of their MCT programs with their students in a variety of ways. The ways in which MCT programs have been implemented with students in general and with hearing impaired students in particular are summarized here with respect to each of seven program elements discussed by Brickell (1978). The seven "key notes" identified by Brickell are (a) the competencies to be measured, (b) how to measure them, (c) when to measure them, (d) the number of minimums that will be set, (e) the levels at which minimums will be set, (f) whether the minimums will be for students or for schools, and (g) the consequences of failing to meet the minimums. The issues involved in implementing MCT programs with hearing impaired students are addressed for each of these seven elements of MCT policy.

Competencies to Be Measured

The competencies to be measured in an MCT program may consist of school skills (those needed to succeed later in school), life skills (those needed to succeed later in life), or basic skills (used in both school and life). These skills may be applied in selected school subjects or in specific life areas (e.g., citizenship, work, family).

A choice of life skills for testing might raise serious substantive due process and equal protection questions, according to Tractenberg (1980). If life skills are not taught in the schools, the MCT program could be challenged as arbitrary under due process. A given selection of life skills may be relevant only to certain groups of students, but not others, and an MCT based upon such a selection would be discriminatory.

The prospects for a legal challenge based on substantive due process would be minimized in choosing basic skills as the focus of an MCT program, for they are certain to be taught in all schools. The importance of testing what has been taught cannot be overemphasized. Beckham (1980) warns that "nowhere is the risk of arbitrariness potentially greater than in the area of congruence between that which is taught and the content of a minimum competency test" (p. 29). Further, basic skills are likely to be perceived as neutral toward all groups within a school and less likely to foster a discrimination charge based on equal protection. Concerns about meeting the educational quality standards of state constitutions, statutes, and regulations could be minimized by selecting basic skills that are relevant to the state's education goals, such as effective citizenship and preparation for the labor market.

A major consideration relevant to the hearing impaired student tested in a state's MCT program is the inclusion of the tested skills in that student's IEP (Beckham, 1980; Olsen, 1980). In Vermont all IEPs are written relative to state mandated competencies (Olsen, 1980). In Alabama the decision regarding whether an exceptional student's program includes the state's basic competencies must be reviewed on an annual basis, and exceptions from the state competencies must be documented fully in the student's IEP (Akers-Adams and Halpin, 1985). Florida has adopted special performance standards and skills for the hearing impaired, passage of which qualifies a student for a special diploma (Randall, 1984). The status of each hearing impaired student with regard to the regular standards and the special standards is to be addressed by the student's IEP (Grisé, 1980).

How to Measure the Competencies

Brickell (1978) mentioned a range of possibilities for measuring the competencies in an MCT program, including testing through (a) experience in actual performance situations, (b) simulated performance situations, (c) school products and performances, and (d) paper-and-pencil tests. Because tests must satisfy standards of objectivity, reliability, and validity in order to comply with due process and equal protection requirements, paper-and-pencil tests (which are more likely to meet those requirements) would be associated with fewer legal problems (Tractenberg, 1980).

Paper-and-pencil tests can pose special problems to some handicapped students, however. Although many MCT programs allow special administration procedures for all handicapped students or for selected categories of handicapped students, hearing impaired students are often required to take the regular test. It cannot be assumed that a test designed for "regular" students, even if administered by using special procedures, will not in some way disadvantage the hearing impaired test taker.

First, the validity of the test for the hearing impaired student must be maintained (McCarthy, 1983, p. 161; Morrissey, 1980, p. 207). That handicapped students must be individually accommodated is widely accepted (Riegel and Lovell, 1980, p. 21), but controversy prevails over "where the line should be drawn in designing accommodations to maintain the validity of the tests" (McCarthy, 1983, p. 161). The validity for special students of tests designed for a nonhandicapped population is currently receiving research attention (e.g., Bennett and Ragosta, 1984; Bennett, Ragosta, and Stricker, 1984).

Accommodation for hearing impaired students varies from state to state. In Alabama the IEP Committee is responsible for "determining accommodations which are appropriate without being excessive or too minimal" (Akers-Adams and Halpin, 1985, p. 11). The Alabama High School Graduation Examination has gone through review by several special task forces, including one for the hearing impaired, and has incorporated suggested editorial changes. For hearing impaired students in Alabama the regular print edition of the test is used, along with test directions that underwent only minor word changes to make them acceptable for that population. In North Carolina a videotape edition of the competency test can be made available for any deaf or hard of hearing student in the public schools. A test administrator or proctor trained in communicating with hearing impaired students should be available to repeat or clarify directions and to answer questions, according to that state's guidelines for competency testing of exceptional students. Florida, as mentioned earlier, has developed and validated a separate special test for its hearing impaired students.

A second issue associated with how the competencies are measured relates to the kind of certification associated with passing the test. A "regular" diploma may be contingent upon passing the "regular" MCT, and students passing a special administration may receive a differentiated diploma. This is the case in several states. In Florida only those students who pass the regular test receive a standard diploma. Those who pass the special test developed for hearing impaired students receive a special diploma that is very similar in appearance and terminology to the standard diploma. Those who do not pass the special test receive a certificate of completion if they meet all course requirements. Deaf students in Florida are regarded as high school graduates if they earn either a standard or special diploma. A problem exists, though, in that the special diploma may become known as a diploma that only mentally retarded children receive upon graduation from high school (Watson, 1979, pp. 8–9). Special tests have been developed in Florida for the educable and trainable mentally retarded, the learning disabled, and the emotionally handicapped, as well as for the hearing impaired. Mentally retarded students represent 80 percent of the population of this special group. According to Watson, "if 80 percent of the students who receive this special diploma are either educable or trainable mentally retarded students, the danger naturally exists that this special diploma could become known as the diploma for the mentally retarded high school graduate. This would be grossly unfair to the hearing impaired student" (1979, p. 9).

On the other hand, meeting the IEP requirements may qualify a special student for a regular diploma in a program that exempts handicapped students from taking the state's MCT. In California and Utah local districts set graduation standards, and students meeting either regular or differential standards may be granted a diploma at the discretion of the local district. This appears to be the kind of situation that Morrissey (1980) warned can lead to a reverse discrimination complaint. In the same vein, McCarthy (1983) maintained that "if graduation requirements are waived only for the handicapped, nonhandicapped students might allege an equal protection violation" (p. 163).

In summary, programs vary widely with regard to inclusion or exclusion of handicapped students in testing, allowing these students to take special administrations of the test or special tests, and granting regular diplomas or certificates differing in some way from the regular diplomas. Local school boards are allowed substantial discretion in these regards in some states.

When to Measure the Competencies

The timing of testing is associated primarily with two major legal issues: the adequate notice aspect of procedural due process and the outcome aspects of the states' educational quality requirements (Tractenberg, 1980). With regard to adequate notice, "a sound program would involve periodic testing of competencies beginning early in a student's educational career," recommends Tractenberg (1980, p. 95). State educational quality requirements likewise are consistent with early testing: "Waiting until the end of the last year in school to assess those competencies, without allowing a meaningful opportunity for improvement, would seem an ineffective and perhaps irrational means of carrying out the state mandate" (Tractenberg, 1980, p. 95).

A legal requirement for all students, adequate notice is of special concern with regard to hearing impaired students. The amount of time judged to be adequate for hearing students may not be adequate for hearing impaired students, especially with regard to language skills of reading and writing. According to Beckham (1980):

> The length of time required for adequate notice to students and parents depends in part upon the time required to make necessary curricular or instructional changes. . . . Where the consequences of a testing program could result in denial of the diploma or other substantial harm to the student, a program providing notice beginning with the first grade might be required, but at least one court has ruled that a minimum of six-years notice is compulsory before a diploma can be denied. (p. 40)

Citron (1982) noted that, as judged in *Board of Education v. Ambach*, "the time frame for notice to [handicapped children] is much more crucial than that for nonhandicapped students in conventional programs" (p. 11). According to McCarthy (1983), the New York trial judge in *Ambach* "indicated that early notice of graduation requirements is particularly critical for handicapped children to allow proper consideration of whether the goals of the students' IEPs should include preparation for the MCT and to afford 'appropriate time for instruction aimed at reaching that goal'"

224 C. A. Bloomquist

(p. 156). He concluded that 3 years' notice of the MCT requirement was inadequate to satisfy due process mandates. Unlike the trial court, however, the *Ambach* appeals court found that 3 years' notice satisfies the due process clause, observing that it is not "of such brief duration so as to prevent school districts from programming the IEPs of such children to enable them to pass the [MCT]. . ." (cited in McCarthy, 1983, p. 157).

In another case dealing with a handicapped student, the appellate court in *Brookhart v. Illinois State Board of Education* (1983) found that "eighteen months' notice of an MCT requirement was constitutionally inadequate because it did not allow enough advance warning for MCT objectives to be incorporated into IEPs" (McCarthy, 1983, p. 157).

The issue of how much notice is adequate has not been resolved. McCarthy (1983) stated,

> Since the Supreme Court has not yet addressed students' due process rights in connection with MCT mandates, the procedural requirements remain somewhat unclear. While several courts have condoned the use of proficiency tests as a diploma prerequisite if students have been advised two to four years before instituting the requirements, the Seventh Circuit Court of Appeals indicated in *Brookhart* that even four years' notice may not be sufficient to protect handicapped students' due process rights. (p. 159)

The IEP committee for a hearing impaired student who will eventually take an MCT will do well to give especially early attention to the student's mastery or growth in the competencies to be tested, as well as to the legal standards of adequate notice that prevail in the state.

Number of Minimums to Be Set

Usual practice ranges from a single minimum competency level, or cutoff score, for all students at a particular grade level throughout the state to multiple statewide or district standards for groups of students categorized by one or more criteria, such as facility with English or existence of a handicap. Both a single standard and differential standards may be associated with legal concerns.

A single standard may be considered to be too high and its fairness and rationality challenged on grounds of due process; one that is considered low could raise questions about the conformity to state constitutional and statutory educational quality requirements.

On the other hand, multiple standards could result in a due process challenge charging arbitrariness or irrationality in their establishment, focusing on the mechanisms by which the standards were established (Tractenberg, 1980). Where state education clauses require the provision of both equality of educational opportunity and a specific minimum quality and extent of education, challenges may also arise when multiple standards are used. Differential standards may not be seen as congruent with equality of educational opportunity. If performance standards for some students are set below proficiency levels reasonably necessary for effective functioning as a citizen or in the job market, educational quality may be in question.

Hearing impaired students may elect, especially with the support of their IEP committees, to be tested against the standard used for hearing students to qualify for regular diplomas. (The procedure varies by state. In some states the hearing impaired student must petition to take the MCT; in others, the student must petition to be exempted from it.) As noted earlier, programs vary widely with regard to diploma requirements for handicapped students, with some states denying standard diplomas to those whose education differs even in a small way from the education of non-handicapped students. A handicapped student wishing to attempt to meet the regular test standard can challenge equality of educational opportunity if denied the chance to take the regular test.

Levels at Which Minimums Are Set

Although Riegel and Lovell (1980) deemed the establishment of the cutoff score or minimum standard to be primarily a political decision, Tractenberg (1980) warned that a political or fiscal approach to setting levels is subject to serious legal challenge from the point of view of students' educational rights. A political or fiscal decision is made to allow an acceptable proportion of students to pass; as a result it sustains public support of the MCT program or is linked with available funds that are sufficient to provide adequate remediation to the students who fail. On the other hand, Tractenberg (1980) argued, setting levels via an approach in which the policymakers decide upon the desired and necessary educational outcomes and education authorities work backwards to establish standards is likely to be viewed by the courts as "more compatible with the states' educational obligations" (p. 99). This approach applies both to a single statewide standard and to standards set for groups of students.

Whether the Standards Are for Schools or Students

If a state's constitution, statutes, or regulations require educational quality directed to the rights of each student, MCT standards for students would be reasonable. Otherwise, the thrust of a state's MCT program could be toward school or school district accountability, with inadequate performance triggering a programmatic or personnel-oriented response. The choice of approach—standards for schools or standards for students—implies many differences in MCT program implementation:

It [the choice] determines whether you will write test items all students can pass or only most students can pass; whether you will test everybody or only a sample; whether you will report results to each individual parent or only to the general public; whether you will settle for a school program that reaches 70% of the students even if that 70% misses, for example, every single "disadvantaged" child; and whether you will modify every unsatisfactory program or fail and recycle every unsatisfactory graduate. . . . [The choice is associated with a] difference in costs, types of tests, demands on the professional staff to teach every student, pressures on each student to succeed, and political action by parents of each student who fails.

(Brickell, 1978, p. 592)

Fenton (1980) argued:

The need to address the potential consequences of [MCT] programs for the individual is eliminated if competency testing focuses on the system rather than the individual. That is, if schools or districts are used as the unit of analysis for test scores, the system's success at imparting minimum competencies to the students can be assessed. . . . [Still, these MCT programs] should be designed to coordinate the curriculum and criterion-referenced tests, based on state and local competency goals. (p. 187)

Consequences of Failing to Meet Minimums

Six possible consequences for students who fall below minimum competency standards, along with six parallel consequences for schools whose students fail to perform adequately, are suggested by Brickell (1978):

1. Verify the findings independently.
2. Provide several more chances.
3. Lower the standard to meet their performance.
4. Remediate so that they can pass (or redesign school programs to match successful programs).
5. Refuse to promote or graduate them (or refuse to let schools operate until they can meet the standard).
6. Promote or graduate them with a restricted diploma or a certificate of attendance (or let schools operate but refuse to accredit them).

Some of these consequences, especially remediation, are written into state MCT programs; indeed, remediation is considered the cornerstone of many.

Of these consequences, Tractenberg (1980) singled out the third with a warning comment: Lowering MCT standards is an unacceptable response for both public policy and legal reasons. If students who fail to meet the standards are given appropriate remediation (and if the program is otherwise fair and rational) then

Ultimately they could be refused promotion or graduation, or be promoted or graduated with a restricted diploma or a certificate of attendance. From a due process perspective, these students may have been deprived of a liberty or property interest by that action, but the state is permitted to do so if it acts fairly and rationally. From an educational quality perspective, the state cannot be required to guarantee educational results for all students. The state can be held, however, to provision of an appropriate educational opportunity for all students. Educational results, as measured by an effective minimum competency testing program, are relevant to a determination of whether the educational opportunity is appropriate. In legal terms, evidence of inadequate pupil performance should shift to the education authorities the burden of demonstrating that, nonetheless, they have been providing all students with appropriate educational opportunities. The result is consistent with sound public policy and with the discharge by educators of their professional responsibility.

(Tractenberg, 1980, pp. 100–101)

CONCLUSION

The courts may be expected to continue their scrutiny of MCT mandates and practices to ensure that both handicapped and nonhandicapped students' rights are protected. In particular, several issues are likely to receive further legal attention and definition. For example, how early in a hearing impaired child's school career must notice be given for it to be considered adequate notice? When accommodations for hearing impaired students are made in test instruments or in test administration, is test validity maintained? Are individualized or standardized diploma criteria appropriate for hearing impaired students and their nonhandicapped peers? By assuring that academic standards and student evaluation practices are fair, the law may be considered a partner with the MCT movement to improve education by promoting more responsible and effective teaching, administering, and studying.

Faced with widespread legal acceptance of states' rights to require passage of a state MCT for graduation of even their handicapped students, educators of hearing impaired students have much indeed to consider in determining the best action for an individual student in an MCT program. For the student there are myriad consequences that are related to a series of considerations. Program differences abound in the competencies required, how and when they are measured, the number and levels of minimum standards available to the hearing impaired student, and the consequences of failure to meet the minimum standard. No single recommendation can be made for hearing impaired students that would be consistent from state to state, or even from school to school within a state.

Further, individual differences in motivation and achievement of the students in question interact with factors regarding the specific MCT program to complicate the educator's task. Nevertheless, among the several questions especially relevant to educators of hearing impaired students who wish to make effective use of MCT programs are the following: What procedures are available for selecting and administering minimum competency tests to hearing impaired students? For what kind of diploma or certificate can a hearing impaired student qualify by passing the test? To what extent is the test valid for hearing impaired students? To what extent are remediation and reevaluation available for hearing impaired students who fail the test? How are the mandated competencies related to instructional materials and methods? How does the student's IEP relate to the competencies required?

The view that the IEP process is best suited to bring the MCT movement into accordance with the needs and legal rights of hearing impaired students appears to be widely held. In fact, Danielson (1980) and Olsen (1980) considered the IEP, in which goals and objectives based on individual needs are stated, to be the appropriate model for *all* children. It is hoped that the information presented in this chapter will give order to the educator's task and shed light upon the paths available to hearing impaired students in MCT programs.

REFERENCES

Akers-Adams, S., and Halpin, G. (1985, August). *Minimum competency testing and the exceptional student*. Paper presented at the meeting of the American Psychological Association, Los Angeles.

Beckham, J. (1980). *Legal implications of minimum competency testing*. Bloomington, IN: Phi Delta Kappa.

Bennett, R. E., and Ragosta, M. (1984). *A research context for studying admissions tests and handicapped populations* (Studies of Admissions Testing and Handicapped People, Report No. 1). Princeton, NJ: Educational Testing Service.

Bennett, R. E., Ragosta, M., and Stricker, L. J. (1984). *The test performance of handicapped people* (Studies of Admissions Testing and Handicapped People, Report No. 2). Princeton, NJ: Educational Testing Service.

Board of Education v. Ambach, 436 N.Y.S.2d 564, 574, 575 (S. Ct. Albany County, 1981), 485 N.Y.S. 2d 680, 688 (App. Div. 1982).

Brickell, H. (1978). Seven key notes on minimum competency testing. *Phi Delta Kappan, 59,* 589–592.

Brookhart v. Illinois State Board of Education, 697 F.2d 179, 187 (7th Cir. 1983).

Citron, C. H. (1982). Competency testing: Emerging principles. *Educational Measurement: Issues and Practice, 1*(4), 10–11.

Citron, C. H. (1983). *Legal rules for student competency testing* (ECS Issuegram 36). Denver: Education Commission of the States.

Danielson, L. C. (1980). Educational goals and competency testing for the handicapped. In R. M. Jaeger and C. K. Tittle (Eds.), *Minimum competency achievement testing* (pp. 201–204). Berkeley: McCutchan.

Donohue v. Copiague School District, Donohue 64 A.D. 2d 29, 407 N.Y.S. 2d 874 (App. Div. 1978) aff'd 47 N.Y. 2d 440, 418 N.Y.S. 2d 375, 391 N.E. 2d 1352 (Ct. App. 1979).

Fenton, K. S. (1980). Competency testing and the handicapped: Some legal concerns for school administrators. In R. M. Jaeger and C. K. Tittle (Eds.), *Minimum competency achievement testing* (pp. 182-188). Berkeley: McCutchan.

Goss v. Lopez, 419 U.S. 565 (1975).

Grisé, P. J. (1980). Florida's minimum competency testing program for handicapped students. *Exceptional Children, 47*(3), 186-191.

Hoffman v. Board of Education, City of New York, 64 A.D. 2d 369, 410 N.Y.S. 2d 99 (App. Div. 1978).

McCarthy, M. M. (1983). The application of competency testing mandates to handicapped children. *Harvard Educational Review, 53*(2), 146-164.

McClung, M. S. (1978). Are competency tests fair? Legal? *Phi Delta Kappan, 59,* 397-400.

Morrissey, P. A. (1980). Adaptive testing: How and when should handicapped students be accommodated in competency testing programs? In R. M. Jaeger and C. K. Tittle (Eds.), *Minimum competency achievement testing* (pp. 205-210). Berkeley: McCutchan.

National Association of State Directors of Special Education. (1979). *Competency testing, special education and the awarding of diplomas.* Washington, DC: Author.

National Institute of Education. (1981, July 8-10). *Issues Clarification Hearing on Minimum Competency Testing.* Washington, DC.

Olsen, K. R. (1980). Minimum competency testing and the IEP process. *Exceptional Children, 47*(3), 176-183.

Olson, L. (1985, September 18). Connecticut panel recommends against high-school exit tests. *Education Week,* p. 9.

Peter W. v. San Francisco Unified School District, 60 Cal. App. 3d 814, 131 Cal. Rptr. 854 (Ct. App. 1976).

Pipho, C. (1978). Minimum competency testing in 1978: A look at state standards. *Phi Delta Kappan, 59*, 585-588.

Pipho, C. (1983). *Student minimum competency testing* (ECS Issuegram 20). Denver: Education Commission of the States.

Pipho, C. (1985, November). *State activity: Minimum competency testing* (Clearinghouse Notes.) Denver: Education Commission of the States.

Popham, W. J., and Lindheim, E. (1981). Implications of a landmark ruling on Florida's minimum competency test. *Phi Delta Kappan, 63,* 18-22.

Randall, K. D. (1984). The application of minimum competency testing to deaf students. *American Annals of the Deaf, 129,* 95-99.

Riegel, R. P., and Lovell, N. B. (1980). *Minimum competency testing.* Bloomington, IN: Phi Delta Kappa.

San Antonio Independent School District v. Rodriguez, 411 U.S. 1 (1973).

State of Florida. (1977). *Minimum student performance standards for Florida schools: Exceptional students.* Tallahassee: Department of Education.

Tractenberg, P. L. (1979). *Legal implications of minimum competency testing: Debra P. and beyond* (Final Report NIE-G-79-0033). Newark: Rutgers School of Law.

Tractenberg, P. L. (1980). Testing for minimum competency: A legal analysis. In R. M. Jaeger and C. K. Tittle (Eds.), *Minimum competency achievement testing* (pp. 85-107). Berkeley: McCutchan.

Watson, P. (1979). *The impact of the minimal competency testing movement on the hearing impaired.* Paper presented at the Conference of American Instructors of the Deaf, Austin, TX.

Chapter **10**

Postsecondary Educational Opportunities for Deaf Students

Brenda W. Rawlings
Susan J. King

For almost a century deaf students seeking specialized educational training at the postsecondary level were limited in the choice of institutions they could attend. The courses of instruction available to them were similarly limited. For most deaf students the only postsecondary option was the liberal arts curriculum offered by Gallaudet College in Washington, DC. Founded in 1864, Gallaudet continues to be the only liberal arts college established with the primary purpose of educating deaf students.

Although the availability of postsecondary training opportunities increased among the general hearing population during the first half of the twentieth century, educational opportunities for deaf high school graduates did not expand accordingly. Gallaudet College tripled its enrollment between 1900 and 1960, growing from 107 students to over 350; enrollment in universities and colleges for the hearing in 1960, however, was 16 times what it had been in 1900 (Schein and Bushnaq, 1962).

For those deaf students seeking advanced training but not interested in Gallaudet's liberal arts education, for those not able to relocate to the Washington D.C. metropolitan area, or for those unable to meet Gallaudet's admission requirements, the only alternative was to attend a postsecondary program at a college for hearing students. In 1955, a survey of more than 1800 colleges and universities found only 65 deaf students enrolled at these programs for hearing individuals (Bigman, 1961). The need for educational support services made this alternative impractical for many deaf students (Crammatte, 1968; Quigley, Jenne, and Phillips, 1968).

Deaf students in the 1980s have a wide range of career training oppor-tunities open to them. There are currently more than 100 special post-secondary programs for deaf students located across the United States, giving them more geographical choices in selecting a program. In addi-tion, the training offered at these programs extends from 1-year certifi-cate awards to advanced degrees at the doctoral level. The career areas available for study include such options as agricultural sciences, media technology, business, and medicine. The quality and quantity of special support services provided, however, varies widely from program to pro-gram; students must try to match their career interests and needed sup-port services with the available program options.

Economic, social, and legislative factors contributed to the establish-ment and growth of postsecondary programs for deaf students over the last two decades. Historically, the secondary education programs at the state residential schools for deaf students had been able to provide voca-tional training to high school students, enabling them to compete in the job market. As society has become more technically oriented and the labor force requirements have called for more highly skilled employees, deaf students have wanted and needed to seek additional higher educational training (Moores, 1982).

The 1960s saw a greater concern for minority groups, among them the physically handicapped. Combined with this was increased recogni-tion of the capabilities of handicapped people. For deaf persons this meant that educators, government agencies, and other groups began to evaluate and discuss the need for alternative special education programs.

In 1968, U.S. Public Law 89-36 established the National Technical Institute for the Deaf (NTID) at the Rochester Institute of Technology in New York. This program offers technical training to deaf students in a campus setting in which deaf students can be integrated with hearing students. Like Gallaudet, this institution serves deaf students from all parts of the country; the educational emphasis is on technical and vocational fields. Although the majority of degrees are awarded at the certificate and associate level, baccalaureate and graduate training is also available.

The decade of the 1960s also saw the enactment of legislation creat-ing federally funded regional programs to serve deaf persons. These were established in St. Paul, Minnesota, at the St. Paul Technical Vocational Institute; in New Orleans, Louisiana, at Delgado Junior College; and in Seattle, Washington, at the Seattle Community College. California State University at Northridge, which had begun offering programs to deaf stu-dents in the early 1960s, became one of these federally mandated regional programs in 1976.

Legislation in 1968 amending the Vocational Education Act con-tributed to the expansion of services to deaf students at the postsecondary level. This legislation required that at least 10 percent of the funds to each state be allocated to handicapped programs. Stuckless (1973) indicated, however, that whereas the use of funds was at the discretion of the individual states, the programs and services developed were not well coordinated. He attributed this in large part to the limited guidance offered by the U.S. Office of Education, the U.S. Rehabilitation Services Administration, and professional organizations concerned with handicapped individuals.

Another contributing factor to the expansion of programs is Section 504 of the Rehabilitation Act of 1975 (U.S. Public Law 93-112), which protects the rights of handicapped individuals by requiring that any institution receiving federal funds not discriminate against handicapped persons by denying them access to their services. Some postsecondary institutions have complied with these requirements by meeting the needs of handicapped students on an ad hoc basis. Other institutions have been even more assertive and have established offices to provide a broad range of special services to all handicapped students on their campuses. Still others have established programs specifically designed for deaf students and then have actively recruited these students.

Colleges and universities have sought out handicapped students not only because of the legislation encouraging them to serve this population but also in response to economic pressures. Because of the national decline in higher education enrollment occurring in the 1970s, many institutions needed to broaden their enrollment to students other than the 18- to 22-year-old age group traditionally served (Frankel and Sonnenberg, 1978). Numerous colleges and universities have sought out older individuals, encouraging them either to initiate or to return to postsecondary studies. Similarly, to increase or maintain enrollments, some colleges have turned to previously underserved segments of the population such as the handicapped.

The best current estimates suggest that between 8000 and 11,000 individuals with hearing losses attend institutions of higher education. Some of these students are enrolled at institutions that provide special services and where the deaf student population may number in the hundreds. Other deaf students attend institutions where they receive no special adaptive services; in some instances the deaf student may be the only physically disabled student on the campus.

These estimates are based on data collected by the National Center for Education Statistics (NCES) (Wulfsberg and Petersen, 1979) and by the Gallaudet College Planning Office (Armstrong and Schneidmiller, 1983). Based on a national sample survey conducted in 1978, the NCES estimated there were approximately 11,000 "acoustically impaired" students attending institutions of higher education. Armstrong and Schneidmiller resurveyed some of the NCES respondents and found that there was considerable overreporting of the acoustically handicapped enrollments in certain programs.

PROGRAM TYPES

The postsecondary educational alternatives available to deaf students can be conceptualized in terms of a cascade model or continuum of services (Reynolds and Birch, 1977). This model has, at one end, very specialized programs or educational environments targeted solely for a unique population; at the opposite end are programs that do not offer any special adaptive services but provide a regular education program only. At one end of the model of postsecondary programs for deaf students would be Gallaudet College and NTID. These two programs enroll few, if any, hearing students and were established with the primary mission of educating a hearing impaired population.

Further along the continuum are the four federally funded regional programs for deaf students mentioned before. These programs offer comprehensive support services for deaf students and are located at facilities designed primarily for hearing students. More than 90 other colleges and universities have been identified as having special programs specifically designed for deaf students. Special services coordinated by program directors in these schools make the curriculum offerings and the institutions' general services accessible to deaf students.

There are other colleges and universities with well-established services to meet the general needs of handicapped individuals (Liscio, 1986; McGeough, Jungjohan, and Thomas, 1983). These services may include some that would be of use to deaf students, but they are available for a more diverse group of handicapped persons. Typically, these institutions have specially trained staff to provide and coordinate services to handicapped students and to the faculty who have such students in their classrooms.

Another type of educational alternative is the regular education setting in which college personnel attempt to meet the needs of individual students on an ad hoc basis. In these situations there is no central office with sole responsibility for delivery of services to deaf students, but a student may be able to obtain assistance from a general academic counselor or a dean's office.

The final educational option possible for deaf college students is to attend a program in which no special services are made available by the college. Students at these programs may not require any special services or may themselves try to arrange the assistance of tutors or notetakers.

Gallaudet College and NTID at the Rochester Institute of Technology have monitored the growth in the number of postsecondary programs specially designed for deaf students and the services offered since 1972. Gallaudet and NTID have conducted numerous surveys to gather information on programs for deaf students, the special services offered, and student enrollment patterns. The results of these surveys include five editions of a directory of institutions with college and career programs for deaf students (Rawlings, Karchmer, and Decaro, 1983; Rawlings, Trybus, and Biser, 1978, 1981; Rawlings, Trybus, Delgado, and Stuckless, 1975; Stuckless and Delgado, 1973).

The comparisons presented in the following sections are based on the Gallaudet and NTID surveys conducted in the fall of 1972 and the fall of 1982. In both years, all institutions known to have a postsecondary program specially designed for deaf students were contacted and asked to complete a detailed questionnaire. A program for deaf students was defined as a program located at an established postsecondary institution, accredited by a recognized educational agency, and organized to provide special services to deaf students.

As national longitudinal data become available from these surveys, it is possible to examine the changes that have occurred in postsecondary educational programs for deaf students over 10 years. As in all studies, certain qualifications and limitations apply to the information reported. The data collected represent all programs known to the researchers at the time the studies were conducted. It is possible there were other programs in existence that had not come to the attention of the project staff. Every effort, however, was made in each survey to reach all postsecondary programs for deaf students.

The most current data reflect the status of postsecondary education just prior to 1985, when large numbers of rubella-deafened youth were beginning to enter postsecondary programs. The rubella epidemic of 1964 to 1965 resulted in almost twice as many children being born with significant hearing impairments than had been born in nonepidemic years. The applicant pool for postsecondary programs in the mid-1980s is not only larger but also contains a group of students more likely to have additional educationally significant handicaps than those whose deafness is attributable to causes other than maternal rubella (White, Karchmer, Armstrong, and Bezozo, 1983). Many postsecondary programs are increasing their enrollments to meet this larger demand, and some are modifying the special services offered for students with additional handicaps.

Since the collection of data in 1983, other postsecondary programs have been established. Most notable is the establishment in 1983 of the new federally funded Postsecondary Education Consortium at the University of Tennessee. Data on this comprehensive program and the hearing impaired students served there are not reflected in the analysis in this chapter.

GROWTH OF POSTSECONDARY PROGRAMS SINCE 1960

As already mentioned, the growth in the number of postsecondary programs for deaf students is a rather recent phenomenon. Before 1960 Gallaudet College had the only established program for deaf students. Several additional programs became available in the 1960s, but it was during the decade of the 1970s that the most significant growth in the number of programs for deaf students occurred (Figure 10–1). Between 1960 and 1964 the number of programs grew to 6; during the last half of the 1960s an additional 12 programs were established. In the next 5 years the programs available for deaf students more than tripled with the establishment of 40 additional postsecondary programs. A similar increase occurred between

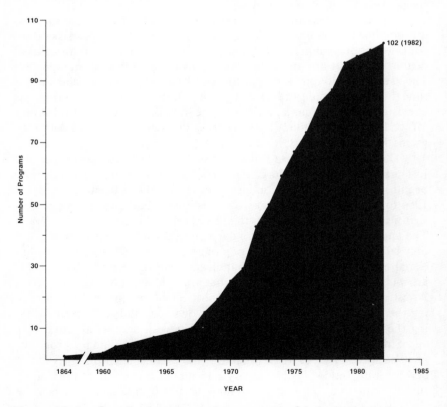

Figure 10–1.   Growth of postsecondary programs for deaf students.

1975 and 1979 when 38 new programs were established. By the fall of 1982, six more institutions were offering organized programs for deaf students, bringing the total to 102.

In the decade preceding 1982, 14 other institutions reported having programs serving deaf students. However, by 1982 the programs at these institutions either were no longer in existence or chose not to report information to the survey. In most cases the programs had very minimal enrollments of deaf students or had, in fact, ceased to exist.

GEOGRAPHICAL DISTRIBUTION

The two national federally funded programs are located in the East, in New York and the District of Columbia. The other 100 programs are widely dispersed across the United States (Figure 10–2). California has the largest number of postsecondary programs with 24; Texas reports 7 programs. Florida follows with 6 and Illinois and North Carolina each has 5 programs for deaf students.

This distribution of postsecondary programs for deaf students is similar to the distribution of all institutions of higher education. Three of the states mentioned—California, Illinois, and Texas—are also among the top five states in the nation in having the largest number of higher educational institutions (Grant and Snyder, 1983).

ENROLLMENT

Current Enrollment

In the fall of 1982 more than 5500 deaf students were enrolled at 102 postsecondary programs for deaf students in the United States (Table 10–1). The vast majority of students, 4586, were reported to be enrolled as full-time students; an additional 983 deaf students attended on a part-time basis.

Enrollment at the 102 postsecondary programs for deaf students can best be examined by dividing the programs into three categories: national programs, regional programs, and state and local programs. The basis for this categorization includes the general constituency served and the manner in which the programs were established. The federally funded national programs are Gallaudet and NTID. Established by federal legislation, these two programs receive substantial federal funding and serve a national constituency. In 1982 the four programs for deaf students at St. Paul Technical and Vocational Institute, California State University at Northridge, Delgado Community College in New Orleans, and Seattle Community College were funded primarily by the government to func-

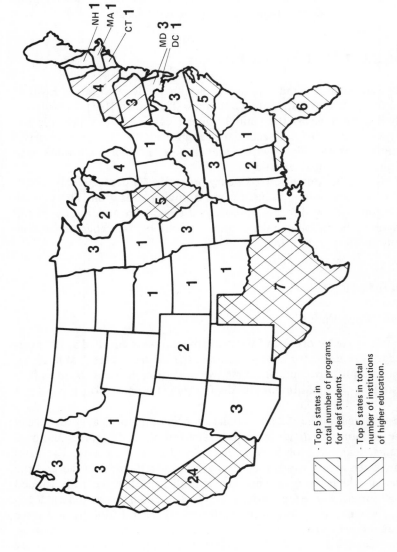

Figure 10–2. Geographical distribution of postsecondary programs for deaf students: Fall, 1982.

- Top 5 states in total number of programs for deaf students.

- Top 5 states in total number of institutions of higher education.

Table 10–1.   Enrollment at Postsecondary Programs for Deaf Students, Fall 1982

Type of Program	Number	Total Enrollment		Total Enrollment Full-time		Total Enrollment Part-time	
		N	%	N	%	N	%
Total	102	5,569	100	4,586	82	983	18
Federally-funded national programs	2	2,135	100	2,070	97	65	3
Federally-funded regional programs	4	497	100	434	87	63	13
State and local programs	96	2,937	100	2,082	71	855	29

tion as regional programs. (As previously mentioned, in 1983 the Post-secondary Educational Consortium at the University of Tennessee became the recipient of federal funds as the southern regional program. The program for deaf students at Delgado Community College has been discontinued.) Ninety-six other programs are included in the third category of state and local programs. These programs were established primarily with state monies or private donations and generally serve state and local residents.

In 1982–1983 the 2 national programs served 2070 hearing impaired students on a full-time basis, almost half (45 percent) of all students attending the 102 postsecondary programs on a full-time basis. Full-time enrollment in the 96 state and local programs slightly exceeded the enrollment at the 2 federally funded national programs, accounting for another 45 percent of the total enrollment. The remaining full-time students (434) attended the 4 federally funded regional programs.

Full-time enrollment figures provide only a partial picture of the student population being served. Students who attend on a part-time basis constitute a large segment of the student population. This is true not only at postsecondary programs for deaf students but also among higher education programs in general. Nationally, 42 percent of students attend institutions of higher education on a part-time basis (Grant and Snyder, 1983).

The proportion of part-time students in postsecondary programs for deaf students, however, was much lower than for the general undergraduate population. Only 18 percent of deaf students enrolled in 1982 at programs for deaf students attended on a part-time basis (Table 10-1). Only 3 percent of deaf students at the national federally funded programs and 13 percent at the regional programs were enrolled part-time; a larger proportion (29 percent) of the deaf students at state and local programs attended on a part-time basis.

Change in Full-Time Enrollment Over 10 Years

The full-time enrollment at postsecondary programs for deaf students almost doubled between 1972 and 1982, growing from 2338 students to 4586 students (Figure 10–3). This increase occurred mainly in the state and local programs. Full-time enrollment in the state and local programs in the Midwest tripled during this 10-year span; in the West the state and local full-time enrollment jumped to 2.6 times what it had been. The state and local programs in the South increased full-time enrollment almost fivefold between 1972 and 1982.

Two of the four federally funded regional programs reported at least a 30 percent growth in their full-time student body enrollment; the other two programs noted a decline in the number of deaf students enrolled fulltime. Both of the federally funded national programs reported an increase in full-time enrollment: Gallaudet grew by 14 percent, NTID by 155 percent.

STUDENT CHARACTERISTICS

As indicated before, it is estimated there were between 8000 and 11,000 deaf students attending postsecondary educational programs in 1982–1983. About 6 out of 10 of these deaf students were enrolled at postsecondary programs designed specifically for deaf students. Other deaf students selected colleges and universities providing limited or no special services.

Three recent studies suggested that deaf students enroll in postsecondary programs at rates similar to or higher than hearing students (Armstrong and Schneidmiller, 1983; Kerstetter, 1985; White et al., 1983). The estimates ranged from a conservative 30 percent to as high as 53 percent of all deaf students graduating from special education secondary programs.

Kerstetter (1985) conducted a national study of deaf students previously enrolled in secondary programs across the United States. The purpose was to determine what student characteristics were predictors of attendance at postsecondary programs and the relationship of these characteristics to the types of postsecondary institutions selected by deaf high school graduates of 25 different school programs. These high school programs represented mainstream educational settings as well as full-time special education programs at residential schools for deaf students.

Two of the characteristics of deaf students found to be the most significant predictors of attendance at postsecondary programs were reading ability and region of the United States in which the student resided. Those deaf students most likely to enroll in postsecondary programs had above average reading skills compared to their high school peers. A higher

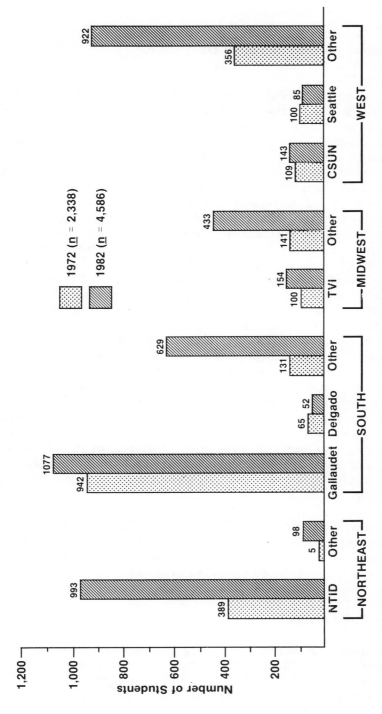

Figure 10-3. Regional distribution of students enrolled full-time at postsecondary programs for deaf students, 1972 and 1982.

percentage of graduates of secondary programs in the West and Midwest enrolled in postsecondary programs than did graduates from other regions of the U.S.

Other characteristics of deaf students appearing to have an influence on postsecondary attendance included sex, ethnic origin, and additional handicapping conditions. Male students were more likely than females to enroll in postsecondary programs. Similar to the general population, white students were more likely than minority students to continue their education after high school. Students with no educationally significant additional handicaps were also more likely to attend postsecondary programs than those students with such handicaps.

For those deaf students enrolled in postsecondary programs, Kerstetter (1985) examined the students' characteristics in relation to the types of postsecondary programs selected. Those deaf students enrolled at the national federally funded programs were more likely to have attended full-time special education programs at the secondary level and to be above average in academic ability. Students at these programs were also more likely to have more severe hearing losses, no additional handicaps, and at least one parent with a hearing loss.

Students selecting the regional and state and local programs for deaf students had less severe hearing losses and were more likely to have parents with normal hearing. The above-average students from mainstream secondary programs were likely to attend these regional and state and local postsecondary programs, as were the students with lower academic abilities who completed full-time special education high school programs.

The students who continued their education at institutions not having programs specifically designed for deaf students also had some significant demographic characteristics. Compared to other deaf students in the sample, these students had less severe hearing losses and more educationally significant additional handicaps.

Although deaf students now have a number of higher educational options available to them, the data suggest that certain students prefer some types of postsecondary programs over other types. The students' previous educational experiences as well as their specialized needs appear to influence their selection of these programs.

PROGRAM SIZE

The majority of postsecondary programs for deaf students in 1982 enrolled small numbers of students in their programs. More than half (61 percent) of the programs enrolled 20 or fewer students on a full-time basis. Thirty-three programs served less than 11 students, and 29 programs enrolled 11 to 20 deaf students (Figure 10–4).

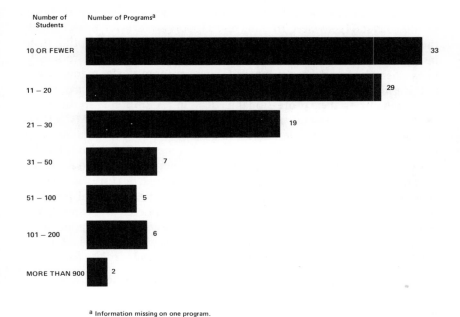

Number of Students | Number of Programs[a]

- 10 OR FEWER — 33
- 11 – 20 — 29
- 21 – 30 — 19
- 31 – 50 — 7
- 51 – 100 — 5
- 101 – 200 — 6
- MORE THAN 900 — 2

[a] Information missing on one program.

Figure 10–4. Full-time enrollment at postsecondary programs for deaf students: Fall, 1982.

Program size is related to the type of program. State and local programs were relatively small, the national programs large; the regional programs, by comparison, were moderate in size. All of the 88 programs with 50 or fewer students were state and local programs. The 4 regional programs enrolled between 52 and 154 full-time hearing impaired students. Gallaudet and NTID each enrolled more than 900 deaf students.

SPECIAL SERVICES

The unique characteristic of postsecondary programs for deaf students is that they all have an established system for providing specialized services intended to meet the individual needs of deaf students. Special services are provided to enable these students to participate fully in the academic and vocational offerings of the college. The scope of services is not limited, however, to the classroom; many offer services that allow deaf students to participate in the extracurricular activities that are an important part of a student's college experience. Support services provide the opportunity to participate in social, cultural, and athletic events sponsored by the college.

244   B. W. Rawlings & S. J. King

Often it is not the deaf student only who requires special services; faculty and staff may need training and support services for working with these students. These services aid the faculty and staff in adapting their instructional methods, curriculum, and materials for use in classroom settings where deaf students are enrolled. Some programs offer manual communication training for personnel who work with deaf students.

Recognizing their professional leadership responsibility in this area, the Conference of Executives of American Schools for the Deaf (CEASD) prepared a publication that addressed a number of issues in establishing postsecondary education programs for deaf students. They also listed the basic support services that should be a core part of any postsecondary program (Stuckless, 1973). CEASD noted that not all deaf students would require all these services, and they also cautioned educational planners that the recommended services should not be considered as a comprehensive listing. Colleges might want or need to offer additional support services based on their student population and the nature of the courses being offered. The support services outlined by CEASD included the following:

Special credit-bearing classes designed specifically for deaf students
Individual tutoring
Voice-to-sign and sign-to-voice interpreting
Notetaking
Vocational counseling of deaf students
Personal counseling services by professionals knowledgeable about the
    development needs of deaf students
Vocational placement services
Diagnostic and clinical speech and hearing services
Communication training for deaf students
Communication training for instructors
Social and cultural activities primarily for deaf students
Supervised housing

Obviously, the quality and quantity of the special services provided to deaf students may vary from program to program and may be a function of the location of the program. For example, a program for deaf students located at a small, rural community college may not be able to provide speech and hearing clinical services because they are not available at the college or within the community. On the other hand, a large urban university with a program for deaf students may either have a speech and hearing clinic on campus or be able to refer students to a facility within the city.

Similarly, the size of the deaf student enrollment may affect availability of the special services offered. If a program has only a few deaf students who need notetakers, these students may be able to make informal arrangements with hearing classmates to share lecture notes. At programs with larger deaf student enrollments, however, the need may be such that coordinated notetaking services that use salaried notetakers are necessary.

The availability of many of the services at the programs for deaf students was found to be related to the number of deaf students enrolled at the programs (Table 10-2). These data also provide some measures of the quality of the service. For example, paid notetakers or paid interpreters may provide more comprehensive and dependable services than those serving on a volunteer basis.

Although fewer than half (39 percent) of the programs offered special classes for deaf students, availability of this service was more likely in the larger programs. In programs enrolling fewer than 11 students, only 21 percent of the programs offered this classroom setting. Of the programs enrolling more than 30 deaf students, 55 percent provided special classes specifically designed for deaf students.

Almost all (98 percent) of the programs offered the services of interpreters who were skilled in both voice-to-sign and sign-to-voice interpreting. Two programs, however, indicated they provided interpreters only when a minimum number of students enroll for the same class, an important consideration if students choose to major in a career area in which there are few or no other deaf students enrolled.

Although widely available, the quality of interpreting services may vary among the programs. Interpreters have various skill levels, and some are certified by professional groups such as the Registry of Interpreters for the Deaf (RID) or other certification agencies. Interpreters may be employed by certain colleges; at other programs interpreters serve on a volunteer basis.

Paid interpreters were widely used by programs (90 percent); all programs with more than 30 students provided paid interpreters. Also, salaried interpreters were more likely to be certified than volunteer interpreters. Ninety percent of the salaried interpreters had some type of interpreting certification; only 21 percent of the volunteer interpreters were certified.

Some postsecondary programs serving deaf students have very structured systems for coordinating notetaking services. NTID, for example, provides training and instruction to those individuals employed as notetakers. At other programs notetaking services are coordinated through the program for deaf students, but the notetakers are volunteers who agree to share their personal notes with a deaf classmate.

The vast majority (93 percent) of the programs offered notetaking services for deaf students. Programs provided these services in a variety of ways. More than one half (53 percent) of the programs used salaried notetakers, and about one fourth supplemented their salaried notetakers with volunteers. Volunteer notetakers were used at only 17 percent of the programs.

Table 10–2. Percentage of Postsecondary Programs for Deaf Students Offering Support Services, by Program Size, 1982

Support Services	All Programs (N = 101)	10 or Fewer Students (N = 33)	11–20 Students (N = 29)	21–30 Students (N = 19)	More Than 30 Students* (N = 20)
Classroom Services					
Special class for deaf students	39	21	45	47	55
Interpreters (paid or volunteer)	98	97	100	95	100
Paid interpreters	90	82	97	89	100
Tutors	84	76	83	84	100
Notetakers (paid or volunteer)	93	88	100	89	95
Paid notetakers	53	39	48	84	55
Clinical and Counseling Services					
Vocational counseling	96	97	97	89	100
Counselors who sign	59	39	55	68	90
Personal counseling	96	94	93	100	100
Counselors who sign	64	36	69	74	90
Vocational placement	87	85	86	84	95
Counselors who sign	38	15	28	58	70
Speech and hearing clinical services	69	61	72	79	70
Services through program or host institution	32	18	24	47	55
Other					
Manual communication training for students	84	70	90	95	95
Manual communication training for instructors	81	67	86	85	85
Social and cultural activities	55	27	69	47	90
Preparatory activities	54	36	48	58	90
Supervised housing	47	42	48	53	50

*Information is missing on one program.

Counseling services were provided to students in several ways (e.g., through counselors skilled in manual communication or by counselors who used an interpreter in sessions with the students). Vocational counseling and personal counseling were offered by 96 percent of the programs. More than one half of the programs provided vocational (59 percent) and personal (64 percent) counseling services with counselors skilled in manual communication. Eighty-seven percent of the programs offered vocational placement services, but only 38 percent of the programs used counselors skilled in manual communication for this service.

Counseling services provided by counselors skilled in manual communication were more likely to be available at the larger programs. Ninety percent of programs with 31 or more students reported that they provide vocational counseling and personal counseling services by counselors skilled in manual communication. Seventy percent of the programs enrolling 31 or more students used vocational placement counselors skilled in manual communication.

Because deaf students have various degrees of speech and hearing problems, speech and hearing clinical services are frequently required. Not all programs offered these services; of the 73 programs that did, the services were provided in various manners. Twenty-five programs reported that both the diagnosis of the speech and hearing of entering students and the clinical services of speech therapists and audiologists were either directly coordinated by the program for deaf students or offered by the host institution. It was much more common that programs referred students to organizations outside the institution for diagnosis and for clinical services. This referral pattern was reported by almost two thirds of the programs providing these services.

The ability to communicate effectively is an important consideration for deaf students. Because most of these programs serve students who sign, CEASD suggests that entering students be evaluated on their expressive and receptive manual communication skills; for those who need to develop or improve their manual communication skills they recommend that sign language instruction be provided. Although 84 percent of the programs offered sign language training, only one third offered the assessment services.

Similarly, to enhance student-teacher communication, it is often beneficial that instructors in programs for deaf students receive manual communication training. Classes in manual communication training for instructors were offered at 81 percent of the programs, and 23 percent of the programs required that those who regularly taught deaf students without the use of interpreters take manual communication training or otherwise demonstrate proficiency in this area.

Social and cultural activities especially designed for deaf students were available in only 55 percent of the programs. This service would most likely depend on having a large enough group of deaf students to be able to offer such activities.

Often students arrive at college and have a need for remedial work in specific academic areas or for more general preparation in adjusting to college life. Deaf students also may need these preparatory services in order to take full advantage of the total college program. Availability of preparatory activities was related to program size: Only one third (36 percent) of the programs with 10 or fewer deaf students provided preparatory programs; 90 percent of the larger programs made this service available.

CEASD cites the availability of supervised housing as a consideration in establishing programs for deaf students because they believe deaf high school graduates may need supervision in adjusting during the transition from adolescence. Obviously the presence or absence of supervised housing is related to the general population served by the host institution. Although supervised housing was available at fewer than half (47 percent) of these institutions, it appears that most of those without supervised housing were programs operating in community colleges serving commuter students.

MAJOR AREAS OF STUDY

In 1968 Crammatte noted that "almost since establishment, schools for the deaf have trained their pupils in the manual trades. As the blind were taught to weave and to make brooms, so the deaf were trained in printing, carpentry, cooking and sewing" (p. vii). As the numbers and enrollment levels of postsecondary programs for deaf students have grown, so has the variety of careers pursued by students in these programs. Crammatte's observation clearly does not apply to the majority of today's deaf students.

The major areas of study of deaf students are grouped here into 15 categories for analysis. These categories or career clusters provide a framework for the types of curriculum studied at the time the programs reported data. Many institutions opened all of their courses of instruction to deaf students; others limited deaf students to selected classes. Some institutions allowed deaf students to enroll only in curriculum areas in which previous deaf students had succeeded or in which special adaptations had been made to the program. By reporting the specific majors currently studied by deaf students, a clearer picture of the career aspirations of and opportunities available to deaf students emerges.

Table 10–3. Career Areas of Study for Deaf Students in Postsecondary Programs Surveyed in Both 1972 and 1982

Career Clusters	1972		1982	
	Programs	*Students*	*Programs*	*Students*
Total	23*	1536†	23*	2171†
Agriculture	1	2	4	6
Business and office	19	402	22	751
Communication and media	12	186	17	225
Construction	10	136	8	43
Consumer and homemaking	3	34	10	84
Environment and natural resources	2	6	4	33
Fine arts and humanities	5	287	11	306
Health	11	51	7	78
Hospitality and recreation	6	47	11	46
Manufacturing	17	159	17	345
Marketing and distribution	2	2	1	4
Personal services	4	9	2	4
Product services	10	92	5	19
Public services	10	70	12	193
Transportation	10	53	10	34

*Clusters add up to more than 23 programs because programs generally offered more than one career cluster area.
†Total students who declared a major area of study.

In 1972 deaf students in 23 programs enrolled in curriculum areas in each of the 15 career clusters (Table 10–3). Several of the curriculum areas, however, had very few deaf students enrolled, and the number of programs enrolling deaf students in these areas was limited. For example, only two students majored in agriculture, both at the same postsecondary program; two students at 2 different programs enrolled as majors in marketing and distribution.

Ten years later, these same 23 programs reported they had more deaf students enrolled in a majority of the career cluster areas. Also, in 8 of the 15 areas of concentration there were increased numbers of postsecondary programs enrolling deaf students in these majors. For example, in 1972, 12 programs enrolled deaf students in communication and media-related majors; in 1982, among these same 23 postsecondary programs, 17 programs enrolled deaf students in this field. The career area that showed the most expansion over the 10 years was that of consumer and homemaking majors: 3 programs enrolled deaf students in this major in 1972; in 1982 there were 10 programs.

The number of programs with deaf students enrolled, however, does not adequately reflect the growing interest of deaf students in particular career areas. The number of students enrolled in the particular majors must be considered also. Between 1972 and 1982 the number of programs enrolling deaf students in business and office careers increased from 19

Table 10–4.   Career Areas of Study by Deaf Students in 97 Postsecondary Programs, 1982

Career Clusters	Programs		Students	
	N	%	N	%
Total	97*	—	3439†	100
Agriculture	13	13	25	1
Business and office	76	78	1147	33
Communication and media	54	56	348	10
Construction	21	22	60	2
Consumer and homemaking	20	21	100	3
Environment and natural resources	9	9	42	1
Fine arts and humanities	43	44	464	13
Health	27	28	129	4
Hospitality and recreation	31	32	87	3
Manufacturing	57	59	500	15
Marketing and distribution	4	4	7	‡
Personal services	5	5	9	‡
Product services	11	11	27	1
Public services	44	45	380	11
Transportation	27	28	114	3

*Clusters add up to more than 97 programs because programs generally offered more than one career cluster area; 5 programs did not report majors for deaf students.
†Students who declared a major area of study.
‡Less than 1%.

to 22. The number of deaf students enrolled in these programs in this area of study almost doubled, from 402 to 751 students. Although the number of programs enrolling students in manufacturing-related majors over the 10 years remained the same (17), the number of deaf students enrolled more than doubled, growing from 159 to 345 students.

The data in Table 10–3 reflect changes in the 23 programs reporting in both the 1972 and 1982 surveys. A more complete picture of the current career choices of deaf students is found by looking at the majors selected by deaf students at the programs reporting in 1982 (Table 10–4). Nearly all (95 percent) of the postsecondary programs reported information on this topic. One third of the deaf students with a declared major chose to study for business and office-related careers. This was also the most widely offered major; 78 percent of the postsecondary programs indicating they had deaf students enrolled in this major.

This growth in business and office career training is not unique to the deaf student population. The NCES reported in 1983 a dramatic shift in the selection of majors by the general student population. Over a 10-year period from 1971 to 1982, degrees in business-related careers doubled (Grant and Snyder, 1983).

Deaf students in 1982, however, did not confine their interests to business and office-related areas. Manufacturing (500 students), fine arts and

Table 10–5. Distribution of Postsecondary Programs for Deaf Students by Type of Program Offered, 1982

Type of Program	N	%
Total Programs	102*	—
Vocational or certificate program	73	72
2-year technical program	57	56
4-year technical program	9	9
2-year liberal arts program	61	60
4-year liberal arts program	25	25
Rehabilitation program	9	9
Other (including graduate)	9	9

*Program types total more than 102 because some programs offered a number of levels of training.

humanities (464), public service (380), and communication and media (348) majors were also fields in which large numbers of deaf students enrolled.

More than one half (59 percent) of the programs enrolled students in manufacturing majors, and 56 percent of the programs trained communication and media majors. Forty-five percent of the programs had deaf students with declared majors in the public service field; 44 percent of the programs had deaf students majoring in fine arts and the humanities.

DEGREES CONFERRED

All of the programs for deaf students were located at degree or certificate granting institutions: deaf students completing their course of instruction might receive a certificate, or an associate or baccalaureate degree. Several of the programs for deaf students also offered advanced degrees at the master's or doctorate level. The type of certificate or degree available to deaf students is clearly important because it relates to the level of training of the instructional course.

Although programs offered a wide variety of levels of training, a large majority (72 percent) were vocational or certificate programs (Table 10–5).

Like hearing students, not all deaf students complete their studies. Students may withdraw from programs for a variety of reasons, including the inability to maintain the academic standards required. They may decide their studies are not meeting their career needs or interests; dissatisfaction with the social life or financial concerns may contribute to a student's decision to withdraw from a program. In the case of deaf students, they may also find that the special services provided by the program are still not sufficient to enable them to succeed or receive the maximum benefit from instruction.

Most programs for deaf students are newly established and therefore have graduated few students. The number of degrees awarded by these programs since their formation, however, provides some measure of the success deaf students have achieved in completing training. In the spring of 1982, 24 programs indicated that they had awarded a total of 4505 baccalaureate degrees to deaf students over the history of their programs. Gallaudet College awarded 88 percent of these degrees, NTID 6 percent, and California State University at Northridge granted 4 percent of these degrees. Twenty-one programs awarded the remaining 3 percent of the baccalaureates.

Six percent (261) of these baccalaureate degrees were granted during the 1981–1982 academic year alone. Gallaudet (65 percent), NTID (11 percent), and California State University at Northridge (8 percent) continued to be the institutions awarding the majority of these degrees (Figure 10–5). Historically, only a limited number of programs awarded baccalaureate degrees to deaf students.

A similar picture emerges at the associate degree level. Fifty-four programs reported granting 2083 associate level degrees to deaf students since their programs were established. Two programs awarded more than one half (62 percent) of these degrees: NTID with 33 percent and the federally funded regional program at the St. Paul Technical Vocational Institute with 29 percent.

In the 1981–1982 academic year, NTID and the St. Paul Technical Vocational Institute still led the nation in granting the majority of these degrees to deaf students. A total of 245 deaf students received associate degrees that year, with 33 percent from NTID and 25 percent from St. Paul. Thirty-nine other programs awarded 102 associate degrees.

During this same academic year 87 students enrolled in programs for deaf students received master's degrees. Four institutions granted 87 percent of these degrees: Western Maryland College (30 percent), California State University at Northridge (28 percent), Gallaudet College (21 percent), and New York University (8 percent). Seven other programs for deaf students granted the remaining 14 percent of the master's degrees given that year.

Over the years these 102 programs have been in existence, 5074 deaf students received certificate or diploma level awards. Although 49 programs granted these certificates, three institutions granted 60 percent of them: Alabama Institute for the Deaf and Blind (33 percent), West Valley Occupational Center (16 percent), and NTID (11 percent).

Of those deaf students completing their postsecondary programs during the 1981–1982 school year, 360 received certificates or diplomas, the most frequently granted award (38 percent) given to graduates of programs for deaf students in 1981–1982. NTID awarded 25 percent of these cer-

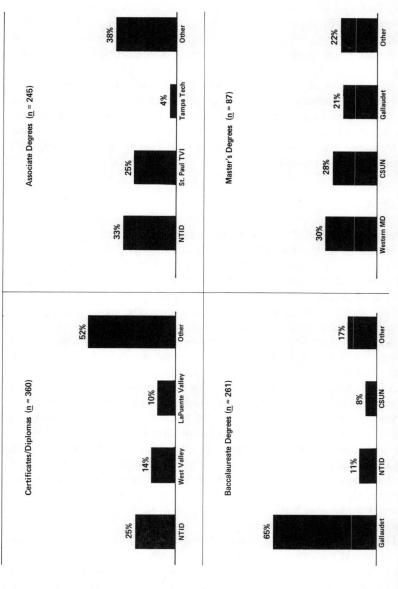

Figure 10–5. Distribution of postsecondary programs by type of degrees awarded, 1982. NTID = National Technical Institute for the Deaf, TVI = Technical Vocational Institute, CSUN = California State University at Northridge.

tificates or diplomas, West Valley Occupational Center 14 percent, and LaPuente Valley Adult School 10 percent of this level degree to deaf students. Twenty-nine other programs awarded the remaining 52 percent of the certificates or diplomas.

Although large numbers of deaf students enrolled in more than 100 postsecondary programs for these students, six institutions were responsible for granting the majority of degrees. This trend may change in the future as newly established programs gain more experience in meeting the needs of deaf students. It may also be that many of these programs will continue to enroll deaf students and provide them with training but will not graduate large numbers. The role of these programs may become that of retraining, remedial, or transfer programs that prepare deaf students to enroll in other institutions.

SUMMARY

Between the 1960s and 1980s the number of postsecondary programs for deaf students increased greatly. This expansion provided options to many more deaf students completing their high school programs than had previously been available. Deaf students could select from programs with different levels of degrees and various career training areas. The postsecondary programs were also more widely distributed across the United States, offering students more choices in where they studied.

Although there were more than 100 postsecondary programs for deaf students in 1982, several programs served most of the deaf students. Gallaudet College and the National Technical Institute for the Deaf enrolled nearly half of the 4586 students attending these programs full-time. Three programs, NTID, West Valley Occupational Center, and LaPuente Valley Adult School awarded 49 percent of all the certificates or diplomas granted to deaf students in 1982; NTID and the St. Paul Technical Vocational Institute awarded 58 percent of all associate degrees. Gallaudet, NTID, and California State University at Northridge granted 84 percent of the baccalaureate degrees granted to deaf students enrolled in special programs during this same period. Clearly, the postsecondary educational options were varied, but the majority of deaf students were completing programs at only several sites.

Depending on funding, the next decade may well see an expansion of the alternatives available to deaf students seeking postsecondary education. A 1983 study completed by McGeough and colleagues reported information on more than 2000 colleges and universities providing facilities and services to handicapped students in the United States and Canada. Their data showed that 1091 colleges and universities in the United States reported that they served hearing impaired or deaf students (Table 10–6).

Table 10–6. Number and Size of Institutions Enrolling Hearing Impaired or Deaf Students, United States, 1983

Number of Students Enrolled	Colleges and Universities	
	N	%
All programs	1,091	100
1–5	730	67
6–11	157	14
12–17	70	6
18–25	52	5
26–50	49	4
51–75	9	1
76 or more	24	2

Source: McGeough, C., Jungjohan, B., and Thomas, J. (Eds.). (1983). *Directory of college facilities and services for the handicapped*. Phoenix: Oryx Press.

McGeough and colleagues (1983) asked respondents to report "hearing impaired or deaf" enrollments in various categories. Two thirds (730) of the programs enrolled 5 or fewer hearing impaired or deaf students. Twenty-four colleges and universities, however, reported hearing impaired or deaf enrollments of 76 or more students.

These colleges and universities also reported availability of specific support services to hard-of-hearing and deaf students, services that may telecommunication devices (TTY/TDD), telephone amplification, and visible warning systems. Only two of the colleges and universities enrolling 76 or more students reported offering all six of these services. The most frequently reported services for the 24 programs enrolling 76 or more students were notetaking services, the availability of telecommunication devices, and interpreter services.

Most of the programs with established programs for deaf students were included in the McGeough study. The McGeough data, however, suggested that more and more colleges and universities are offering limited support services to hard of hearing and deaf students, services that may or may not be sufficient for students with hearing handicaps to be successful in a college program. Increased awareness among educators at the postsecondary level of the needs of these students and of the need for the provision of special services may attract students with minimal hearing handicaps to these programs.

Organizations such as the Higher Education and the Handicapped Resource Center (HEATH) serve as clearinghouses for information on postsecondary education for handicapped individuals, and through various publications, such as *The Deaf Student in College* (1979, 1983), college educators are becoming sensitized to the educational and social implications of deafness and more aware of ways to aid prospective students with hearing impairments.

In the future, options for students with hearing handicaps may expand, but significant numbers of students with severe and profound hearing losses will continue to need the established postsecondary programs for deaf students. These special programs offer more comprehensive support services and provide an environment with significant numbers of deaf peers for social activities. The training programs offered by these postsecondary programs may change to meet new labor force demands and the desire of deaf students for additional educational training. The relatively large pool of college-age deaf students will be much smaller in the late 1980s as rubella-deafened youth complete their secondary education. This will most likely lead to increased competition among these programs for a more limited number of students. All of these factors will contribute to changes in postsecondary education for deaf students over the next decade.

REFERENCES

Armstrong, D. and Schneidmiller, K. (1983). *Hearing impaired students enrolled in U.S. higher education institutions: Current status of enrollments and services* (Institutional Studies Report 83-3). Washington, DC: Gallaudet College.

Bigman, S. (1961). The deaf in American institutions of higher education. *Personnel and Guidance Journal*, 39, 743–749.

Crammatte, A. (1968). *Deaf persons in professional employment*. Springfield, IL: Charles C. Thomas.

The deaf student in college. (1979). Washington, DC: Gallaudet College Press.

The deaf student in college: Beyond the classroom. (1983). Washington, DC: Gallaudet College Press.

Frankel, M., and Sonnenberg, W. (1978). Enrollment. In M. Frankel (Ed.), *Projections of education statistics to 1986–87* (pp. 7–29). Washington, DC: National Center for Education Statistics.

Grant, W., and Snyder, T. (1983). *Digest of education statistics: 1983–84.* Washington, DC: National Center for Education Statistics.

Kerstetter, P. (1985). *Demographic predictors of postsecondary program choice of hearing impaired secondary school students.* Unpublished doctoral dissertation, Gallaudet College, Washington, DC.

Liscio, M.A. (Ed.). (1986). *A guide to colleges for hearing impaired students.* Orlando: Academic Press.

McGeough, C., Jungjohan, B., and Thomas, J. (Eds.). (1983). *Directory of college facilities and services for the handicapped.* Phoenix: Oryx Press.

Moores, D. (1982). *Educating the deaf: Psychology, principles, and practices* (2nd ed.). Boston: Houghton Mifflin.

Quigley, S., Jenne, W., and Phillips, S. (1968). *Deaf students in colleges and universities.* Washington, DC: A. G. Bell Association.

Rawlings, B., Karchmer, M., and Decaro, J. (Eds.). (1983). *College and career programs for deaf students.* Washington, DC: Gallaudet College.

Rawlings, B., Trybus, R., and Biser, J. (Eds.). (1978). *A guide to college/career programs for deaf students.* Washington, DC: Gallaudet College.

Rawlings, B., Trybus, R., and Biser, J. (Eds.). (1981). *A guide to college/career programs for deaf students*. Washington, DC: Gallaudet College.

Rawlings, B., Trybus, R., Delgado, G., and Stuckless, E. (Eds.). (1975). *A guide to college/career programs for deaf students*. Washington, DC: Gallaudet College.

Reynolds, M., and Birch, J. (1977). *Teaching exceptional children in all America's schools*. Reston, VA: Council for Exceptional Children.

Schein, J., and Bushnaq, S. (1962). Higher education for the deaf in the U.S.: A retrospective investigation. *American Annals of the Deaf, 107,* 416–420.

Stuckless, E. (Ed.). (1973). *Principles basic to the establishment and operation of postsecondary education for deaf students*. Washington, DC: Conference of Executives of American Schools for the Deaf.

Stuckless, E., and Delgado, G. (Eds.). (1973). *A guide to college/career programs for deaf students*. Rochester, NY: National Technical Institute for the Deaf.

White, C., Karchmer, M., Armstrong, D., and Bezozo, C. (1983). Current trends in high school graduation and college enrollment of hearing impaired students attending residential schools. *American Annals of the Deaf, 128,* 125–131.

Wulfsberg, R. and Petersen, R. (1979). *The impact of Section 504 of the Rehabilitation Act of 1973 on American colleges and universities*. Washington, DC: National Center for Education Statistics.

Conclusion

The introduction to this volume noted the demographic nature of most of the chapters: They deal with numbers and facts about hearing impaired children and their education, as reported to the Annual Survey of Hearing Impaired Children and Youth. This compilation of a uniform set of national data was the purpose of the organization recommended by the 1964 meeting of educators and researchers in deafness referred to in the introduction of this book. It was envisaged that this data collection would serve as a sound information base for decision making at both the national and local levels.

One of the most difficult tasks of professionals working in any field is to translate the researcher's quantified data and the demographer's numbers into policy and program planning and to bridge the gap between the data and what the data mean. Demography may be destiny, as the saying goes, but to determine what that destiny may be—and perhaps to modify it and by so doing reject the saying—is often very frustrating.

For editors of a book who are reviewing its contents, there are two temptations. On the one hand, the temptation is simply to allow the numbers to speak for themselves and to let readers interpret them as they will, both for meaning and for any practical consequences that may result from that interpretation. In this case, no conclusion to this book would be needed. On the other hand, editors may search diligently for an overall meaning in the book, reaching for applications of the information presented. That search is often elusive.

The conclusion of this book attempts to avoid both these temptations. There does appear, however, to be a common thread running through the chapters, a central theme upon which they focus: the education of deaf children. There are also implications of the data presented here, both for policy and program planning and for future research.

Deaf children, as a group, share certain characteristics that should influence decisions about their educational placement and the type of education they receive. Over the years of its existence, the Annual Survey has shown, in many areas (e.g., achievement levels, speech intelligibility, additional handicaps) a consistency in the characteristics reported about deaf children. It is a consistency that most of the chapters of this book have attempted to describe and analyze. It is also a consistency that strongly suggests trends for the future of the education of deaf children.

Chapter 1 attempts to establish the boundaries of the subject, the number and characteristics of deaf children in the United States, which the other chapters discuss in more detail. It also indicates that the data reported to the Annual Survey are fairly representative of deaf children receiving special educational services in the United States. Although population trends are often difficult to predict, Chapter 2 suggests that, barring unforeseen circumstances, there probably will not be any substantial increase in the number of hearing impaired children and youth entering the educational system in the near future. On the basis of these chapters, the following is a discussion of certain issues concerning the education of deaf children and youth that have been raised in this book.

The first issue concerns that of educational placement. Public residential schools for deaf students, long the bastion of the education of deaf children, are facing a declining student enrollment. It is difficult to envisage what the future of these schools will be, but many of them are in the process of change. Some are implementing innovative programs for students not previously served by these schools. Others are becoming resource centers on deafness and education of deaf children in their states. Some of them appear to be on their way to becoming large day programs. At the same time, hard questions are being asked of the residential schools. Do the outcomes of a residential education justify the costs involved? What are the social and emotional consequences of a residential school education? Do residential schools prepare deaf students for a work world composed largely of hearing individuals?

About the same time that the residential school population was decreasing, the number of hearing impaired students enrolled in schools or classes with hearing students began to increase, a movement strongly encouraged by the enactment of U.S. Public Law 94-142 in 1975. Annual Survey data show that less than 40 percent of the students reported to the survey in 1980 were mainstreamed in some fashion with hearing students; by 1984 that number had risen to almost 50 percent. Mainstreaming of handicapped children and youth is not going to disappear. Some communities have had effective mainstream programs for years, and the educational and political climate at present is such that the movement toward mainstreaming appears to be accelerating.

As Chapter 5 suggests, there are several concerns about the quality of the mainstreaming experience that deaf children and youth may encounter. Will they be mainstreamed in physical education and shop or the lunchroom, but not in reading and mathematics classes? Will they be socially integrated as well as physically integrated, especially in those schools in which very few deaf children are enrolled? Will the local communities, in this period of fiscal austerity, be able to provide the specially qualified teachers and counselors, the interpreters and tutors and notetakers for meeting the needs of many deaf children?

A related issue is that of multiply handicapped students. Chapter 3 indicates that 30 percent of the children and youth reported to the Annual Survey have one or more handicaps in addition to their hearing impairment. The planning and implementation of appropriate educational programs for deaf students—whether within a residential or day setting or within a local school district—must take into account this large number of multiply handicapped deaf students and their diverse needs.

The issue of placement, then, is an extremely important area for further discussion and research. It is an area of concern to both the residential schools and the integrated settings.

Another issue concerns communication. Communication is a critical element in the educational process: communication with teachers and counselors and fellow students, inside and outside the classroom. How will the mainstream programs and schools provide appropriately in this area for the communication needs of deaf students—for those who rely upon some system of signing (Chapter 6) and for those who have poor speech (Chapter 7)? The whole area of communication needs to be carefully examined by those involved in placement decisions and classroom planning. It, too, is an area in which more careful research by knowledgeable professionals is needed.

The communication issue is, of course, much broader than school placement, leading back, as it does, to the central problem of language development. How is language developed in deaf children? Whatever the answer to that question may be, the encouragement of that development— or the lack of such encouragement—has very great effects on all aspects of the child's life and that of the family. It is not only the academic progress of deaf children that is involved in the communication-language issue, but also the development of the whole individual, including the person's social and emotional growth. This aspect of the deaf child's education is one that has not been covered in this book, but it is, obviously, an extremely important area.

Another important issue discussed in these chapters is the academic achievement of deaf children and youth. Chapter 8 on achievement test results of hearing impaired students who took the Stanford Achievement Test reveals that, on the average, deaf students seriously lag behind hearing students, especially in reading and language and to a lesser degree in mathematics. The average achievement levels of deaf students in these academic areas, whether in residential schools or in local school settings, are not encouraging, although the chapter points to the higher achievement scores in 1983 as compared to those in 1974. How will 12- and 13-year-old deaf students not previously mainstreamed be integrated into academic classes with hearing students when they are 4 years behind their age group in reading skills? How does the communication method used by the student within the school setting affect academic achievement?

The achievement of deaf high school students is relevant to their ability to pass minimum competency examinations in those states requiring such examinations (Chapter 9). Achievement also determines whether a student can enter a postsecondary program, either a special program for deaf students or regular classes with hearing students (Chapter 10). Without adequate mastery of basic academic skills, there is little chance deaf students will be successful in either of these areas. Without such success, job opportunities for many deaf students will certainly be limited.

Thus, a third area for ongoing research suggested by this book is the achievement of deaf children and youth. For years research has shown that the average 18-year-old deaf student receiving special education reads at the fourth grade level. That statement has been heard and read over and over again. It is time now to go beyond that statement and discover ways to remedy it.

Much of the previous discussion has centered on educational placement and the roles of the residential schools and mainstream programs in the education of deaf children. Whether this is the most important issue for the education of hearing impaired children is very questionable; it has certainly loomed large in discussions among professionals over the past decade.

There is no more destructive and divisive issue for the education of hearing impaired students than the one over whether the residential or day school or the mainstream setting is the better environment for deaf children and youth. (The "oral/manual" controversy has demonstrated how divisive and unproductive such an issue can be. (It is destructive precisely because it does not take into account the fact that hearing impaired children, like everyone else, are individuals. What "works" with some individuals does not work with other individuals; the classroom setting best suited for one deaf child may not be the best educational environment for another deaf child.

The chapters of this book do not examine individual deaf children. By the very nature of the analyses, these chapters deal in cumulative data or in averages: They do not say *all* deaf children have poor speech intelligibility or poor reading levels, that *all* deaf children use signs. The kind of summary data presented in this book says nothing about individual deaf children or about the educational decisions that should be made regarding these individuals. Rather these data set the context for decision making. They can serve as signposts alerting educators and parents of deaf children and youth to issues needing consideration in any educational decision. The chapters of this book highlight evidence that, it is hoped, will illuminate some of the complexity involved in educating deaf children and youth.

Although it is necessary to stress the individuality of deaf children, it is also important, especially at the policy and planning levels, to consider the interdependence, the interrelatedness of many of the characteristics of these children. For example, two characteristics, degree of hearing loss and age at onset of loss, strongly influence most aspects of the lives of deaf children, especially the three educational issues just discussed in this conclusion: placement in a school program, communication (speech intelligibility and use of a sign system), and achievement level. The consistency with which this interdependence has been shown over the years, in data from both the Annual Survey and other research, has been overwhelming. It is a relationship that educators and public officials at the federal, state, and local levels should take into consideration before setting general policy or establishing programs for deaf children in the United States.

Appendix A
Form, 1982–1983 Annual Survey of Hearing Impaired Children and Youth

PLEASE RETURN THIS
COPY BY APRIL 15 TO:
Center for Assessment
and Demographic Studies
Gallaudet College
7th & Florida Avenue, N.E.
Washington, D.C. 20002

ANNUAL SURVEY OF HEARING IMPAIRED CHILDREN & YOUTH
1982-1983 SCHOOL YEAR

CONFIDENTIAL: Information
which would permit
identification of any
individual or institution
will not be released.

I. This form is for **new** students and for **previously reported** students. FOR FURTHER INSTRUCTIONS SEE BACK OF PAGE.

II. For items marked with an **asterisk (∗)**, please try to complete, as they were left blank in the previous survey

III. **Questions 11 and 12** are new for this year's survey and should be completed for all students.

IV. Please use a **NO. 2 PENCIL** to complete this form, **NOT** ink, ballpoint, or felt-tip pen.

1. STUDENT NAME or SCHOOL-ASSIGNED CODE

NAME OR SCHOOL-ASSIGNED CODE

2A. PRESENT SCHOOL OR AGENCY

School _____

Location _____
(city/state)   NAME

B. (OPTIONAL) Actual location where services are received, if different from 2A:

Name of school _____

3. FOR PREVIOUSLY REPORTED STUDENTS

Is this student still enrolled in the program named in 2A?

○ NO (If "NO," there is no need to complete remainder of this form, but return it to Survey office)

○ YES (If "YES," please complete remainder of this form)

○ TRANSFERRED TO ANOTHER SCHOOL WITHIN OUR SYSTEM (Complete remainder of this form):

NAME OF SCHOOL IN YOUR SYSTEM TO WHICH THIS STUDENT TRANSFERRED

4. DATE OF BIRTH

Previously reported	MO.	Ⓙ Ⓕ Ⓜ Ⓐ Ⓜ Ⓙ Ⓙ Ⓐ Ⓢ Ⓞ Ⓝ Ⓓ
	DAY	⓪①②③ ⓪①②③④⑤⑥⑦⑧⑨
	YR.	④⑤⑥⑦⑧ ⓪①②③④⑤⑥⑦⑧⑨

5. SEX

Previously reported   ○ Male   ○ Female

6. ETHNIC BACKGROUND

PREVIOUS
○ White   ○ Asian/Pacific American
○ Black   ○ Other
○ Hispanic   ○ Cannot Report
○ American Indian ○ Unknown

7. PRESENT TYPE OF EDUCATIONAL PROGRAM (Please answer all items)

A. Does this hearing impaired student receive special education classroom instruction (e.g., residential or day school, full or part-time special ed classes, resource room, itinerant teacher, etc.)?

○ YES   ○ NO

If YES, the student receives this instruction in a setting designed for or with: (MARK ALL THAT APPLY)

○ Hearing impaired students who are not multiply handicapped

○ Multiply handicapped hearing impaired students

○ Students with various handicaps, not all of whom are hearing impaired

○ This student receives instruction at home

B. Does this student receive regular classroom instruction with hearing students, either full or part-time?

○ YES   ○ NO

If YES, indicate services this student receives in support of this regular classroom instruction:

                    ○ (IF NONE, MARK HERE)
○ INTERPRETER   ○ TUTOR OR SPECIAL AIDE
○ NOTE-TAKER   ○ OTHER (specify _____)

C. Is speech and/or auditory training provided on a routine basis to this student?

○ YES   ○ NO

D. Is student in parent/child program?   ○ YES   ○ NO

E. Does student-live at school during week?   ○ YES   ○ NO

8. AGE AT ONSET OF HEARING LOSS

○ At-birth or under 3 years of age

○ 3 years of age or older

○ Unknown

9. CAUSE OF HEARING LOSS (Complete only one section, either A or B or C or D)

A. If onset at birth, what was the probable cause(s)?

○ MATERNAL RUBELLA
○ TRAUMA AT BIRTH
○ HEREDITY
○ PREMATURITY
○ Rh INCOMPATIBILITY
○ OTHER COMPLICATIONS OF PREGNANCY
○ OTHER

B. If onset after birth, what was the probable cause(s)?

○ MENINGITIS
○ HIGH FEVER
○ MUMPS
○ INFECTION
○ MEASLES
○ OTITIS MEDIA
○ TRAUMA
○ OTHER

C. ○ CAUSE CANNOT BE DETERMINED (though attempt was made)

D. ○ DATA NOT AVAILABLE IN STUDENT'S RECORD

10. UNAIDED AUDIOLOGICAL FINDINGS

(If unaided air conduction results are not available in 10B, complete in C the category which describes student's hearing loss without amplification.)

AIR CONDUCTION TEST

A. Previously reported test year:

NEW OR UPDATED TEST YEAR
⑥⑦⑧
⓪①②③④⑤⑥⑦⑧⑨

B. AUDIOLOGICAL RESULTS

PREVIOUSLY REPORTED DATA			NEW STUDENT OR UPDATED		
500	1000	2000	500	1000	2000
RIGHT			RIGHT		
LEFT			LEFT		

C. Fill in the category below which best describes the student's unaided loss.

○ NORMAL LIMITS (Less than 27 dB. ISO)   ○ MODERATELY SEVERE (56-70 dB. ISO)
○ MILD (27-40 dB. ISO)   ○ SEVERE (71-90 dB. ISO)
○ MODERATE (41-55 dB. ISO)   ○ PROFOUND (91 dB plus. ISO)

11. HEARING AID USE

Does this student currently wear a personal hearing aid for at least one hour a day?

○ YES   ○ NO

12. COMMUNICATION

A. Does the student use sign language?

○ YES   ○ NO

B. Does the student's instructional program incorporate the use of sign language?

○ YES   ○ NO

C. Is sign language used by the student's family in the home?

○ YES   ○ NO   ○ Data Not Available

13. ADDITIONAL HANDICAPPING CONDITIONS

Does this student have an educationally significant handicapping condition in addition to hearing impairment?

○ YES   ○ NO

If "YES," mark all educationally significant additional handicaps.

GROUP 1
○ Legal Blindness
○ Uncorrected Visual Problem (but not Legally Blind)
○ Brain Damage or Injury
○ Epilepsy (Convulsive Disorder)
○ Orthopedic (other than cerebral palsy)
○ Cerebral Palsy
○ Heart Disorder
○ Other Health Impaired

GROUP 2
○ Mental Retardation
○ Emotional/Behavioral Problem
○ Specific Learning Disability
(includes perceptual-motor problem)
○ Other

Thank You.

265

INSTRUCTIONS

1. SEE INSTRUCTION SHEET ACCOMPANYING THESE FORMS FOR COMPLETING INDIVIDUAL QUESTIONS.

2. THIS MACHINE-SCANNABLE FORM IS FOR BOTH NEW OR PREVIOUSLY UNREPORTED STUDENTS AND ALSO FOR STUDENTS PREVIOUSLY REPORTED TO THE ANNUAL SURVEY. A few questions require written answers - e.g., name of present school.

3. FOR NEW OR PREVIOUSLY UNREPORTED STUDENTS: Please complete all questions on this form.

4. FOR PREVIOUSLY REPORTED STUDENTS: Note that all previously reported information on this student is printed out in each section.

   A. Update old information or correct previously reported wrong information simply by filling in the correct circle: e.g., if "white" is the previously reported wrong ethnic info, fill in the circle for the correct info (e.g., "black").

   B. If you wish to add information to previously reported info which is correct, fill in the circle for the new info and also mark the circle(s) for the previously reported correct information. E.g., if you wish to add "epilepsy" to the previously reported "heart disorder" in the additional handicaps section, fill in the circles for BOTH "epilepsy" and "heart disorder."

   C. If the printed info on an item is up-to-date and correct, no response is needed on your part.

5. QUESTIONS 11 and 12 ARE NEW QUESTIONS FOR THIS YEAR'S SURVEY. These questions should be completed for all students.

USE A NO. 2 PENCIL ONLY		EXAMPLE: Year is 1981
• DO NOT USE INK, BALLPOINT OR FELT TIP PENS • MAKE CLEAN ERASURES		YEAR
• MAKE NO STRAY MARKS ON THE ANSWER SHEET • MARK IN DESIGNATED AREAS ONLY		8 ⓪①②③④⑤⑥⑦●⑨
• CORRECT MARKS ●●●●● • INCORRECT MARKS ○⊙⊙⊘⊗		1 ⓪●②③④⑤⑥⑦⑧⑨

PLEASE DO NOT FOLD OR BEND THIS FORM.
THANK YOU.

FOR OFFICE USE ONLY — NEW OR CURRENT: RIGHT EAR / LEFT EAR, FREQUENCY 500, FREQUENCY 1000, FREQUENCY 2000; SCHOOL TO WHICH STUDENT TRANSFERRED

Appendix B
Selected Readings: Center for
Assessment and Demographic Studies

The following selected readings, written mainly by staff of the Center for Assessment and Demographic Studies, have been grouped into the major categories discussed in this book: demographics, communication, and achievement (plus an *other* category). The list is not an exhaustive one and obviously does not include many excellent articles by other educators and researchers in the field of hearing impairment.

DEMOGRAPHICS

Gentile, A., and McCarthy, B. (1973). *Additional handicapping conditions among hearing impaired students—United States: 1971–72* (Series D, No. 14). Washington, DC: Gallaudet College, Office of Demographic Studies.

Gentile, A., and Rambin, J. (1973). *Reported causes of hearing loss for hearing impaired students—United States: 1970–71* (Series D, No. 12). Washington, DC: Gallaudet College, Office of Demographic Studies.

Jensema, C. (1974). The distribution of hearing loss among students in special educational programs for the hearing impaired. *Asha, 16,* 682–685.

Jensema, C. (1974). Post-rubella children in special educational programs for the hearing impaired. *Volta Review, 76,* 466–473.

Jensema, C. (1975). Children in educational programs for the hearing impaired whose impairment was caused by mumps. *Journal of Speech and Hearing Disorders, 40,* 164–169.

Jensema, C., and Mullins, J. (1974). Onset, cause, and additional handicaps in hearing impaired children. *American Annals of the Deaf, 119,* 701–705.

Jensema, C., and Trybus, R. (1975). *Reported emotional/behavioral problems among hearing impaired children in special educational programs: United States, 1972–73* (Series R, No. 1). Washington, DC: Gallaudet College, Office of Demographic Studies.

Karchmer, M. (1983). Hearing-impaired students and their education: Population perspectives. In W. Northcott (Ed.), *Introduction to oral interpreting, principles and practices* (pp. 41–59). Baltimore: University Park Press.

Karchmer, M. (1984). Demographics and deaf adolescence. In G. Anderson and D. Watson (Eds.), *Proceedings of the National Conference on the Habilitation and Rehabilitation of Deaf Adolescents* (pp. 28–47). Washington, DC: The National Academy of Gallaudet College.

Karchmer, M. (1985). A demographic perspective. In E. Cherow, R. Trybus, and N. Matkin (Eds.), *Hearing impaired children and youth with developmental disabilities* (pp. 36–56). Washington, DC: Gallaudet College Press.

Karchmer, M., Milone, M., and Wolk, S. (1979). Educational significance of hearing loss at three levels of severity. *American Annals of the Deaf, 124,* 97–109.

Karchmer, M., and Petersen, L. (1980). *Commuter students at residential schools for the deaf* (Series R, No. 7). Washington, DC: Gallaudet College, Office of Demographic Studies.

Karchmer, M., Petersen, L., Allen, T., and Osborn, T. (1981). *Highlights of the Canadian Survey of Hearing Impaired Children and Youth, Spring 1979* (Series R, No. 8). Washington, DC: Gallaudet College, Office of Demographic Studies.

Karchmer, M., Petersen, L., Allen, T., and Quaynor, A. (1982). Hearing impaired children and youth in Canada: Student characteristics in relation to manual communication patterns in four special education settings. *American Annals of the Deaf, 127,* 89–104.

Karchmer, M., Rawlings, B., Trybus, R., Wolk, S., and Milone, M. (1979). *Educationally significant characteristics of hearing impaired students in Texas, 1977–78* (Series C, No. 4). Washington, DC: Gallaudet College, Office of Demographic Studies.

Karchmer, M., and Trybus, R. (1977). *Who are the deaf children in "mainstream" programs?* (Series R, No. 4). Washington, DC: Gallaudet College, Office of Demographic Studies.

Karchmer, M., and Wolk, S. (1980). *Louisiana State Survey of Hearing Impaired and Deaf-Blind Children and Youth, 1978–79.* Washington, DC: Gallaudet College, Office of Demographic Studies.

Murphy, N. (1972). *Characteristics of hearing impaired students under six years of age—United States: 1969–70* (Series D, No. 7). Washington, DC: Gallaudet College, Office of Demographic Studies.

Murphy, N., and Trybus, R. (1975). Hearing impaired school leavers. *American Annals of the Deaf, 120,* 86–91.

Rawlings, B. (1970). *Summary of selected characteristics of hearing impaired students—United States: 1969–70* (Series D, No. 5). Washington, DC: Gallaudet College, Office of Demographic Studies.

Rawlings, B. (1973). *Characteristics of hearing impaired students by hearing status—United States: 1970–71* (Series D, No. 10). Washington, DC: Gallaudet College, Office of Demographic Studies.

Rawlings, B., and Gentile, A. (1970). *Additional handicapping conditions, age at onset of hearing loss, and other characteristics of hearing impaired students—United States: 1968–69* (Series D, No. 3). Washington, DC: Gallaudet College, Office of Demographic Studies.

Rawlings, B., and Jensema, C. (1977). *Two studies of the families of hearing impaired children* (Series R, No. 5). Washington, DC: Gallaudet College, Office of Demographic studies.

Rawlings, B., and Trybus, R. (1978). Personnel, facilities, and services available in schools and classes for hearing impaired children in the United States. *American Annals of the Deaf, 123,* 99–114.

Ries, P., Bateman, D., and Schildroth, A. (1975). *Ethnic background in relation to other characteristics of hearing impaired students in the United States* (Series D, No. 15). Washington, DC: Gallaudet College, Office of Demographic Studies.

Ries, P., and Voneiff, P. (1974). Demographic profile of hearing impaired students. *Deafness Annual, 4,* 17–42.

Rubella and non-rubella deaf students by region and by state. (1980). In *Deafness and rubella: Entrants in the 60's, adults in the 80's* (Highlights of a national conference on Eisenhower College Campus, Rochester Institute of Technology), Rochester, NY: Rochester Institute of Technology.

Schildroth, A. (1980). Public residential schools for deaf students in the United States, 1970–1978. *American Annals of the Deaf, 125,* 80–91.

Schildroth, A. (in press). Hearing impaired children under 6: 1977 and 1984. *American Annals of the Deaf.*

Spragins, A., Karchmer, M., and Schildroth, A. (1981). Profile of psychological service providers to hearing impaired students. *American Annals of the Deaf, 126,* 94–105.

Trybus, R. (1975). Socioeconomic characteristics of hearing impaired students in special educational programs. In C. Williams (Ed.), *Proceedings of the First Gallaudet Symposium on Research in Deafness: The Role of Research and the Cultural and Social Orientation of the Deaf* (pp. 181–186). Washington, DC: Gallaudet College Press.

Trybus, R. (1976). National baseline data for education of the deaf: Problems and prospects. *Proceedings of the Forty-Eighth Meeting of the Conference of Executives of American Schools for the Deaf, Inc.* (pp. 53–55). Fulton, MO: Missouri School for the Deaf.

Trybus, R., Karchmer, M., Kerstetter, P., and Hicks, W. (1980). The demographics of deafness resulting from maternal rubella. *American Annals of the Deaf, 125,* 977–984.

Trybus, R., Rawlings, B., and Johnson, R. (1978). *Texas State Survey of Hearing Impaired Children and Youth: A new approach to statewide planning, monitoring, and evaluation of special education programming.* Washington, DC: Gallaudet College, Office of Demographic Studies.

Voneiff, P. (1971). *Audiological examinations of hearing impaired students—United States: 1969–70* (Series D, No. 6). Washington, DC: Gallaudet College, Office of Demographic Studies.

Voneiff, P., and Gentile, A. (1970). *Type and size of educational programs attended by hearing impaired students—United States: 1968–69* (Series D, No. 4). Washington, DC: Gallaudet College, Office of Demographic Studies.

White, C., Karchmer, M., Armstrong, D., and Bezozo, C. (1983). Current trends in high school graduation and college enrollment of hearing-impaired students attending residential schools for the deaf. *American Annals of the Deaf, 128,* 125–131.

Wolk, S., Karchmer, M., and Schildroth, A. (1982). *Patterns of academic and nonacademic integration among hearing impaired students in special education* (Series R, No. 9). Washington, DC: Gallaudet College, Center for Assessment and Demographic Studies.

COMMUNICATION

Jensema, C. (1977). Classroom communication and achievement test scores: A preliminary report. In C. Williams (Ed.), *Proceedings of the Third Gallaudet Symposium on Research in Deafness: Educational Development Research Problems.* Washington, DC: Gallaudet College Press.

Jensema, C., Karchmer, M., and Trybus, R. (1978). *The rated speech intelligibility of hearing impaired children: Basic relationships and a detailed analysis* (Series R, No. 6). Washington, DC: Gallaudet College, Office of Demographic Studies.

Jensema, C., and Trybus, R. (1978). *Communication patterns and educational achievement of hearing impaired students* (Series T, No. 2). Washington, DC: Gallaudet College, Office of Demographic Studies.

Jordan, I.K., Gustason, G., and Rosen, R. (1976). Current communication trends at programs for the deaf. *American Annals of the Deaf, 121,* 527–532.

Jordan, I.K., Gustason, G., and Rosen, R. (1979). An update on communication trends at programs for the deaf. *American Annals of the Deaf, 124,* 350–357.

Karchmer, M., Cairns, G., and Butterfield, E. (1977). Longitudinal observations of deaf and hearing infants' vocalizations. In C. Williams (Ed.), *Proceedings of the Third Gallaudet Symposium on Research in Deafness: Educational Development Research Problems.* Washington, DC: Gallaudet College Press.

Woodward, J., Allen, T., and Schildroth, A. (1985). Teachers and deaf students: An ethnography of classroom communication. In S. Delancy and R. Tomlin (Eds.), *Proceedings of the First Pacific Coast Conference on Linguistics.* Eugene, OR: University of Oregon Press.

ACHIEVEMENT

Allen, T. (1984). *Out-of-level testing with the Stanford Achievement Test (7th edition): A procedure for assigning students to the correct battery level.* Paper presented at the annual meeting of the American Educational Research Association, New Orleans, LA.

Allen, T. (1984). Test response variations between hearing-impaired and hearing students. *Journal of Special Education, 18,* 119–129.

Allen, T. (1986). *Understanding the scores: Hearing-impaired students and the Stanford Achievement Test (7th Edition).* Washington, DC: Gallaudet College Press.

Allen, T., and Karchmer, M. (1981). Influences on academic achievement of hearing impaired students born during the 1963–1965 rubella epidemic. *Directions, 2,* 40–54.

Allen, T., and Osborn, T. (1984). Academic integration of hearing-impaired students: Demographic, handicapping, and achievement factors. *American Annals of the Deaf, 129,* 100–113.

Allen, T., White, C., and Karchmer, M. (1983). Issues in the development of a special edition for hearing impaired students of the seventh edition of the Stanford Achievement Test. *American Annals of the Deaf, 128,* 34–39.

Buchanan, C., Ries, P., Sepielli, P., and Trybus, R. (1973). *Further studies in achievement testing, hearing impaired students—United States: Spring 1971* (Series D, No. 13). Washington, DC: Gallaudet College, Office of Demographic Studies.

DiFrancesca, S. (1972). *Academic achievement test results of a national testing program for hearing impaired students—United States: Spring 1971* (Series D, No.

9). Washington, DC: Gallaudet College, Office of Demographic Studies.

DiFrancesca, S., and Carey, S. (1972). *Item analysis of an achievement testing program for hearing impaired students—United States: Spring 1971* (Series D, No. 8). Washington, DC: Gallaudet College, Office of Demographic Studies.

DiFrancesca, S., Trybus, R., and Buchanan, C. (1973). *Studies in achievement testing, hearing impaired students—United States: Spring 1971* (Series D, No. 11). Washington, DC: Gallaudet College, Office of Demographic Studies.

Gentile, A., and DiFrancesca, S. (1969). *Academic achievement test performance of hearing impaired students—United States: Spring 1969* (Series D, No. 1). Washington, DC: Gallaudet College, Office of Demographic Studies.

Gentile, A., and DiFrancesca, S. (1970). *Item analysis of academic achievement tests, hearing impaired students—United States: Spring 1969* (Series D, No. 2). Washington, DC: Gallaudet College, Office of Demographic Studies.

Hoemann, H., Andrews, C., Florian, V., Hoemann, S., and Jensema, C. (1976). The spelling proficiency of deaf children. *American Annals of the Deaf, 121,* 489–493.

Jensema, C. (1975). A note on the achievement test scores of multiply handicapped hearing impaired children. *American Annals of the Deaf, 120,* 37–39.

Jensema, C. (1975). A note on the educational achievement of Oral Deaf Adult Section members. *Volta Review, 77,* 135–137.

Jensema, C. (1975). *The relationship between academic achievement and the demographic characteristics of hearing impaired children and youth* (Series R, No. 2). Washington, DC: Gallaudet College, Office of Demographic Studies.

Jensema, C. (1978). A comment on measurement error in achievement tests for the hearing impaired. *American Annals of the Deaf, 123,* 496–499.

Trybus, R. (1978). What the Stanford Achievement Test has to say about the reading abilities of deaf children. In H. Reynolds and C. Williams (Eds.), *Proceedings of the Gallaudet Conference on Reading in Relation to Deafness* (pp. 213–221). Washington, DC: Gallaudet College Press.

Trybus, R., and Jensema, C. (1975). The development, use, and interpretation of the 1973 Stanford Achievement Test, Special Edition for Hearing Impaired Students. *Report of the Proceedings of the Forty-Seventh Meeting of the Convention of American Instructors of the Deaf* (pp. 73–78). Washington, DC: U.S. Government Printing Office.

Trybus, R., and Karchmer, M. (1977). School achievement scores of hearing impaired children: National data on achievement status and growth patterns. *American Annals of the Deaf Directory of Programs and Services, 122,* 62–69.

Wilson, K., Karchmer, M., and Jensema, C. (1978). Literal vs. inferential item analysis of reading achievement in hearing impaired students. In H. Reynolds and C. Williams (Eds.), *Proceedings of the Gallaudet Conference on Reading in Relation to Deafness* (pp. 154–170). Washington, DC: Gallaudet College Press.

Wolk, S., and Allen, T. (1984). A 5-year follow-up of reading comprehension achievement of hearing-impaired students in special education programs. *Journal of Special Education, 18,* 161–176.

Wolk, S., and Schildroth, A. (1984). Consistency of an associational strategy used by hearing-impaired students. *Journal of Research in Reading, 7,* 135–142.

Wolk, S., and Schildroth, A. (1985). A longitudinal study of deaf students' use of an associational strategy on a reading comprehension test. *Journal of Research in Reading, 8,* 82–93.

OTHER

Anderson, R., and Sisco, F. (1977). *Standardization of the WISC-R performance scale for deaf children* (Series T, No. 1). Washington, DC: Gallaudet College, Office of Demographic Studies.

Belmont, J., and Karchmer, M. (1976). Instructed rehearsal strategies' influence on deaf memory processing. *Journal of Speech and Hearing Research, 19,* 36–47.

Belmont, J., and Karchmer, M. (1978). Deaf people's memory: There are problems testing special populations. In M. Gruneberg, P. Morris, and R. Sykes (Eds.), *Practical aspects of memory* (pp. 581–588). London: Academic Press.

Belmont, J., Karchmer, M., and Bourg, J. (1983). Structural influences on deaf and hearing children's recall of temporal/spatial incongruent letter strings. *Educational Psychology, 3,* 261–276.

Goulder, T., and Trybus, R. (1977). *The classroom behavior of emotionally disturbed hearing impaired children* (Series R, No. 3). Washington, DC: Gallaudet College, Office of Demographic Studies.

Jensema, C. (1974). An application of latent trait mental test theory. *British Journal of Mathematical and Statistical Psychology, 27,* 29–48.

Jensema, C. (1974). The validity of Bayesian tailored testing. *Educational and Psychological Measurement, 34,* 757–766.

Jensema, C. (1975). Reliability of the 16PF Form E for hearing impaired college students. *Journal of Rehabilitation of the Deaf, 8,* 14–18.

Jensema, C. (1975). A statistical investigation of the 16PF Form E as applied to hearing impaired college students. *Journal of Rehabilitation of the Deaf, 9,* 21–29.

Jensema, C. (1976). Bayesian tailored testing and influence of item bank characteristics. In *Proceedings of the First Conference on Computerized Adaptive Testing*. Washington, DC: U.S. Civil Commission, Personnel Research and Development Center.

Jensema, C. (1977). Three characteristics of teachers of the deaf who are hearing impaired. *American Annals of the Deaf, 122,* 307–309.

Karchmer, M., and Belmont, J. (1976). *On assessing and improving deaf performance in the cognitive laboratory.* Paper presented at the American Speech and Hearing Association meeting, Houston, TX.

Karchmer, M., and Kirwin, L. (1977). *Usage of hearing aids by hearing impaired children in the United States* (Series S, No. 2). Washington, DC: Gallaudet College, Office of Demographic Studies.

Rawlings, B. (1977). The 1975 survey of postsecondary programs for deaf students. In C. Williams (Ed.), *Proceedings of the Third Gallaudet Symposium on Research in Deafness: Educational Development Research Problems.* Washington, DC: Gallaudet College Press.

Rawlings, B., Karchmer, M., DeCaro, J., and Eggleston-Dodd, J. (Eds.). (1986). *College and career programs for deaf students.* Washington, DC: Gallaudet College.

Rawlings, B., Karchmer, M., King, S., and Brown, S. (1985). *Gallaudet College Alumni Survey, 1984* (Gallaudet Research Institute Monograph No. 2). Washington, DC: Gallaudet College, Center for Assessment and Demographic Studies.

Rawlings, B., and Rubin, F. (1978). *A survey of media equipment available in special educational programs for hearing impaired students, 1977–78* (Series C, No. 3). Washington, DC: Gallaudet College, Office of Demographic Studies.

Rawlings, B., and Trybus, R. (1976). Update on postsecondary programs for hearing impaired students. *American Annals of the Deaf, 121,* 541–546.

Sachs, B., Koch, H., Trybus, R., and Falberg, R. (1974). Current developments in the psychological evaluation of deaf individuals. *Journal of Rehabilitation of the Deaf, 8,* 132–133.

Schildroth, A. (1976). The relationship of nonverbal intelligence test scores to selected characteristics of hearing impaired students. In C. Williams (Ed.), *Proceedings of the Third Gallaudet Symposium on Research in Deafness: Educational Development Research Problems.* Washington, DC: Gallaudet College Press.

Summers, H., Rubin, F., and Rawlings, B. (1977). *Selected statistics on deaf and hearing impaired students: A source book for developers and disseminators of instructional materials.* Washington, DC: Gallaudet College, Pre-College Programs.

Trybus, R. (1973). Personality assessment of entering hearing impaired college students in using the 16PF, Form E. *Journal of Rehabilitation of the Deaf, 6,* 34–40.

Trybus, R., and Hewitt, C. (1972). The mini-mult in a nonpsychiatric population. *Journal of Clinical Psychology, 28,* 371.

Trybus, R., and Murphy, N. (1974). Utilization of the data bank of the Annual Survey of Hearing Impaired Children and Youth for rehabilitation planning. *Journal of Rehabilitation of the Deaf, 8,* 98–104.

Wolff, A. (1985). Cognitive strategies and processes. In D. Martin (Ed.), *Cognition, education, and deafness: Directions for research and instruction* (pp. 79–81). Washington, DC: Gallaudet College Press.

Wolff, A. (1986, August). *Neurophysiological differences among deaf children with different etiologies of deafness.* Paper submitted to the meeting of the American Psychological Association, Washington, DC.

Wolff, A. (1986, June). *Neurophysiological differences between deaf and hearing children.* Paper to be presented at the meeting of the International Neuropsychological Society, Veldhoven, The Netherlands.

Author Index

A

Ahuja, E. M., 11
Akers-Adams, S., 221
Allen, T., 61, 114, 115, 126, 130,
    141, 142, 161, 170, 193
Anderson, R., 93
Andrews, F. M., 128n
Armstrong, D., 89, 233–234, 235,
    240
Auxter, D., 76

B

Band, J. D., 38
Baud, H., 97
Beckham, J., 215, 217, 219, 220,
    221, 223
Bell, A. G., 107
Belmont, J. M., 76
Bennett, R. E., 221
Bergstrom, L., 39
Bersoff, D., 110
Bezozo, C., 89, 235, 240
Bigman, S., 231
Birch, J., 234
Biser, J., 235
Bishop, M., 113
Boughman, J. A., 36
Bourg, J. W., 76
Brentari, D., 141, 155
Brickell, H., 220, 226
Brill, R., 91
Broome, C. V., 38
Brown, S. C., 38
Budetti, P. P., 77
Burke, J., 101
Bushnaq, S., 231

C

Calvert, D. R., 36
Chadwick, O., 58
Chess, S., 76
Citron, C. H., 215, 223
Cochi, S. L., 38
Conneally, P. M., 38
Conrad, R., 62, 76, 140, 141
Craig, W., 91
Crammatte, A., 231, 248

D

Danielson, L. C., 228
Davis, H., 11, 11n, 42
DeCaro, J., 235
Delgado, G., 235
Delk, M. T., 14
Denhoff, E., 58
Dolman, G., 100
Dunn, L., 109

E

Edelstein, T. J., 77
Engel, A., 9
Evans, A., 83

F

Fenton, K. S., 215, 226
Fernandez, P., 76
Frankel, M., 233
Fraser, D. W., 38
Freeman, L., 140
Frisina, D., 90

G

Gaffney, R., 140
Gardner, E. F., 161
Gardner, H., 111–112
Geers, A., 140
Geffner, D., 140
Gentile, A., 5, 52, 61, 63, 87
Gerald, D., 97
Goetsch, E. A., 76
Gordon, J., 106–107
Gordon, L. K., 38
Grant, W., 237, 239, 250
Gregg, N. M., 36
Grisé, P. J., 221
Gruenewald, L., 75
Gustason, G., 125

H

Haase, K. W., 5
Halpin, G., 221
Harvey, J., 109–110
Hicks, W., 62
Hightower, A. W., 38
Hinman, A. R., 38, 50
Holden, R. H., 58
Horstmann, D. M., 39
Howarth, J., 140
Huber, P., 11

J

Jacobson, J. W., 60
Janicki, M. P., 60
Jenne, W., 231
Jensema, C, 38, 39, 74, 76, 125,
     129, 130, 136, 140, 141, 144
Jensema, C. K., 77
John, J., 140
Johnson, D., 101
Johnson, R., 101
Jordan, I. K., 125
Jungjohan, B., 234, 255

K

Kanner, L., 106

Karchmer, M. A., 59, 61, 62, 63,
     65, 76, 89, 90, 101, 112,
     114, 115, 129, 130, 136, 137,
     140, 141, 144, 145, 161, 168,
     235, 240
Karlsen, B., 161
Kaskowitz, D., 20
Kauffman, J., 106
Kaufman, N., 100
Kennedy, J., 144
Kenyon, N., 36
Kerstetter, P. P., 62, 240
Kessner, D. M., 39
Kindred, E., 113
Kluwin, T. N., 101
Knapp, W., 107

L

Lepow, M. L., 38
Levitt, H., 140
Lezak, M. D., 58
Libbey, S., 112, 113, 117
Lim, D. J., 39
Lindheim, E., 215
Ling, D., 139
Liscio, M. A., 234
Lovell, N. B., 217, 221, 225

M

MacDougall, J. C., 76
Madden, R., 161
Maruyama, G., 101
Masland, R. L., 36
Massey, J. T., 9
Maurer, K., 9
McCarthy, B., 61, 63, 87
McCarthy, M. M., 215, 216, 217,
     221, 223–224
McClung, M. S., 215
McDaniel, E., 76
McDowell, A., 9
McEldowney, D., 39
McGeough, C., 234, 255
McInnes, J., 77
McManus, P., 77
Meadow, K., 64, 76
Merwin, J. C., 161

Messenger, R. C., 128n
Metz, D., 140
Milone, M. N., 130, 140, 145, 161
Mohanakumar, T., 36
Monsen, R., 140
Moog, J., 140
Moores, D., 59, 60, 62, 76, 101, 105, 106, 107, 108, 121, 139, 232
Morrissey, P. A., 221, 222

N

Naiman, D., 75
Nance, W. E., 35, 36, 38
Noel, M., 101
Norwood, C., 20
Noyes, J., 83

O

Olsen, K. R., 210, 217, 221, 228
Olson, L., 209
Osborn, T., 114, 115, 141, 161

P

Palmer, P., 77
Paparella, M. M., 38
Paquin, M. M., 136
Patterson, D., 97
Petersen, L. M., 61, 63, 90, 130
Petersen, R., 233
Phillips, S., 231
Pipho, C., 208, 209
Popham, W. J., 215
Pronovost, W., 112, 113, 117
Pugh, G., 142

Q

Quaynor, A., 61, 63, 130
Quigley, S., 90, 231

R

Ragosta, M., 221

Rambin, J. B., 52
Rawlings, B., 28, 61, 63, 87, 235
Rehnquist, J., 111
Reynolds, M., 234
Riegel, R. P., 217, 221, 225
Ries, P. W., 1n, 5, 13, 45, 61
Roberts, J., 11
Rose, S. P., 38
Rosen, R., 125
Rudman, H. C., 161
Rush, M. L., 76
Rutter, M., 58

S

Salem, J., 91
Samuelson, J. S., 38
Schein, J., 5, 13, 14, 42, 231
Schiavetti, N., 140
Schildroth, A. N., 59, 85, 86, 91, 93, 101, 112, 113, 114, 115, 126, 129, 145
Schlech, W. F., 38
Schneidmiller, K., 233–34, 240
Schrier, A. J., 43
Schroeder, J., 75
Shaver, K. A., 36
Shroyer, C., 76
Siantz, J., 109–110
Silverman, S. R., 11
Singer, J. T., 43
Sitler, R., 140
Smith, C., 140
Smith, J. M., 43
Smith-Davis, J., 101
Snyder, T., 237, 239, 250
Solomon, G., 58
Sonnenberg, W., 233
Spragins, A. B., 59, 77, 101
Stearns, M. S., 20
Stein, L., 77
Stevens, G., 93
Stewart, L., 59
Stricker, L. J., 221
Stuckless, E. R., 38, 50, 233, 235, 244
Stuckless, R., 93
Sweeney, A., 35

T

Terman, L., 106
Thomas, J., 234, 254
Tomberlin, J., 43
Tractenberg, P. L., 215, 216, 217,
    218, 219, 220, 221, 223, 224,
    225, 226–227
Treffry, J., 77
Trybus, R., 62, 76, 114, 115, 125,
    129, 130, 136, 137, 140, 141,
    144, 161, 168, 235

V

Veltman, E., 110
Vernon, M., 38, 52, 59, 63, 68
Voneiff, P., 45

W

Ward, J. I., 38
Watson, P., 210, 222
Weinberg, B., 77
White, C., 89, 235, 240
Williams, P. 89
Wolff, A. B., 38
Wolk, S., 112, 113, 114, 115, 129,
    130, 140, 141, 145, 154, 161
Woodward, J., 126
Wulfsberg, R., 233

Y

Yoder, D., 75

Subject Index

Italic page numbers refer to figures and tables.

A

Academic achievement patterns, hearing impaired students, 161–168, 203–205, 261–262
 conversion table validity, 189–193, *191*
 mathematics, 161–164, *163,* 166–7, *168, 172, 181,* 182, *183, 188*
 1974 and 1983 test scores comparison, 161–165, *163, 170, 172*
 additional handicap, 178
 age at hearing loss onset, 178
 cause of deafness, 178
 degree of hearing loss, 177–178
 demographic variables, 175–179, *176–177*
 group, 175
 sex, 175
 reading comprehension, 161–164, *163, 164, 167, 172, 180, 181, 183, 188*
 statistical analysis, 179–182
 biasing factors, 182, *183*
 subgroups, 1983 norming project, 193–203
 additional handicap, 201–203, *203, 204*
 degree of hearing loss, *201,* 201, *202*
 education program type, 197, *197, 198*
 ethnic group, 197–201, *199, 200*
 region of the country, 194–197,

 195, 196
 test level assignment, 183–189, *186, 187*
 test scores gains, 169, 193
 school representation, *174*
 stratification variables, *170, 172*
Academic degrees, deaf students, 251–254, *253*
Academic integration, as variable in speech intelligibility, 151–152, *152,* 154, 159
Additional handicapping conditions (AHC), 55–56, *64,* 261
 age distribution, 70–71, *70, 71, 72, 73*
 comparison with general population, 66
 definition, 56
 disability groupings, 65
 ethnic background relationship, 67
 geographical distribution, 71–74
 prevalence, 62, *63,* 64, *65*
 residential school enrollment, 93–96, *94, 95*
 future trends, 100–101
 sex distribution, 68–69, *69*
 use on Annual Survey, 56, *57,* 58–59
 variables of speech intelligibility, *145, 146, 147,* 152–153, *153,* 154, 156–157, 159
Age, as factor in sign usage, 128–130, *129, 132*
Age distribution, in hearing loss

279

onset, 40–41, *42,* 45–46
academic achievement
     relationship, 178
mainstreaming placement
     relationship, 114
with additional handicapping
     condition, 70–71, *70, 71,*
     72, 73
Age distribution in residential
     schools, 87–89, *89*
future trends, 98–99
geographical statistics, 88–89, *89*
Alabama High School Graduation
     Examination, 221–222
American Sign Language, 126
Annual Census. See *Annual Survey*
     of Hearing Impaired Children
     and Youth.
Annual Survey of Hearing
     Impaired Children and
     Youth, xi, xii, xiii, xiv, 15,
     34–36, 55, 116–117, 265–266
additional handicapping
     condition factor, 56
data reliability, 78
definition and use, 56, *57,*
     58–59
incidence rates, 59, 61, *64, 65,*
     93
data usefulness, 15–18, 259
etiological reporting trends,
     46–47
funding, xiv
growth, xiv
handicap categories, 43–46, *44*
hearing loss cause questions,
     34–35
profoundly hearing impaired
     overrepresentation, 27–28
residential school enrollment
     patterns, 84, 102
sign use data, 125, 126–127, *127*
special education estimates, 23–24
speech intelligibility data, 142
survey questions, 34

B

Bell, Alexander Graham, influence
     on residential schools, 107
Better-ear averages, equation
     attempts, 10–11
as measurement factor, 15–16,
     17, 117
Bilateral hearing loss, as

distinguished from unilateral
     hearing loss, 5, 7, *7*
incidence, 28–29
Black population, handicap
     overrepresentation, 67–68,
     75, 78
Brain damage or injury, as
     additional handicapping
     condition, *57,* 58
age distribution, *72*
Bureau of Education for the
     Handicapped of the Office
     of Education, xiii–xiv

C

Career opportunities, deaf students,
     248–251, *249, 250, 251*
Census statistics, deaf population,
     xiii
Center for Assessment and
     Demographic Studies, xiii,
     xiv, 126, 140
Annual Survey, xiv
special education estimates, 23–24
special projects, xv
speech intelligibility norming
     project, 142
Cerebral palsy, as additional
     handicapping condition, *57*
age distribution, *72*
Certification, in minimum
     competency testing (MCT)
     programs, 222–223
Classroom instruction, as variable
     in sign usage, 130–131, *132,*
     135, 136–137
Clerc, Laurent, 106
Cognitive-behavioral handicaps,
     definition, 43, 45, 64
prevalence, 66
Committee on the Conservation of
     Hearing Loss, 11
Communication method, as
     variable of speech
     intelligibility, 141, *145, 146,*
     147, *147, 148,* 148–151, *149,*
     150, 154, 159, 259
Conference of Executives of
     American Schools for the
     Deaf, xiii, 244
Congenital cytomegalovirus, 53
Congenital rubella syndrome
     (CRS), as hearing loss cause,
     35, 36, 49

geographical distribution, 40
incidence decrease, 49-50

D

Data collection, deaf population,
    xi, 2-3
Deaf students, postsecondary
    educational opportunities,
    231-234, 254-255
attendance statistics, 233
program types, 234-236
    career areas, 248-251, *249,
        250, 251*
    degrees, 251-254, *253*
    enrollment, 237-240, *239*
    geographical distribution, 237,
        238
    growth, 236-237, *236*
    program size, 242-243, *243,
        255*
    specialized services, 243-248,
        246, 254
    student characteristics,
        240-242, *241*
Degree of hearing loss, as factor in
    sign use, 129-130, *132, 135*
as factor in speech intelligibility,
    145, 146-147, *146, 147,*
    154, 159
*Diagnostic and Statistical Manual of
    Mental Disorders* (DSM III),
    59

E

Education for All Handicapped
    Children Act. See *U.S.
    Public Law 94-142.*
Educational malpractice litigation,
    219
Educational placement, 260. See
    also *Residential schools for
    deaf students.*
Emotional or behavioral problem,
    as additional handicapping
    condition, *57,* 59, 62, 64, 68
age distribution, *73*
geographic distribution, 73
prevalence, 76-77
Epilepsy, as additional
    handicapping condition, *57,*
    58
age distribution, *72*
Ethnic background, handicap
    relationship, 67

placement factor, 118-119
in residential schools, 91-92, *91,*
    95-96
future trends, 99-100
Ethnic background, as variable of
    speech intelligibility, *145,*
    146, 147, 151, 154, 156-157,
    159
Ethnic status, as factor in sign use,
    130, *132, 135,* 136
Etiology of hearing loss, trends, 33,
    46-50
demographic aspects, 40-42

F

Fourteenth Amendment, in relation
    to minimum competency
    testing programs, 215

G

Gallaudet College, educational
    opportunities, 231, 234, 236,
    237, 254
support of Annual Survey of
    Hearing Impaired Children
    and Youth, xii
Gallaudet Hearing Scale, 4-5, *5,*
    7-8, 10
comparison with National Health
    and Nutrition Examination
    Survey results, 11-15, *12*
Geographical distribution, hearing
    impaired children, 40-41
additional handicapping
    condition, 71-74

H

Handicapped education programs,
    historical perspective,
    105-107
Handicapping condition, percentage
    of total U.S. school
    enrollment, *67.* See also
    *Additional handicapping
    conditions.*
Health Examination Survey. See
    *National Health and
    Nutrition Examination
    Survey.*
Health impairment, as additional
    handicapping condition, *57,*
    61
age distribution, *73*
Hearing impaired students,

implementation of state
minimum competency testing
(MCT) programs, 220
competencies to be measured,
220–221
failure consequences, 226–227
measurement methods, 221–223
minimums levels, 225
minimums to be set, 224–225
program standards, 225–226
timing of testing, 223–224
Hearing impaired youth aged 6–17
years in the U.S., number
and percent distribution, 6,
7, 8–9, 16, 17, 25–28, 26,
29–30
males and blacks
overrepresentation, 26, 27,
28
sampling errors, 8, 14–15, 18
Hearing impairment, term use, 1
Hearing impairments, causes and
distribution, 33, 36–40, 37,
39, 48, 51
additional handicapping
conditions, 43–46, 44,
66–67
Annual Survey of Hearing
Impaired Children and
Youth questions, 34
Hearing loss, unknown cause,
34–35, 39
Hearing loss terminology, 1–2
defining criteria, 2–3
Heart disorder, as additional
handicapping condition, 57
age distribution, 73
Hemophilus influenzae type B,
vaccine, 38, 50, 52
Heredity, as cause of hearing loss,
35, 36, 38, 39, 49, 52
additional handicapping
conditions, 44, 45
degree of hearing loss, 43
geographical distribution, 40, 41
incidence increase, 47, 50

I

Individualized education plan
(IEP), 208, 222–224, 228

J

Judicial rulings, handicapped

education issues, 216–217,
219, 223–224

K

Knapp Institute, 107

L

Learning disability, as additional
handicapping condition, 57,
59, 64, 68
age distribution, 73
prevalence, 75–76
Legal blindness, as additional
handicapping condition, 57,
61
age distribution, 72
prevalence, 77
Legal provisions, as related to
minimum competency testing
(MCT) programs, 214–219
common law, 219
due process, 215–216
equal protection, 216–217
state education clauses, 217
state education regulations,
218–219
state education statutes, 218
Legislation, in handicapped
educational program
creation, 232–233
Log-linear analysis, as data analysis
technique, 143–144
use in speech intelligibility study,
144–153, 145, 246

M

Mainstreaming, 105, 109, 258–259
advantages and disadvantages,
120–121
historical perspective, 106–107
placement issues, 112–115
social adjustment, 114
speech intelligibility level
importance, 141
urban school placement, 115–120
variable in sign usage, 131, 136
Maternal rubella, as cause of
hearing loss, 36, 38, 39, 49,
52, 62
additional handicap cause, 43,
44, 45
definition, 36
degree of hearing loss, 43

geographical distribution, *41*
incidence decrease, 47, 50, 53
Mathematics achievement levels,
    hearing impaired students,
    161–164, *163, 165, 168, 172,
    181,* 182, *183, 188*
Meadow/Kendall Social-Emotional
    Assessment Inventory for
    Deaf and Hearing Impaired
    Students, 116, 117, 118
Measles, as cause of hearing loss,
    39, 47
Meningitis, as cause of hearing
    loss, 36, 38, 39, *49,* 52
  additional handicapping
      conditions, *44,* 45
  definition, 38
  degree of hearing loss, 43
  geographical distribution, 40, *41*
  incidence increase, 47, 50
Mental retardation, as additional
    handicapping condition, *57,*
    58–59, 64
  age distribution, *73*
  geographic distribution, 73
  prevalence, 74–75
*Mills v. Board of Education of the
    District of Columbia,* 109
Minimum competency testing
    (MCT) programs, 207–229
  associated legal provisions,
      214–219, 227–228
    common law, 219
    due process, 215–216
    equal protection, 216–217
    state education clauses, 217
    state education regulations,
        218–219
    state education statutes, 218
  focus shift, 209
  state mandates, 208–214,
      211–213, 213
  state program implementation,
      220
    competencies measured,
        220–221
    failure consequences, 226–227
    measurement methods, 221–223
    minimums levels, 225
    minimums to be set, 224–225
    program standards, 225–226
    timing of testing, 223–224
Moderate-to-profound hearing loss,

defining criteria, 2
Multiple Classification Analysis, as
    sign usage measure, 128, 133
Multiply handicapped children,
    implications for U.S.
    educational system, 55. See
    also *Additional handicapping
    conditions.*
Mumps, as hearing loss cause, 39,
    47

N

National Health Interview Survey
    (NHIS), 3–8
  hearing ability supplement, 4–5,
      5
    comparison with National
        Health and Nutrition
        Examination Survey
        results, 11–15, *12*
    ear rating scale, 4, 5
    Gallaudet Hearing Scale, 4–5,
        5
  hearing aid use question, 4
  special education estimates,
      21–23, *22*
National Health and Nutrition
    Examination Survey
    (NHANES), 3–4
  comparison with the Gallaudet
      Hearing Scale results,
      11–15, *12*
  decibel levels and speech
      comprehension
      correspondence, 11
  description, 8–9, *10*
  sampling errors, 9
National Institute of Education
    Issues Clarification Hearing
    on Minimum Competency
    Testing, 208
National Institute of Neurological
    Diseases and Blindness
    (NINDB), 1964 national
    meeting, xiii
National Technical Institute for the
    Deaf, 232, 234, 235, 254
New York State Office of Mental
    Retardation and
    Developmental Disabilities,
    mentally retarded
    developmentally disabled
    population survey, 60

O

Office of the Annual Census of
    Hearing Impaired Children.
    See *Center for Assessment
    and Demographic Studies.*
Office of Demographic Studies. See
    *Center for Assessment and
    Demographic Studies.*
Orthopedic, as additional
    handicapping condition, *57*
    age distribution, *72*
Otitis media, as cause of hearing
    loss, 36, 39, 52
    additional handicapping
        conditions, 44–45
    definition, 39
    degree of hearing loss, 43
    geographical distribution, 40, *41*
    incidence increase, 47, 50

P

*Pennsylvania Association for
    Retarded Citizens (PARC) v.
    Commonwealth of
    Pennsylvania,* 109
Physical handicaps, definition,
    43–45
Postsecondary educational
    alternatives, deaf students,
    234–236, 254, 255
    career areas, 248–251, *249, 250,
        251*
    degrees, 251–254, *253*
    enrollment, 237–240, *239*
    geographical distribution, 237
    program size, 242–243, *243, 255*
    program growth, 236–237, *236*
    specialized services, 243–248, *246,
        255*
    student characteristics, 240–242,
        241
Profound hearing loss, defining
    criteria, 2, 42–43
    Annual Survey incidence, 69

R

Race differences, in hearing loss,
    41–42
Reading comprehension
    achievement levels, hearing
    impaired students, 161–164,
    163, 164, 167, 172, 180, 181,
    183, 188

Residential schools for deaf
    students, 83–84
    age distribution, 87–89, *89*
        geographical statistics, 88–89,
            89
    enrollment patterns, 85–87, *85,
        86*
        geographical statistics, 86–87,
            86
        sex ratio, 87
    ethnic backgrounds, 91–92, *91,*
        99–100
    future trends, 96–102
    multiply handicapped students
        enrollment, 93–96, *94, 95,*
        97–98, 100–101
    nineteenth century rationale, 83
    resident to day student ratios,
        89–91, *90*
        geographical patterns, 89–90
Rubella epidemic, 15, 35, 38, 40,
    65, 70, 88, 98, 108, 175, 235

S

School integration, urban settings,
    115–120
    academic results, 119–120
    class placement by subject
        matter, 117–118, *117*
    data sources, 116–117
School placement, historical
    perspective, 105–112
    nineteenth and early twentieth
        centuries, 105–107
    post-World War II
        developments, 107–109
Seguin, Edouard, 106
Sex distribution, in hearing loss, 41
    additional handicapping
        condition, 68, *69,* 78
Sign communication, synonymous
    terms, 126
Sign communication use increase,
    125–126
Sign language, student usage,
    126–128, *127, 261*
    classroom instruction, 130–131,
        132
    home and school variables,
        127–128, 134–137, *135*
    signing in the home, 133–134,
        135, 136–137
Sign usage, age factor, 128–130,
    129

degree of hearing loss factor,
129–130, 132, 135
student characteristics, 129
Special education,
minimum competency testing
program development, 210
precedent-establishing court
cases, 109, 110–111
Special education for the hearing
impaired, 18–19, 29–30, 47,
49
data sources, 19–20, 21–23,
23–24
statistical estimates, 19–24
Speech intelligibility, 139–141, 154
definition and measurement, 140
degree of hearing loss
relationship, 140, 154
educational placement
relationship, 141
facet of communication, 139
nonauditory factors relationship,
140–141
primary communication method
relationship, 141, 154
Speech intelligibility sample,
educational, demographic,
and communication
characteristics, 144–153, *145,*
154
conclusions, 154–155
implications, 155–157
Stanford Achievement Test,
procedures and special
norms development, xiv,
116, 117
academic achievement measure,
161–162, *163*

speech intelligibility measure,
142–143
Student characteristics, in sign use,
129–130, *129*
age at onset, 129, 130
classroom instruction variable,
130, 131, *132, 135,* 136
degree of hearing loss, 129–130,
136
ethnic status, 130
signing in the home variable,
133–134

U

Uncorrected visual problem, as
additional handicapping
condition, *57,* 58, 61, 64–65
age distribution, *72*
prevalence, 77
U.S. Department of Education,
special education estimates,
19–20, 25, 66
U.S. Division of Health Interview
Statistics, 21
U.S. National Center for Health
Statistics (NCHS), hearing
impairment data source, 3–4
surveys, 3–4
U.S. Public Law, 89-313, 210
U.S. Public Law 93–112, 207, 233
U.S. Public Law 94–142, 19, 56,
66, 75, 83, 97, 107, 109–112,
207, 210, 260

V

Vaccines, against meningitis, 38
against rubella, 38, 50, 52